MACEDC

.

Anthropology, Culture and Society

Series Editors:
Dr Richard A. Wilson, University of Sussex
Professor Thomas Hylland Eriksen, University of Oslo

MACEDONIA
The Politics of Identity and Difference

Edited by
JANE K. COWAN

Pluto Press
LONDON • STERLING, VIRGINIA

First published 2000
by PLUTO PRESS
345 Archway Road, London N6 5AA
and 22883 Quicksilver Drive,
Sterling, VA 20166–2012, USA

www.plutobooks.com

British Library Cataloguing in Publication Data
A catalogue record for this book is available from
the British Library

ISBN 0 7453 1594 1 hardback
ISBN 0 7453 1589 5 paperback

Library of Congress Cataloging in Publication Data
Macedonia : the politics of identity and difference / edited by Jane
Cowan.
    p. cm.— (Anthropology, culture, and society)
Includes bibliographical references.
    ISBN 0–7453–1594–1 — ISBN 0–7453–1589–5 (pbk.)
    1. Nationalism—Macedonia. 2. Macedonian question. I. Cowan, Jane
K., 1954– II. Series.
    DR2192 .M34 2001
    305.891'819—dc21

                                                            00–009742

    09 08 07 06 05 04 03 02 01 00
    10   9   8   7   6   5   4   3   2   1

Designed and produced for Pluto Press by Chase Publishing Services
Typeset from disk by Stanford DTP Services, Northampton
Printed in the European Union by Antony Rowe Ltd, Chippenham, England

For my mother and father,
Norma Jane Dent Cowan and Paul Richard Cowan

CONTENTS

LIST OF MAPS, FIGURES AND TABLES

MAPS

FIGURES

TABLES

LIST OF ABBREVIATIONS

CCE	Cultural Capital of Europe
DAN-MAK	*Dansk–Makedonsk Venskabsforening* (Danish–Macedonian friendship association)
DPA	Democratic Party of Albanians
ELAS	*Ellinikos Laikos Apeleftherotikos Stratos* (Greek People's Liberation Army)
EU	European Union
FAEV	Forum Against Ethnic Violence
FYROM	Former Yugoslav Republic of Macedonia
GCP	Greek Communist Party
IMRO	Internal Macedonian Revolutionary Organisation
MCIC	Macedonian Centre for International Cooperation
MGRC	Minority Groups Research Centre
MMS	Museum of the Macedonian Struggle
NGO	Non-governmental organisation
NOF	*Narodno Osloboditelen Front* (People's Liberation Front)
OAED	*Organismos Apascholisis Ergatikou Dynamikou* (Organisation for the Employment of Human Resources)
OSCE	Organisation for Security and Cooperation in Europe
PDP	Party of Democratic Prosperity
PRM	People's Republic of Macedonia
SDSM	Social Democratic Alliance of Macedonia
SNOF	*Slavianomakedonski Narodno Osloboditelen Front* (Slavo-Macedonian People's Liberation Front)
UN	United Nations
VMRO-DPMNE	Internal Macedonian Revolutionary Organisation/Democratic Party of Macedonian National Unity

PREFACE

The impetus for the present volume dates from November 1994 when the Forum Against Ethnic Violence (FAEV), a group of anthropologists alarmed at the rise in ethnic violence throughout the world, organised a conference on 'Macedonia' at University College, London. The war in Bosnia and other parts of the former Yugoslavia had escalated horrifically by then, and it was not clear whether conflict would break out in Macedonia as well. The still fledgling ex-Yugoslav republic was facing a series of refusals of recognition from Yugoslavia, Bulgaria and Greece. By far the most strident opposition came from Greece, which was seeking to rally world opinion to the justice of its claims for exclusive rights to the Macedonian name and heritage. An economic blockade which Greece had instituted against the new republic – already blocked from the north due to the UN Security Council's embargo against the new Yugoslavia – was having complex and not altogether intended effects. The worsening economic conditions were only making the ethnic Macedonian population dig in their heels against the demanded changes to the republic's name, flag and constitution. At the same time, these conditions were also contributing to radicalising the Albanian-speaking population within the republic.

Conference discussions circled around these two related themes: the 'Macedonian Controversy' (the question of who had the right to call themselves, or others, Macedonians) and the question of diversity within and between communities residing in a territory so named. Prominent in the discussion, alongside academics, journalists, artists and some political figures, were representatives of non-governmental organisations (NGOs), based in the republic, addressing these problems on a day-to-day level. They described such projects as a cross-border friendship association for Greeks and Macedonians conceived as a symbolic counter-weight to diplomatic-level hostility, local environmental projects attempting to build cooperation among diverse groups of Macedonian citizens, and an NGO devoted to problems of women within the republic's Albanian community.

Three contributors to the present volume gave papers at the conference (Loring Danforth, Jonathan Schwartz and Riki Van Boeschoten), and others participated as active audience members. However, this volume has followed its own independent trajectory. When it became clear that publication as conference proceedings was not feasible, the volume was reconceptualised. I took the opportunity to invite as additional contributors individuals whose research on Macedonia I find especially innovative, many of them younger scholars just establishing their careers. I was keen to put their work together and see what kinds of resonances, and tensions, the juxtaposition elicited. The volume has evolved over four years of preparation. The initial hope to include a chapter on the NGO projects did not prove feasible, though Jonathan Schwartz's contribution offers a glimpse of their work from an anthropologist-activist's perspective. The spirit of cooperation across boundaries that NGO representatives articulated has also remained a guiding notion for the volume.

I wish here to acknowledge the efforts of those associated with initial attempts at publishing the conference papers: Predrag Zivkovic, who provided a full transcription of the papers and discussions and Glenn Bowman, who initiated the editing process, before I agreed to take over as editor in spring 1996. The FAEV, while relinquishing to me total control over the newly defined project, generously provided financial support toward production costs, the translation of one paper, and editorial assistance in the final stages. On behalf of the FAEV organisers, I am happy to thank the co-administrators of the 'Conference on Macedonia', Predrag Zivkovic and Sandra Squires, as well as several organisations which subsidised it: Christian Aid, Dutch Inter-Church Aid, Charity Know-How Fund, the Royal Anthropological Institute, the Association of Social Anthropologists, and the Anthropology Departments of Goldsmith's College and University College, London. I am also delighted to thank the Centre for the Study of South-Eastern Europe of the University of Wales, which provided additional financial support at a critical moment.

During the long gestation of this project I incurred many debts. I warmly thank all the contributors, who tolerated with patience my editorial interventionism and my requests for repeated revisions. Many of them pressed me toward the same high standards by offering astute and, in some cases, quite lengthy comments on the introduction; Loring Danforth deserves particular mention. For help with maps, photographs and electoral statistics, I am grateful to Iakovos Michailidis, Jonathan Schwartz and Georgios Agelopoulos. Very special thanks go to Keith Brown, with whom I co-authored the introduction. Keith's expertise on society and history in the republic, both before and after independence, complemented my own more Greek-based expertise; together, we were able to craft an introduction which frames the contemporary politics of identity and difference in and of Macedonia in much broader than usual terms. In the larger editorial process, too, I relied a lot on his sense of things; he also kept me laughing. Sarah Green read the entire manuscript in January 2000 and provided an unusually detailed and immensely stimulating reader's report. Inspired by her rigour and insight, we were able, alas, to follow up on only a portion of her many suggestions. Richard Wilson, series editor and greatly valued Sussex colleague and friend, provided acute substantive and organisational advice, as well as moral support. With her quiet efficiency, Lysbeth Gehrels helped me draw together the multiple strands of the manuscript in the final few weeks of preparation, working miracles with her excellent copy-editing skills. I thank also the staff at Pluto Press, especially the managing editor, Anne Beech, for their flexibility and professionalism.

My family has lived with this project as long as I have. With Charlie I have puzzled over 'Macedonia' through the course of many years, and whatever sense I have made of it owes much to his wisdom, ethical sensitivity and analytical grasp. I thank our sons, Isaac and Andrew, for not being infinitely patient with my preoccupation with this text and for interrupting me at my computer with demands for a story, a bike ride or a game of Uno. Their energy and zany humour many a time lifted my spirits when I was feeling burdened by a project I feared would never be finished. Finally, I thank my parents, Dick and Norma Cowan. Though perplexed, I am sure, by their Scots-Irish, midwestern American daughter's inexplicable fascination for lands in the southeastern corner of Europe, they have always encouraged me to follow my own dreams and projects. Only now that I am myself a parent do I understand what a gift their openness has been. In gratitude for this, and for their love and support along the way, I dedicate this book to them.

A NOTE ON NAMES AND TERMS

An index of the contestation surrounding Macedonia – what it is and what it means – is the bewildering diversity of names and terms for the 'same' thing: places, persons, language. Of course, this 'sameness' does not really survive that diverse naming. Imagine three second-cousins – Kyril (a Macedonian citizen), Kole (a Bulgarian citizen) and Kostas (a Greek citizen) – whose grand-fathers were three brothers living, until the First World War, in a small village near to the town that Greeks call Kastoria, and that Macedonians and Bulgarians call Kostur. When, nowadays, Kyril uses a different name for 'x' from Kole or Kostas, he signals that he sees 'x' differently from them, and he simultaneously constructs that difference in the very act of naming. To complicate the situation even more, Kyril, Kole and Kostas may not be absolutely consistent in the words they choose for 'x'; what they choose may depend on the context. Conversely, the 'same' word – 'Macedonia' or 'Macedonians' – means different things to Kyril, Kole and Kostas.

The contributors to the volume have made their own choices about names and terms. These may reflect their own personal views. As anthropologists, though, they are usually careful to distinguish their own views from those of the people they are describing. As a guide to those unfamiliar with the historical and political nuances of terms in this semantic battleground, I outline some basic points.

The term 'Macedonia' refers to a territory whose boundaries are matters of dispute. Citizens of the Republic of Macedonia, and many immigrants from northern Greece now living in diaspora communities around the world, use the term 'Macedonia' in several ways. Firstly, they use it to refer to an ancient kingdom. Secondly, they use it to refer to a historically established (but vaguely bounded) territory 'partitioned' between Greece ('Aegean Macedonia'), Serbia ('Vardar Macedonia') and Bulgaria ('Pirin Macedonia') in 1913. Thirdly, they use the word 'Macedonia' for the new Republic of Macedonia. Many Greeks, on the other hand, following their government's unwillingness to recognise the new republic under this name, use the appellation 'Former Yugoslav Republic of Macedonia' (FYROM). Even prior to the 1990s controversy, they referred to the land north of their borders as 'Yugoslavia' or 'Serbia', not 'Macedonia', and to the language spoken by the people there as *Servika* or *Slavika*. Greeks today tend to use the term

'Macedonia' for the northern region of their nation-state, or (like many others) in reference to a less precisely demarcated ancient kingdom of Macedonia.

Who is a 'Macedonian'? The word may be used for an inhabitant, or former inhabitant, of a region called Macedonia, irrespective of ethnicity; for a citizen of the Republic of Macedonia, again, irrespective of ethnicity; or for a member of the Macedonian nation or ethnic group. It is the third, apparently most 'natural' usage, which is most controversial.

Outside the borders of Greece (that is, in diaspora communities, in the Yugoslav republic after the Second World War and in the present independent republic) many who originated from communities in 'Greek Macedonia' were able to develop, or consolidate, an identity as nationally Macedonian. These people call themselves Macedonians, and the slavic language that they speak Macedonian. They also identify their relatives who still live in Greece as Macedonians, or as members of the Macedonian minority.

Within Greece's borders, some of these relatives call themselves Macedonians in this same national sense, refer to themselves as members of the Macedonian minority and call their language Macedonian. A majority, however, do not use these terms or, at least, not in the same way. This population, many of whom used to be called and to call themselves 'Bulgarians', and some of whom later identified as 'Slavo-Macedonians', now tend to call themselves 'locals' (*dopii*) or 'local Macedonians' (*dopii Makedones*). Most of them think of themselves as Greeks in a national sense.

Many of the contributors in this volume use one of the more or less inter-changeable terms for this population within Greece: 'Slav-speakers', 'Slavic-speakers' or its Greek form, 'Slavophones'. This set of terms signals a group distinguished by their knowledge of a non-Greek language. Such designation has its own politics. Slavic dialects widely spoken in northwest-ern Greece for many generations until the mid-twentieth century resemble those codified in Skopje as literary Macedonian after the Second World War. Dialects spoken in north central Greece, south of the Bulgarian border, although part of the same linguistic continuum, contain more Bulgarian elements, while being distinct from standard Bulgarian (based on an eastern dialect). Yet all these dialects were largely intelligible to speakers of standard Bulgarian. There are now few Greek citizens for whom a slavic language is the only medium of communication. Calling them, or descendants of communities in which these dialects were formerly prevalent, by any of these terms (Slav-speakers, Slavic-speakers, Slavophones) arguably allows one to distinguish these persons without making assumptions about their national loyalties, which may be various. It avoids the political charge that 'Macedonian-speaker' or 'Bulgarian-speaker' would have in a climate of nationalist thought which presumes a link between language and nation. But these phrases still cannot claim to achieve perfect neutrality. They are unacceptable to those in this population who do identify themselves as 'ethnically' or 'nationally' Macedonian, who call themselves Macedonians and who perceive the phrase 'Slavic-speaker' as a denial of that affiliation.

The term 'Slavo-Macedonians' is used in one paper (Michailidis) for those Slavophones who opposed the Greek and Bulgarian national projects. The term developed within the context of the international Communist Party in the interwar period, where the Slavo-Macedonians were viewed as a separate people with rights to autonomy. Some Greeks, including scholars, who are unwilling to call the ethnic majority in the new republic 'Macedonians', opt to call them 'Slavo-Macedonians', in reference to the left-wing genesis of their national identity.

As noted above, the Slavic mother tongue spoken by people in this region is called by various names, by the people themselves and by scholars. Linguists generally accept that a continuum of dialects exists across geographical Macedonia, from which three literary languages have been established: Serbian, Macedonian and Bulgarian. Since language has been viewed within European nationalisms as a primary criterion of nationhood, proponents of different national projects have defined the language spoken in geographical Macedonia accordingly. Bulgarian nationalists define it as Bulgarian, and Macedonian nationalists as Macedonian. Greek nationalists, somewhat surprisingly, have used both of these terms at various historical moments (depending on which nationalism they saw as the greatest threat to their own). Nowadays, though, they mostly define it as 'not a real language' at all, but rather a 'Slavic idiom' or 'dialect'. Within the northern region of Greece, people who speak this language use a variety of terms for it: *Vulgarika*; '*Vulgarika* but not the "real" *Vulgarika*'; *Slavika*; *Makedonika*; *Makedonitika*; *Makedonski*; *nash* (our [language]); *ta dopia or ta dopika (the 'local' [language])*; or even simply *i glossa*, (the language). These different terms allow people to make, or to avoid making, national claims. They may use different terms in different contexts.

Places in Macedonia, both human settlements and landscapes, often have a variety of names associated with them. This is a legacy of the multiple linguistic groups which inhabited and still inhabit the region. A good example is the town in northern Greece that Agelopoulos, in this volume, calls Salonica, which is also known by the names Thessaloniki (Greek), Solun or Solon (Macedonian, Bulgarian), and Selanik or Selnik (Turkish). Similarly, the capital of the Republic of Macedonia, officially called Skopje, is also known as Shkup (Albanian) and Uskub (Turkish). The towns within Greek national borders which the Greek authorities call Florina, Edessa and Kastoria, members of Macedonian human rights groups call Lerin, Voden, and Kostur. The town within the borders of the Republic of Macedonia which the republic's authorities call Bitola, its Albanian-speaking citizens call Manastir, while its Greek-speaking families call it Monastir.

Differently inflected, and thus somehow a 'different' place, in each case, Macedonia itself is known also as Macédoine (French), Makedonija (Macedonian, Bulgarian), Makedonia (Greek) and Maqedonia (Albanian).

As part of the process of nation-building in the region, all national governments have tried to establish one name as true and authoritative, and these are the names one sees on official maps. Oppositional movements (counter-nationalisms or minority rights movements), for their part, frequently insist on an equally monolithic set of place names. However, people who live in these places may use several or all of these names in a much more fluid way in the course of their everyday lives.

Finally, a comment on transliteration. Both Greek and Cyrillic have been rendered into latin script with as much consistency as possible. No transliteration system is ideal for all cases, so compromises have had to be made. Thus, both the Cyrillic ć and the č are normally rendered in this text as 'ch'. In a few cases, concerning proper names and places which are well known to English-speaking audiences in something closer to a latinised version of their written Cyrillic form (for example, Milosevic), or in response to the preferences of the persons so named, these familiar spellings have been retained.

Coastlines
Nation-State boundaries
Approximate extent of 'Geographical Macedonia'

* Since the break-up of the former Yugoslavia, Serbia and Montenegro remain constituent republics of the Federal Republic of Yugoslavia.

** As the book goes to press, 'The Former Yugoslav Republic of Macedonia' remains the name by which the state is officially recognised by the UN and other international organisations. However, the name is still disputed and under negotiation. The self-designation of the state in question is 'The Republic of Macedonia'.

Map 1. Geographical Macedonia within contemporary southeastern Europe

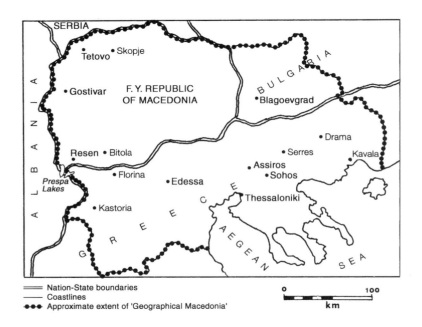

Map 2. Geographical Macedonia in relation to contemporary states in the region

INTRODUCTION: MACEDONIAN INFLECTIONS
Jane K. Cowan and K.S. Brown

THE MACEDONIAN QUESTION REFRAMED

'Why not Macedonia for Macedonians, as Bulgaria for Bulgarians and Servia for Servians?' Posed in *The Times* in 1897, Gladstone's question reflected the concerns of a *fin-de-siècle* Western European ruling elite witnessing the dis-integration of the Ottoman Empire and anxious over the future succession of political control in European Turkey. Already, the new states in the region (Greece, Serbia, Bulgaria), as well as a movement claiming to strive for an autonomous Macedonia, were laying claims on the territory and its population, basing these on whatever criteria best suited their national arguments – language, religion, history, household customs, national consciousness.[1] Britain and the other Great Powers saw in any redistribution of territory, however, the potential for regional instability which might, in turn, provoke wider disputes between alliance blocs. The 'Macedonian Question' thus had high profile, and marked a shift from the politics of empires to that of nation-states. It remained a fraught and contested issue, nationally and internationally, throughout the first half of the century, long after the 1919 Paris Peace Conference redrew national boundaries cutting through the territory.

After the establishment of a federal Yugoslavia in 1944, the Macedonian Question lay dormant in the international imagination. Greek, Yugoslav and Bulgarian historians continued to investigate the turbulent modern history of the region where their frontiers met, but they did so with little contact with each other, and without reaching a wide audience. Since the violent break-up of Yugoslavia in the early 1990s, however, Macedonia has again attracted considerable attention. The Yugoslav Republic which bore the name Macedonia found its bid to recognition and sovereignty blocked when it sought to use the same name for itself as a nation-state. In the period 1992–5 a vigorous campaign, with massive domestic support, was conducted by Greece to safeguard the name as designating exclusively the northern territories incor-porated into the Greek state in 1912–13.

The 1990s controversy, still not fully resolved, is indisputably rooted in nineteenth-century nationalist struggles. The rhetorics of the competing nationalisms heard today echo the romantic nationalism that heralded the 'modern' era in the Balkans a century ago. Even the current involvement of diasporic communities in the politics of Macedonia replicates a familiar pattern. Yet the sense of *déjà vu* these provide easily misleads. The renewed potency of the Macedonian Question – its ability, once again, to capture the imagination and commitment of present-day actors – must be understood in relation to current political and economic conditions within small countries at Fortress Europe's periphery, one formally inside, the others outside. The Macedonian Question's passionate reanimation occurs at the beginning of a new century, in a radically different world from the one in which rival claims were first staked in the region. Social, political, economic, ideological and technological changes have affected not only local conditions, but the very nature of international connections. Those mobilising these rhetorics and engaged in struggles around them are inhabitants of the late twentieth century, active subjects of their own varied histories – not trapped in a Balkan time warp.

In this volume, anthropologists and one historian explore key dimensions of the politics of identity and difference in the context of contemporary Macedonia. The Macedonian controversy involves immigrant communities in Australia, North America and Europe who are themselves caught up in the ethnic politics of their host societies, citizens in three different Balkan states that have followed distinctive nation-building policies (Republic of Macedonia, Greece, Bulgaria), and international and state bodies, non-governmental organisations (NGOs), academics and other interested 'outsiders'. Although a majority of the papers deal directly with the region, we define Macedonia not only as a geographical area, but also as a discursive space of global significance. As territory and as name, Macedonia can be seen as a site where different rhetorics – of civil society, multiculturalism and international cooperation, as well as of ethnic tensions, ancient hatreds and national security – intersect. An examination of this site of collisions and meetings can broaden our understanding of the relationship between different domains of discourse. Beyond that, our examination itself constitutes an intervention, wherein we seek to challenge the explanatory utility of certain stock terms, and suggest new avenues of enquiry.

One of our major concerns is with the dynamics of 'identity' and 'difference' as social processes, in a region of the world where ethnicity has been simultaneously fundamentalised and pathologised. A significant body of opinion in the Western media and political establishment, working from assumptions hardly distinguishable from the claims of nationalist ideologues of the region, has construed ethnic loyalties as more enduring here than elsewhere and as 'naturally' trumping all others. Thus, the argument that the war in Yugoslavia was 'caused' by age-old ethnic hatreds was heard not only from local leaders, who relied on divisive ethno-nationalisms for their power-base, but also from Western journalists and policy-makers.

Along with other critics, we condemn such an approach as deeply flawed. As Susan Woodward insisted in her impressive riposte, *Balkan Tragedy*, 'to explain the Yugoslav crisis as a result of ethnic hatred is to turn the story upside down and begin at its end' (1995: 18; see also Sorabji 1993). The consequences of this sort of explanation have not been negligible. The ethnicising of the conflict within Western, especially NATO, analyses contributed to considerable inter-national indecision (see Gow 1994) and ultimately shaped policy to produce intervention, such as the Dayton Accords, that abetted the process of carving out ethnically defined political units. By appearing, moreover, to accept the naturalness and inevitability of ethnic animosity, it ironically facilitated the production, entrenchment and legitimation of *new* (or reinvigorated) and exclu-sivist ethnic and national identities.

Given the real world implications of such reductive approaches to identity and affiliation in 'the Balkans', and especially 'the tinderbox' of Macedonia, an important objective of this volume is to highlight ethnicity as constructed, fluid and variably salient, rather than essential, fixed and already given. Consequently, we take pains to reveal the problems with certain dominant metaphors of Macedonian multiplicity – fruit salads, mosaics and chess-boards – which represent groups as discrete and irreducible 'billiard balls' in collision. Instead, we emphasise the contingent and context-specific ways in which identity and difference are expressed, or eschewed. We also stress dif-ferences *within* categories.

From the extensive debates on identity and difference within studies of gender, sexuality and race in the 1980s (for example, Fuss 1989), however, we are aware that even though identity and difference are 'constructed', they are usually experienced as 'real'. Nonetheless, we argue that the 'reality' of ethnic and national categories is grounded not simply in local ideologies, but in international legal frameworks, as well. The hegemony of these categories is so profound that even resistances are articulated in their terms, whether through counternationalisms (see, for example, Chatterjee 1986) or through appeals to multiculturalism. At the same time, while there is no denying the emotional hold that ideas of the nation can have on individuals, processes of identification are neither straightforward nor a foregone conclusion. As made clear by several chapters in this volume that examine the struggles of individuals confronted by two competing nationalisms, individual agency needs to be acknowledged in our analyses.

CONTINGENT MACEDONIA

'Everyone is interested in the stability of your country except your neighbours.' According to an Internet ironist, this is one of the top ten reasons to be a Macedonian in the territories of the former Yugoslavia in the 1990s. The humour, as so often, is jet black and apposite. After the declaration of Macedonian independence in 1991, Bulgaria recognised the new state, but not the nation to which its majority belong, nor the language that they speak. The new Yugoslavia refused to ratify the frontier between Macedonia and Serbia, while the Serbian Orthodox church denied the status of its Macedonian counterpart. Albania faced its own crises of transition, but

Macedonian citizens self-identified as Albanian were allegedly involved in various armed confrontations with Macedonian police over the rights of the Albanian minority in western Macedonia. And in the best-known neighbourly stand-off, Greece – the northern region of which is also called Macedonia – challenged the republic's status by interpreting its constitution, new flag and very name as expressions of extraterritorial ambitions.[2]

The republic, as a result, has languished in a liminal space. Its internationally recognised name, 'The Former Yugoslav Republic of Macedonia' (FYROM), is an index of its contingency, novelty, and, perhaps uniquely among states, previous status.[3] Yet it has survived, until now: in part, it might be argued, because of the wider world's interventions. United Nations (UN) forces were deployed in a preventive mission in 1993; the Organisation for Security and Cooperation in Europe (OSCE) and other European agencies have, for a long time, had offices in Skopje. Organisations which promote reconciliation and dialogue, such as Search for Common Ground, have developed programmes there, and like other countries in Eastern Europe, the republic has received funding from sources like the Soros Foundation to support the creation of an 'open society'.

These initiatives contribute to a rhetoric in which the Republic of Macedonia appears as a beacon of hope. Although its citizens belong to a number of distinctive linguistic and religious communities, and many can thereby be assumed to have potentially conflicting loyalties, state institutions created and reshaped since the declaration of independence in 1991 have nonetheless endured. The republic has survived border incursions, armed confrontations between police and citizens and government scandals over paramilitary activities. When the charismatic president, Kire Gligorov, was seriously injured in a car bomb attack in 1995, the constitutional provisions for interim rule operated smoothly. Popular dissatisfaction with widespread governmental corruption between 1994 and 1998 was translated into a change of government in the elections of 1998.[4] And, most recently, when over a quarter of a million refugees from Kosovo arrived in the spring of 1999 – one refugee for every eight citizens – the republic somehow managed to continue to function.[5] Events of the last ten years, then, suggest that the Republic of Macedonia is operating as a stable state.

At the same time, though, doomsayers read only a delay of the inevitable. Invoking the ferocity of the fighting and destruction in Slovenia, Croatia, Bosnia and most recently Kosovo, they see in the clear tensions between largely distinct communities in Macedonia – especially between Macedonians and Albanians – the potential for violence. Such analyses also delve into more distant histories to read the future. The period of the Balkan Wars of 1912–13, when those national borders now fraught with such significance were first drawn, has been a touchstone. Witness, for example, the decision of the Carnegie Foundation at the height of the war ravaging Yugoslavia to re-publish, in 1993, under the title *The Other Balkan Wars*, its famous report of 1913 centred on the struggles in Macedonia, rather than commission a new fact-finding mission (see Todorova 1997: 3–7). The reported savagery of all the protag-onists who fought at the century's beginning to control some part of Macedonia – Greeks, Bulgarians, Turks and Serbs – is seen as immanent, and unchanged, in today's inflamed passions.[6]

The re-emergence within Greece of the Macedonian Question in the early 1990s seemed to provide further support for prophecies of renewed cata-strophe. The shrillness of Greece's official campaign against the republic's bid for recognition and sovereignty, and the depth of public support it enjoyed within Greece, gave weight to a rhetoric, among Western commentators, of regional recidivism. That rhetoric rested, in turn, on broader claims about Balkan perspectives of history as fundamentally different from 'our own'. 'In the Balkans,' opined one influential analyst, 'history is not viewed as tracing a chronological progression, as it is in the West. Instead, history jumps around and moves in circles; and where history is perceived in such a way, myths take root' (Kaplan 1993: 58). Thus, even a country acknowledged to be stable, democratic and proud of its European status could be characterised as suffering from this Balkan syndrome. Greeks who expressed outrage or even mere opinion on the subject of the establishment of a new state called Macedonia on their country's border revealed themselves, in the eyes of many observers, as 'Balkan' rather than European, in the pejorative sense described by Maria Todorova (1997) – for a key dimension of this alleged character was an unhealthy concern with the past.

Yet despite the noisy clamour about the 'ownership of history', Greek reactions were not exclusively preoccupied with the past. They were also manifestly connected to concerns about the present and future. In particular, at stake was the potential effect of the recognition of a new Macedonian state on the domestic politics of northern Greece, which exhibits its own demographic plurality. Under the national banner of Greece are immigrants and refugees to the region, from Asia Minor and Bulgaria in the 1920s, and from Epirus in the 1950s, as well as residents settled in the region for far longer. Labelled in the Greek vernacular as *dopii* (locals) those communities of longer standing are, or were in the past, Slavic-speaking. As such, they can perceive themselves or be perceived by others as having a more legitimate claim to the name 'Macedonians' than their more recently settled fellow-Greeks. On the basis of language, custom and kinship, some of them also recognise ties with the Macedonian-speaking residents of the republic. The possible repercussions of such perceptions were the source of considerable anxiety in Greece where national unity and security remain high on the political and societal agenda.

Further concern was generated by the interventions not only of analysts, but also of various activists from the wider world. For just as the Republic of Macedonia (on the territory of the former Yugoslavia) has been targeted by international organisations seeking to investigate and promote good relations between different groups within a state, so the region of Macedonia (on the territory of Greece) has attracted the attention of a similar set of agencies concerned with minority and human rights. As a result, groups making claims on behalf of a Macedonian minority in northern Greece have found a new and broader forum, and a slightly different language, in which to make their case. This, in turn, endows such challenges to the Greek self-image of national unity and purity with a certain authority.

PARTISANSHIP AND DECONSTRUCTION OF MACEDONIAN NATIONALISMS

Macedonia, then, is a term with multiple resonances in the 1990s. It has also generated a significant literature. Entry into this literature demands appreciation of, if not answers to, a slew of questions, which the short account presented above sought implicitly to address. The central one of these is perhaps the thorniest: who are the Macedonians? Hugh Poulton's book of the same title (1995) focused on one possible constituency of bearers of the name: citizens of the new republic. Even this definition of Macedonians leaves open questions of entitlement to citizenship, especially among former Yugoslav citizens who moved out of Kosovo in the 1980s. Should the label, then, refer to *all* those who inhabit the territory of the new Republic of Macedonia? But this would be to ignore strident and historically justified claims that the name should refer to the western and central areas of northern Greece. Should the term be attached to those who inhabit the northern Greek region bearing that name? Or to Bulgarian citizens originating from that region, who for one reason or another left? Or does it refer to an ethnically defined community, a community linked, according to various proponents, by blood, tradition, language or culture?

All of these definitions have their champions who, in turn, contest the truth status of other people's definitions. Consensus can only emerge when the term's ambiguity survives. At a world cup qualifying soccer match in Chicago in 1994, for example, a plane flew over the stadium trailing a banner with the slogan 'Macedonia for the Macedonians'. No one, whatever side they were on, would think to do anything but applaud the sentiment. For any partisan of Macedonia, the slogan expresses their heart's desire. Their disagreement is over the rightful bearers of the name, and the extent of the territory, not over the automatic and proprietary rights of the former over the latter.

A belief in a single true meaning of Macedonia unifies, in a theoretical sense, what might be termed *first-order discourse* about Macedonia. Within this strand of thinking, ontologically equivalent meanings of the term jostle for precedence. Those who put the term 'Macedonia' into this semantic realm include historians, politicians and polemicists in the region and outside, who accept common-sense notions of purity and history. They stake out a clear and partisan position, embracing one or other of the potential definitions alluded to above and denying the validity of others. This has fuelled a considerable debate aimed at establishing the 'correct' use of 'Macedonia' and 'Macedonian' – in both popular and academic circles. This is a literature of claim and counter-claim, which is dominated by an idiom of certainty, fact, and scientific proof, but in which there is also room for passion and outrage. It has the qualities of nationalist discourse, in that there is no room for compromise. Similarly, in the quest for irrefutability, the argument increasingly turns to the same resources beloved of nationalists – including historical descent, residential longevity and linguistic purity. Dominant, in particular, is the idiom of the national community as a natural and enduring entity under permanent physical, as well as less direct forms of, threat.

In this discursive realm are protagonists from the present and the past with varying degrees of academic respectability. The concern with truth status is demonstrated in some representative titles: *The Macedonian Camouflage in the Light of Facts and Figures* (Christides 1949); *The Falsification of Macedonian History* (Martis 1983); *On Scientific Truth about Macedonia* (National Technical University of Athens 1993). The titles emphasise a sharp break between the validity of their authors' own claims, and those of their rivals. Their correlates in a more scholarly vein are more measured in their language, but the conclusions are similarly clear-cut. Douglas Dakin's monumental 1966 work, for example, *The Greek Struggle in Macedonia, 1897–1913*, traces an archival history of Hellenic resistance to non-Greek claimants in the area. Drawing on a different vein of authority, Horace Lunt's sociolinguistic work documents the distinctness of the Macedonian language since the mid-nineteenth century (Lunt, 1984; see also Friedman, 1975).

Such accounts, whose authors make no bones about their political commitment, are objects of suspicion or criticism in a plethora of articles and books by a range of journalists, historians and anthropologists. As a result, another set of literature, which could be called a *second-order discourse*, has developed in which authors have set out to distance themselves from partisanship – and indeed, to take partisanship as part of the object of study (for example, Danforth 1995; Karakasidou 1997). They have sought to deconstruct the teleologies of one or more nation-states in the region, and instead to write more encompassing narratives, in which wider political and economic forces play a part. Such authors lay claim to a position outside the mêlée. Their accounts often focus on the uncertainities and ambiguities in Macedonia's history. In these analyses, disputed periods of history – the empire of Philip II and Alexander III, the rule of King Samuil, the nationalist struggles of the nineteenth century, the Balkan Wars, or the Greek Civil War – are painstakingly reviewed. Most saliently, this strand of analysis emphasises that history is written according to interests in the present, and that national solidarities are the products of willed human agency, not God-given or natural developments.[7]

Such analyses can be termed critical and deconstructionist, in that they denaturalise the nation-state. However, what the debate over Macedonia has demonstrated is how vulnerable deconstructionist analyses are to reappropriation by other, usually counternationalist, projects. The paradoxical 'double-standard of nationalism' noted by Morgenthau in 1957 – such that

a critique of someone else's nationalism is never taken to apply to one's own
– is as much in evidence today as ever. If this is rooted largely in the persuas-
iveness of one's own lived, naturalised/nationalised everyday practices that,
as Herzfeld demonstrates in explorations of 'cultural intimacy' (1997), merely
ideological critiques find 'hard to reach', it is also exacerbated by the method-
ological convention of analysing nationalisms one at a time. A single state's
commitment to homogeneity can easily be read as uniquely perverse, and
its mechanisms uniquely reprehensible, when comparative contextualisation
– historical and regional – is lacking. Studies of single cases may, in addition,
emphasise internal processes of nation-building and national identity
formation, underplaying the wider ideological, political and economic forces
which compel and shape such processes.[8]

Such is the dilemma of much anthropological and historical work which
values thick description of a single case over sometimes problematic comparison.
Accounts which highlight the role that Tito and communist realpolitik played
in the recognition of Macedonian religion, language and sovereignty after
the Second World War (Kofos 1964), for example, are easily made to serve
the agenda of a narrow Greek nationalism that denies historical roots to a
Slavic Macedonian identity. Conversely, analyses which highlight the per-
sistence of senses of solidarity in northern Greece that are expressed in idioms
other than those encouraged by the Greek nation-state apparatus (for example,
Cowan 1997a, Karakasidou 1993, Rossos 1994) may provide fodder to
those Macedonian nationalists who see portions of Greece and Bulgaria as
terra irredenta. To their chagrin, scholars are branded as traitors or pariahs
by one group of nationalists, and heroes by another, while the broader
theoretical implications of their work are lost on many readers.

AN ETHNIC ESSENTIALISM REINSCRIBED?

Even when such analyses escape the clutches of nationalist redeployments,
they often unwittingly contribute to another stereotype of the region. The deconstructionist literature points out that between its life as a powerful ancient
kingdom and its involvement in national struggles in the nineteenth century,
Macedonia's borders remained curiously ill-defined. That territorial ambiguity
remains, as its borders have been and continue to be defined very differently
by mapmakers with different agendas (Wilkinson 1951). Yet in counter-
point to the perceived fuzziness of its outer edges is a conviction of the
sharpness of boundaries between its component parts, both social and territorial (see, for example, McNeil 1992). A controlling trope for this peculiarity
of Macedonia is that of the *macédoine* – or 'fruit salad'. Variously derived
from the far-reaching polyglot empire of Alexander, or the period of religious
and proto-national struggles in the last decades of Ottoman rule, the term is
recycled by authors wishing to stress the heterogeneity of the region.

The *macédoine* has somehow shifted from homely image to home truth. By the magic of nominalism, Macedonia's character as homeland to communities ostensibly as discrete as apples and oranges appears as an essential quality, rather than as a continuously refashioned product of particular histories and politics. From these accounts emerges the suggestion that Macedonia's *contested* status, too, is a product of essential qualities of the region and its inhabitants. So-called ethnic groups – 'Bulgarians', 'Albanians', 'Greeks', 'Turks', 'Gypsies', 'Vlachs', and sometimes 'Macedonians' – remain as the distinctive components of the salad, maintaining their separate but juxtaposed identities or flavours.

In other words, although many accounts of identities in Macedonia do not privilege any specific group's narratives of history, neither do they undermine the idea of the unchanging ethnic group. This has the odd effect of reinscribing a different species of essentialism. For even if the historically contingent 'constructedness' of nations is tirelessly declared, the enduring 'essentiality' of ethnicity is simultaneously reinforced through endlessly reiterated metaphors of *macédoines*, mosaics and chessboards.

Concerns with heterogeneity can be a feature of two quite distinct worldviews. For some analysts, the 'plural society' model from anthropology, developed to conceptualise diversity in colonial contexts, seems apposite for the Balkans. In this view, the Ottoman legacy has given to the region certain qualities perceived in other former imperial or colonial possessions, such as a profound link between ethnicity and class or occupation (Vermeulen 1984; Van Boeschoten, this volume). Some less scholarly but influential accounts tend to employ concepts like 'tribe', and reveal a variant form of what Rosaldo (1989) has called 'imperialist nostalgia', which can at times read like racism, in their vigorous assertion of the incapacity of people in the Balkans to move beyond so-called ancient hatreds (Kaplan 1993). A political consequence of this view is to argue that since no local power has been able to establish a hegemony, the region can only be administered by the intervention of external agencies.[9]

Recognition of enduring diversity also characterises many more liberal political positions. Cultural difference, of course, remains anthropology's key domain, and activists from the discipline are involved throughout the world in the protection or maintenance of indigenous life-ways (Campbell, 1995; Cowan, Dembour and Wilson forthcoming). Macedonia represents a case where state agencies, whether through fear of irredentism from neighbours or through concern with national purity, have sought to assimilate, expel or otherwise control those citizens who represent divergence from the national ideal. In an international climate increasingly infused by a multiculturalist ethos, where the rights of individuals to religious, linguistic and other cultural freedoms are cherished, Macedonia's internal heterogeneity has come to be perceived as a phenomenon that should be preserved. In practical terms, this has led to a situation in which local communities in Macedonia with a distinctive linguistic or religious heritage are labelled as 'minorities' (for example, by human rights NGOs) in a casually *a priori* manner. Such labelling stresses points of difference from majority culture, often without investigating, or with scant concern for, perceptions of similarity and difference within the community concerned. In this sense, multiculturalism and human rights discourses partially construct the minorities they purport merely to describe (see Cowan forthcoming).

The situation outlined above is intended to emphasise the paradoxical challenges that Macedonia poses to any who wish to maintain for the social sciences the capacity to move beyond mere description. Although often seen as a site on which the pernicious effects of virulent nationalism can be challenged head on, those challenges often appear to miss their mark, and leave unaltered, or even strengthened, the core premises on which nationalist thought depends. At their heart is a vision of analytically separable discrete pieces joined together, or bouncing off one another, each demonstrating internal homogeneity and impermeability. These pieces may be defined as nations or tribes, as ethnic groups or minorities; they may be aggressive or unruly, undeveloped or martyred; but even if one or a whole set appear to be banished, others take their place, apparently more firmly ensconced than ever.

Among more recent attempts to assail the reifications of Balkan multiplicity is a critical historiography which privileges the notion of a shared 'Balkan mentality' (Kitromilides 1996). Similar in spirit are accounts that emphasise the lability of categories as individuals and families moved from one group to another, one language to another, one identity to another, according to context, and across the span of a generation or a lifetime (Agelopoulos 1997; Brown 1998b and 1999; Cowan 1997a; Danforth 1995; Gounaris 1996; Karakasidou 1997; Vereni 1996 and this volume). They echo a shift in emphasis within anthropology of the last two decades, summed up powerfully in Eric Wolf's *Europe and the People without History* (1982). Wolf criticised approaches which envisaged cultures and societies as billiard balls in a global pool hall. Writing more recently, Michael Carrithers (1992) has suggested that in Wolf's work we can see the anthropological concept of culture recast. An idiom of museum-going, where the objects of attention are discrete and self-contained tableaux, has been replaced, he suggests, by a turn toward the connections within, and between, societies and their observers.

Carrithers ties this reflexive turn to a metaphor of film, an art form in which the juxtaposition of images is as important as – and some, after Eisenstein, would say *more* important than – the content of the images themselves. Without discounting the significance of institutions, artifacts, and beliefs, then, anthropologists are trying increasingly to foreground the dynamic relations between them, and to illuminate the multiple ways in which contingencies impact upon human society. If the chapters in this volume are linked, it is by a concern to understand Macedonia as a site not of groups in collision, but of processes under way, whose qualities inhere not so much in themselves as in the ways in which they are seen and presented.

A vital first step in this enterprise is to contextualise the history of Macedonia within a broader canvas, and to interrogate the importance of the sites from which Macedonia has been observed.

MINORITY QUESTIONS AND INTERNATIONAL ORDER

For most of the twentieth century, when the nation-state form became consolidated as the 'natural' political form and when mono-ethnic nations were the European ideal, Macedonian multiplicity was perceived as a problematic anomaly. In the aftermath of the First World War, when boundaries were definitively redrawn, Bulgaria was dramatically diminished, while Greece and Yugoslavia each acquired new territories, including portions of Macedonia. These territories contained populations who either did, or might potentially, identify with a so-called 'kin state' across their borders, including the 'Bulgarian minorities' in Greece and Serbia, the 'Greek minorities' in Bulgaria and Serbia and, in all three states, various Muslim minorities assumed to have sentimental ties to Turkey.[10]

Anxious about the dangers this situation posed to their still fragile new states, leaders undertook various policies. Most disruptively, people were literally moved across national borders, first through a voluntary and reciprocal emigration scheme between Bulgaria and Greece, organised by an international 'Mixed Commission' under League of Nations' supervision. This gave members of the respective minority communities – 'Greeks' in Bulgaria, and 'Bulgarians' in Greece – the option to adopt the citizenship of their 'kin state' (while shedding their previous citizenship). Later, in the aftermath of Greece's failed military assault on Turkey in 1922, the Lausanne Treaty of 1923 dictated a compulsory exchange. Making religion the primary criterion of nationality, the treaty compelled Muslim Greek nationals (by the treaty's logic, 'Turks') to 'return' to Turkey, while Orthodox Christians (hence, 'Greeks') in communities across Turkey were forced to abandon their homes for resettlement in Greece. Some 650,000 (out of 1.4 million) of these new Orthodox (and, not infrequently, Turkish-speaking) Greek citizens were sent to Greece's northern territories. The ensuing conflicts between these incomers, and the settled population, largely 'Bulgarian-speaking', over houses, property and rights to land exacerbated the flow of 'Bulgarian' refugees into Bulgaria (see Karakasidou 1997). Although the arrival of so many refugees, among them supporters of an autonomous Macedonia, was politically and economically destabilising for Bulgaria, both state bureaucrats and most Bulgarian citizens considered the refugees their national 'brethren' who they were morally obliged to assist.[11]

Apart from these radical uprootings, states pursued other strategies to defuse the potential use of linguistic or religious differences for irredentist purposes, and at the same time, to 'incorporate' these newly acquired populations into the existing 'national body'. Greece, like many nation-building states in Europe, employed both carrot and stick in this process. It used state institutions – schools, universities, the army, local government – to reorganise daily life and reorient social loyalties. It developed new academic disciplines like folklore and history to elaborate a national mythology of glorious ancient origins, defiant continuity through 'four centuries of slavery' under 'the Turks', and heroic vindication of enduring nationhood through the Greek revolution. Conveying these Hellenic visions through schoolbooks and public rituals, it enjoined the new Greek citizens to see their own past, as well as their present affiliations, in its terms. At the same time, it discouraged and in certain moments (for example, during the Metaxas era of 1936–41, and later during the military dictatorship of 1967–74) prohibited and punished cultural expressions which seemed to indicate 'non-Greek' affiliations (Carabott 1997; Cowan 1997a).

Yugoslavia followed similar strategies in the interwar period, declining to recognise the existence of a 'Bulgarian minority', and insisting on the 'Serbian' affiliation of this population. Tito's postwar reorganisation of the state into a federation of republics changed this official position, however. Macedonia was distinguished as one of the federal republics in 1944, while Macedonians were recognised as a constituent 'people'. Tito's new structure recognised separate 'peoples' and 'nationalities' residing throughout the various republics, and gave them certain rights on that basis. The relation between a 'people' and its territory was less rigid and less exclusivist than in other state models, yet a connection between, say, Croatia and Croatians was not denied. At the same time, the partisan legacy, and a socialist vision of the future which did not discriminate between national groups, were mobilised as the basis for the new Yugoslav slogan of 'brotherhood and unity'; and this provided the foundation of a reconfigured Yugoslav overarching identity.

The policies of these two states over this century to cope with Macedonian multiplicity – in most respects unexceptional in relation to other concurrent national projects within Europe – and the varied responses of the individuals and communities involved, resulted in a range of new subjectivities. National borders separated individuals who shared the same language. Members of the 'same' group became swept up into different national projects which reconfigured the nature, meanings and potency of pre-national identities and affiliations. The category 'Vlach', for instance, had a different valency in the northern Greek context from that in the Federal Republic of Macedonia; hence, the young 'Vlach' woman growing up on the Greek side of the border inhabited that category, and was marked by it, rather differently from her cousin in Krushevo. To account for this difference only in terms of two parallel nation-building processes is to oversimplify, however. Although national institutions were designed to produce a homogenous national citizenry, these processes were mediated by a huge number of local particularities and contingencies, including the active responses of those national subjects themselves. What resulted were numerous, often idiosyncratic, collective and individual 'accommodations' to the national standard. The emigration process was similarly transformative for those who left their home territories for another country, fleeing political persecution, postwar reprisals or economic hardship. The salience and significance of being 'Greek', 'Macedonian', 'Albanian', 'Bulgarian' was always redefined in diaspora, in relation to new neighbours, new state contexts and newly narrated memories.

The contingency, variability and historicity of these labels, as well as the role of individual agency in constructing selves through – or against the grain of – such labels, are rendered invisible in the international community's contemporary discourse about Balkan minorities. This discourse essentialises identities. In effect, minorities are treated as homogenous communities united by a common language, religion, or ethnic or national identity. Typically, minorities are named using national categories, and the sometimes odd equivalences this sets up – Albanians in Albania seen as 'the same' as Albanians in the Republic of Macedonia or in Kosovo or in Copenhagen; Macedonians in Greece seen as 'the same' as Macedonians in the republic or in Australia or in Bulgaria – are rarely queried. Equally, the wide spectrum of responses to the hegemonic national norm *within* such 'minority' groups in a single country, which may range from comfortable accommodation to outright resistance, receives little theoretical consideration. Yet in homeland and diaspora alike, differing orientations to a 'shared' identity are at the centre of intra-group political contestation.

While a more subtle analysis of the dynamics of identity and difference needs to pay attention to intra-group variation and contestation in particular locations, this does not imply that such processes can be analysed in isolation from larger frameworks. The Macedonian Human Rights movement, for example, which emerged in the mid-1980s and which lobbies in international fora on behalf of Greece's Macedonian minority, is but one example of a global proliferation of rights-based movements (see Association of Macedonians in Poland 1992; Cowan forthcoming; Cowan, Dembour and Wilson forthcoming; Danforth 1995; Gounaris 1997; Roudometof 1996). It is a phenomenon structured by global discourses of individualism and human rights, and by the social, political and economic relations between transnational networks of migrants, home communities, and national and international institutions. In a complex and reciprocally constitutive fashion, these movements both compel, and are a product of, the international community's increasing propensity to acknowledge the legitimacy of claims to group recognition and to rights based on them.

This particular movement was developed largely in diasporic contexts by immigrants from the Macedonian region now living in officially 'multicultural' states like Canada and Australia. Among them, 'Macedonianness' has been reconceptualised in terms of a multiculturalist model of the proper relations between a state and its 'cultures' (see for example, Bivell 1995). 'Macedonianness' is, moreover, viewed through the prism of their lived experience within New World settler societies, with their Anglo-Saxon legal traditions and their privileging of individual rights and freedoms as supreme and unassailable cultural goods. Given rather different legal and cultural traditions in Greece (Pollis 1993), such a perspective is undoubtedly alien to many that the Macedonian Human Rights movement claims as its constituency and on whose behalf it speaks. Yet the movement is not wholly a foreign import. It expresses, rather, the coincidence between a diasporic project, and a locally based mobilisation centred in one prefecture, that of Florina, in western Greek Macedonia. This mobilisation draws on, and intentionally reinforces, a recent intensification of 'ethnic' feeling in the local area, whose causes are analysed in Riki Van Boeschoten's paper. Similar cases of mobilisation around minority rights, though each with its distinctive features, abound in the region – Kosovar Albanians, Albanians in the Macedonian Republic, Macedonians in Bulgaria, to name just a few. Indeed, diaspora community involvement in minority politics in the homeland is the rule, rather than the exception – and follows a venerable tradition.

Recent developments within Europe have also been crucial in shaping the ways minority rights activists within Macedonia articulate claims and pursue political objectives. The vision of 'Europe' being negotiated within the framework of the European Union (EU) has opened space to challenge national sovereignty without making explicitly separatist claims. For instance, the notion of subsidiarity allows, in principle, groups or regions within nation-states to enjoy greater autonomy by virtue of direct ties with 'Brussels' and 'European' institutions. Additionally, the rise of minority rights to the top of the European political agenda post-1989, the proliferation of new regional agreements – particularly *vis-à-vis* post-socialist countries, including the Republic of Macedonia – both to promote and to monitor implementation of those rights (see Burgess 1996; Miall 1994), and an expanding NGO sector oriented to the post-1989 Balkans has made it expedient, even imperative, to use a language of human rights in the name of minorities (see Greek Helsinki Monitor and Minority Rights Group – Greece 1998). The institutionalisation of human rights at the global level strengthens the clientelistic relationship between minorities and supranational bodies. This relationship is also reinforced by the current widespread suspicion of states and sympathy toward subalterns among academics and the general public. While minorities still negotiate, or do battle, with states, in recent years minorities have been appealing increasingly to the international community to intervene. Ethnic and national minority politics in the region of Macedonia, thus, should not be seen as the re-emergence of ancient, suppressed but still pristine identities, rooted in the Macedonian soil. Rather, such politics need to be understood as a site where a transnational array of actors are renegotiating identities and making claims within a reconfigured global political context.

THE CHAPTERS

The politics of identity and difference *within* and *about* Macedonia thus span dispersed geographical locations and multiple institutional sites. Moreover, they are a multifaceted phenomenon, which can be approached in many different ways and in relation to varying analytical levels and processes: for example, individual identity formation, relations between groups within and across national boundaries, relations between a group and the state. Though sharing a disciplinary identity (all are anthropologists, apart from one historian), the contributors to this volume bring to their topics a diversity of perspective, writing style, authorial voice and analytical focus, as well as of spatial and temporal scale (ranging from a study which traces the transformations of identity in a small locality over the course of a century to another describing transnational encounters over the past decade). As a result, the volume comprises chapters which are, in any direct sense, incommensurable. In their diversity, they cannot pretend to enable closure on the topic of Macedonia, which is bound to remain contested for some time to come.

For all their differences, the chapters nonetheless share certain common themes. Insofar as Macedonia is a metaphor for internal multiplicity, plurality is an unsurprising preoccupation. Many chapters critically explore the ways this plurality has been depicted descriptively or analytically through a concept of ethnicity, and normatively through a vision or political project of multi-culturalism. Several focus on how individuals position themselves in relation to hegemonic discourses of ethnic and national difference – how they narrate a self in history and thus construct identifications. Finally, a number of the chapters highlight the transnational nature of struggles to define Macedonia and Macedonianness and the (albeit locally inflected) global discourses and international institutions through which those attempts are made.

Several chapters address the question: how useful is ethnicity as an analytical category in making sense of social and cultural phenomena in this region, whether in the past or in the present? They reveal the extent to which the term is a highly contested one, both as a theoretical notion, and as a label which ordinary people use to describe a certain sort of identity. Moreover, they show that it is not always and everywhere an equally salient rubric for organising individual lives, biographies and social relations. In the first of three chapters on the Florina region of northwest Greece, where activism around a non-Greek Macedonian identity and Macedonian human rights has centred, Riki Van Boeschoten, like most anthropologists nowadays, rejects a 'primordialist' approach to ethnicity. Rather, she asks: what are the conditions under which differences defined as 'ethnic' matter? Her question is not so much *what* is the ethnicity in question, but – in an echo of Dimen-Schein's (1975) classic query, 'When is an Ethnic Group?' – *when* and *why* it emerges. Ethnicity in the Western Macedonian region of Florina, she argues, and in contrast to the Central Macedonian community of Assiros recently studied by Karakasidou (1997), has long been 'the modality through which class is lived' (Hall *et al.*

1978: 394). The intensification of ethnic identities around Florina in the past decade or so, however, is a consequence of a complex interrelationship of developments at local, national and international levels.

Whereas Van Boeschoten presents a macro-level analysis of the Florina region, based on fieldwork since 1988 along with wide-ranging survey data, and suggests factors which make ethnicity salient *now*, Piero Vereni's chapter is in its micro-level focus methodologically of the opposite extreme. Vereni zooms in on a single Florina farmer whose mother tongue is Macedonian, exploring how Leonidas attempts to come to terms with the puzzles surrounding his national belonging through his reworking of history in a series of notebooks. Leonidas' strategy is to juxtapose Greater History, the history of the nation, with his own, Lesser History, the specific histories of his family and community. He constructs his own subjectivity not through already given categorical distinctions between ethnic groups, but through a dialogical, and dialectical, encounter between two renderings of history. Leonidas calls himself '*Ellinas Makedonas*' (Greek-Macedonian), but with a personally defined and distinctive sense to the term. Vereni's good fortune in getting access to this unusual treasure trove is amplified for readers by his own theoretical adventurousness in analysing it. He highlights Leonidas' intensely emotional struggle to create a coherent sense of self by using, but necessarily reinterpreting and thereby transforming, the official Greek national narrative.

A third chapter focusing on the Florina region is offered by the historian Iakovos Michailidis, one of a growing number of Greek scholars currently developing a critical challenge to the deeply nationalist mainstream of Greek historiography on Macedonia. Michailidis decries the triumphalism of that historiography and the ways it has refused to acknowledge the aspirations and experience of those on the losing side of various Macedonian struggles, from the original Ilinden uprising against the Ottomans in 1903, through to Slavo-Macedonian resistance in the Greek Civil War. Using conventional historical sources and techniques, he unveils a normally 'hidden' history of the region. He reveals the role of kinship in the continuity of the Macedonian struggle in its different historical incarnations, inferring the importance of narratives of heroism and loss within intimate family and community contexts in creating a commitment to a particular dream for Macedonia. Michailidis notes how the experience of defeat, as well as the rage of multiple refusals of recognition, left its trace in the nationalist narratives composed on behalf of the new republic by those historians originally from the Greek side of the border – from where, in an earlier era, they were forced to flee. He condemns this nationalism as much as he condemns its Greek counterpart, and ends with a call for historians to break the cycle of competitive histories and counter-histories, each wilfully blind to the experience of the other, and to develop greater intellectual independence from their own nation's myths.

The next two chapters, by Loring Danforth and Jonathan Schwartz, address the 'imagined community' (Anderson 1983) of Macedonia as constructed within the Macedonian diaspora. Even when formulated in the homeland, such imaginings are nurtured, reconfigured or thwarted by the specific conditions prevailing in the host countries. A complex interplay between imported dreams and current realities shapes the nature of ethnic or national identity formations at the individual and group level, and the intense links between homeland and diaspora communities. As Danforth's (1995) work shows, Macedonian diaspora communities (who disagree among themselves over what exactly the designation 'Macedonian' refers to) have assumed a vigorous moral and material role in the cultural and political movements of the Balkans. Indeed, these Macedonian networks exemplify the oft-pronounced 'transnational' nature of nationalism. Highly significant for contemporary reformulations of 'Macedonianness' is the fact that the major destinations of emigrants from Macedonia have been several 'New World' countries, which in the 1980s adopted multiculturalism as official state policy. They include, most notably, Australia and Canada, but such policies are being implemented to a lesser extent, as well, in northern European, especially Scandinavian, countries.

Linked with the previous three chapters in his focus on immigrant communities originating from Florina, and resonating with Piero Vereni's chapter in his concern for identity construction at an individual level, Danforth's chapter examines the opportunities created by Australia's multiculturalist policies in making a 'Macedonian' identity a newly viable option. Danforth shows how the Australian multiculturalist discourse has made it possible for emigrants from the Greek portion of Macedonia, who often see themselves as 'Greeks' but with a resentful awareness that they are viewed as somehow 'second class citizens', to abandon this identification and assume a new one as 'Macedonians'. Importantly, such transformations typically are not understood as a matter of choice by the individuals concerned. Rather, they are articulated in terms of a miraculous jump 'from blindness to insight' within a framework of spiritual revelation. They express the conviction that 'then, I believed I knew who I was, but now I *really* know!' In this sense, they resemble religious conversion. Danforth notes the ironies of multiculturalist policies, which are grounded in the same assumptions as nationalisms in that a 'cultural' or 'ethnic' identity is deemed as necessarily singular and mutually exclusive in any one person. He shows how this perpetuates arguments which, even when they involve a recast identity, appeal to birth, blood and kinship as that identity's foundation.

Jonathan Schwartz, an American anthropologist who lives and teaches in Copenhagen, has been involved for many years as both anthropologist and community activist with emigrant workers to Denmark from the Prespa lakes region in the Republic of Macedonia. Both the diaspora community and the homeland have been research sites, and this paper juxtaposes the two places, while also drawing on earlier work in the Macedonian diasporic centre of Toronto, asking questions about how and why relations across ethnic lines operate differently in each place. In Schwartz's experience in Copenhagen, a deterioration of conditions not in the homeland as such, but in the 'imagined

homeland' of Kosovo, led in the late 1990s to a breakdown of previously good
relations between the republic's Albanians and Macedonians. Meanwhile,
back in Prespa, those groups, along with their Turkish and Roma neighbours,
were striving to make sure that the war on their doorstep didn't destroy their
community. Schwartz's account, whilst sobering to starry-eyed enthusiasts
of diasporic hybridity, does suggest that in the homeland, cooperation across
ethnic lines still survives, even if it is much diminished in relation to the past.
Significantly, these current interchanges are rarely a consequence of multiculturalism embraced as a goal in itself; rather, they reflect mutual
interdependencies and the need for strategic cooperation in a harsh physical
and economic environment.

Keith Brown presents a different angle on relations between ethnic groups,
and between each of them and the state in the new republic. If some have
seen the Republic of Macedonia as vindication of one Slavic people's long
struggle for independent nationhood, that republic must also attend to its own
internal diversity if it is to survive. Brown's chapter offers an account of a shifting
politics of identity and difference within the republic across its first decade of
existence. In the early 1990s, architects of the Republic of Macedonia sought
to create a territorial state in which those who were not ethnic Macedonians
– such as Albanians, Roma, Turks, Vlachs, Serbs – would enjoy full citizen
status. They aimed to nurture new loyalties through promoting national
symbols that its multicultural citizenry could rally around. Selecting a symbol
from the ancient past which preceded the ethnic division of the present and
thus transcended it was, indeed, a brilliant unifying strategy. But in choosing
the Vergina 'sun' for its flag, the new government challenged Greek claims
to the heritage that the symbol encoded.

Since 1995, when a compromise concerning the flag was agreed, and
after which overt hostility between Greece and the Republic of Macedonia
subsided considerably, attention has returned to internal politics, especially
the issue of relations between the majority ethnic Macedonians and the large
ethnic Albanian community. Tensions over cultural and educational rights
for Albanian citizens of the republic, already manifest in the Yugoslav period,
have flared again. The war in Kosovo, too, has compelled many of them to
re-evaluate their commitment to the Macedonian republic's project. Tracing
the evolving pattern of confrontation between activists and government
forces, Brown identifies a shift toward 'parapolitics' in which actions carried
out for apparently other-than-political purposes nonetheless entail a challenge
to state legitimacy. For some in the Albanian community, these may be
tactics in a struggle for greater autonomy, or even separate statehood. Yet
for those Albanians who see themselves as having a long-term stake in the
republic, they may equally concern a challenge to ethnically exclusive
meanings of being Macedonian.

In the final chapter, Georgios Agelopoulos looks critically at the recent arrival
of a concept of multiculturalism in Greece, its reformulation in the Greek context
and the ways it influenced the representations of Salonica as a historically

multicultural city within its 1997 Cultural Capital of Europe (CCE) celebrations. Emphasising that the concept of multiculturalism bears the imprint of the consciousness of late modernity, he finds its application to late nineteenth- and early twentieth-century Salonica misleading. Agelopoulos is concerned to warn advocates of multiculturalism not to surrender to romantic visions of the past. More importantly, he insists that they – and we – think more seriously about what such coexistence could, and should, entail in the present. A painless celebration of gastronomic, sartorial and musical multiplicity is not enough. Multiculturalism must acknowledge the real needs of Others in our midst, both citizens and immigrants, whose economic, social and cultural marginalisation too frequently goes unremarked, or at least remains frustratingly unconnected with multiculturalism's wider vision.

TOWARD MORE INCLUSIVE FORMS OF BELONGING

Where so much of the writing about Macedonia (as about the Balkans generally) has privileged local ideas of narrow and exclusive belonging, this volume hopes to contribute to making more visible those initiatives that are attempting to build bridges between communities and to nurture more inclusive forms of belonging. The efforts of the Copenhagen-based Macedonian friendship society, *DAN-MAK* (however ill-fated) and the more informal but more successful cross-ethnic partnerships in the Prespa region, described by Schwartz, are by no means unique. Since the early part of the decade, many NGOs have been established in this region. Although some are devoted particularly to developing smoother relations between ethnically 'divided' communities, or to nurturing 'friendships' across national borders, others are tackling this issue indirectly. They are doing so by involving these groups in projects of common interest (for example, environmental issues, media reporting, women's issues) and letting the experience of cooperation emerge as a 'by product'. The project to provide piped water to villages in the region of Prilep, described by Schwartz in his chapter, is one example, and at the 1994 Forum Against Ethnic Violence (FAEV) 'Macedonia' conference, we heard the voices of several other activists describing analogous projects. Another noteworthy initiative, with which one of our authors is associated, is the Salonica-based Minority Groups Research Centre. This is an association of scholars and researchers that promotes 'the multidimensional study of minority groups, minority languages and every form of religious or cultural diversity at a general theoretical level, as well as with regard to specific minority groups in Greece and elsewhere' (MGRC brochure 1998).

Issues surrounding how the Macedonia of the future should be envisaged and the state's role in relation to diversity are especially urgent for scholars who identify themselves as Macedonians, in whatever sense – among whom we count two of our contributors. Such individuals have not always assumed the role of the 'sacred scholar' defending nationalist agendas (Karakasidou

1994), but sometimes of the critically engaged intellectual. Their verbal and textual interventions bear witness to a shared conviction that intellectuals have a responsibility to speak out, and their involvements have often bridged scholarship and activism. Importantly, though, their definitions of the present and past situation in Macedonia, their hopes for the future and their sense of the appropriate strategies to achieve them are not identical. Our metaphor of 'inflections', rather than evading politics and the taking up of 'a (single) position', facilitates an awareness of this kind of plurality of views among intellectuals from the region, who differ on the basis of many more than just national axes. It fosters, we hope, a respect for dialogue and the values of listening, as well as speaking out.

'Difference' may be a fact of life in Macedonia, but it is not just inherited – it is also produced. The kinds of difference that provoked quips of Macedonian 'fruit salads' at the turn of the last century are not precisely those we find there today. This in itself constitutes a refutation of sorts of the tired parade of adjectives of Balkan difference: 'age-old', 'enduring', 'essential'. Macedonia has been made, and can be remade. In any event, if Macedonia has to live with plurality, it is not immediately obvious what models best serve that end. There are no magic formulas. Danforth, Schwartz, Brown and Agelopoulos have all indicated ambiguities and contradictions in the theory and practice of 'multiculturalism', which Cowan and Brown in this introduction have suggested that the pursuit of 'human rights' is not always politically or ethically straightforward. This does not mean that such visions are not worth striving for, only that they must not be regarded as 'sacred cows', never to be questioned. For Macedonia to flourish, we need all the critical intelligence and good will that can be mustered. We think it unlikely that any single vision of Macedonia will ever be universally persuasive. We have already seen what happens when protagonists care only to promote their own. The recognition of a multiply inflected Macedonia may offer the best chance for the future.

INFLECTIONS

As hinted throughout, this volume is guided by a metaphor of its own, one that is novel for this context: 'inflections'. It draws on the resonances of the term in its multiple conceptual domains. From linguistics, it evokes the ways by which a single word is altered by the particularities of enunciation – tone, colour, voice, emotion – within particular contexts, enabling a rich variability in connotation and, ultimately, denotation. From its musical and theatrical usages, it highlights the performative aspects of specific utterances. Our use of the metaphor was initially inspired, though, by David Mamet's exploration of the craft of film-making (1991). Mamet employs a rather different, implicitly structuralist notion of inflection. For him, an image – 'pure' and 'meaningless' in itself – is inflected not through variations in enunciation, but by placing it, temporally and spatially, alongside other images. A story is created through this chain of inflected images.

All these senses of 'inflection' reject a notion of the signifier as singular and univocal. The first sense of 'inflection' takes the meaning of a word to inhere not in the word itself, but in its enunciation within particular performative contexts. 'Inflection' here can be linked to the epistemological metaphor of 'location', to the idea that what Macedonia *is* depends on where one looks and speaks from, while how it is *represented* also depends on who one is speaking to.

Yet a perusal of media images of the Macedonian conflict suggests that the question of location, and the 'view from somewhere' that it entails, is not merely social, political, disciplinary or theoretical. More prosaically, perspective can quite literally depend on where one stands. One familiar image of the conflict (an example of which, though produced originally in the Greek weekly *Makedoniki Zoi*, was reproduced as the first photograph in Danforth 1995: 31; see also the photograph on page 93, same volume), was a bird's eye view of the huge 14 February 1992 public demonstration in Thessaloniki, the Macedonian port city once coveted by all nationalist movements of the region (who knew it each by a different name: Salonica, Solun, Selanik). In this event, Greek citizens expressed support for their government's position that the name 'Macedonia', as historical heritage, belonged exclusively to the Greek nation. The photograph was taken from a high vantage point, probably from a top floor of a high-rise apartment building, and looks down on a vast sea of demonstrators carrying flags and banners. The crowds, the angularity of the flags, the banners announcing 'Macedonia is Orthodox and Greek' produce an impression of threat, though the faces are too small to ascertain any emotions.

Another photograph of the same event, one among dozens disseminated during the Macedonian conflict, whose origin we have been subsequently unable, alas, to trace, presented a totally different image. Taken at street-level, it showed an amiable cluster of children playing, while a relaxed concatenation of old and young people, a few desultorily holding Greek flags, stood around watching, with mild interest, something off to the left of the frame. It was a scene reminiscent of any ordinary public parade, completely lacking the intensity and implied passion of the first photograph. In the same vein, several Greeks who attended the Thessaloniki demonstration later confided to one of us (Cowan) – in separate and unrelated conversations – their sense of bewilderment at the chasm between their experience of that day and its perception by the outside world. They recalled the high spirits of students and bored office-workers released from duller duties, and stressed the event's festive, ludic atmosphere. People were celebrating Macedonia as 'Greek', they agreed, but not necessarily with aggression or hostility toward those across the border.

Such accounts are, of course, partial. More strident, aggressive protests were occurring elsewhere in the crowd and we know from countless examples across the world that a 'friendly patriotism' can easily slide into an ugly chauvinism. Yet these images and testimonies complicate the dominant media representations, exemplified by the first photograph. In so doing, they should give pause to anyone trying to understand the motivations for this popular manifestation and, more generally, of the dynamics of the Macedonian issue in Greek social and political life (see also Liakos 1993; Mouzelis 1994; Sutton 1997).

The Macedonian multiplicity which we, as editors, want to underline in this volume is not that which is conventionally emphasised: its proverbial, taken-for-granted and presumed-to-be-essential 'ethnic plurality', nor even the ways these supposedly clear-cut ethnic or national locations determine the multiple and irreconcilable 'truths' told about Macedonia. Rather, our interest is in the multiplicity of inflections through which Macedonia is rendered – as a lived or imagined place, a political project, a symbol, a fable about difference, a ground for identity, an academic object. We believe that in exploring these different inflections, our collective work can help to unsettle assumptions of fixed, stable ethnic and national categories, and the constituencies defined by them. It does so by pointing to diversities and tensions *within*; by showing categorisation and identification as dynamic, historically grounded and politically responsive processes; and by revealing their transnational dimensions. This deconstructive move, though, is politically useful only if followed by questions about power. Which agents and institutions have an interest in making an ethnic logic appear natural and inevitable? Through what discourses and practices is this pursued? Who benefits? Who loses? What processes set the parameters within which diversity, and commonality, can be imagined and constructed at this present moment in this part of the world? What can we learn from the cases examined here about the implications of 'recognising' – and 'not recognising' – difference at the political level? Each chapter offers for consideration one or more inflections of the complex, contested reality of Macedonia. Our overall intellectual object, indeed, is the contesting visions and versions themselves, the local and global forces that shape their articulation, and their points of overlap. As a totality, the volume also works, we hope, through Mamet's sense of inflection: each chapter is inflected by, and may be reanimated by or rethought in terms of, the other chapters with which it is juxtaposed.

ACKNOWLEDGMENTS

For helpful comments on an earlier version of this introduction, we would like to thank Georgios Agelopoulos, Loring Danforth, Sarah Green, Vaso Neofotistos, David Sutton, Riki Van Boeschoten and Richard Wilson. We would also like to thank Kostas Kazazis for his input. As should go without saying, the views expressed here are our own.

NOTES

1. We have decided not to provide a 'potted history' of the Macedonian struggle, but to focus on other issues. For a brief but clear summary, see the Introduction to Mackridge and Yannakakis (1997). Two English-language surveys of various struggles in turn-of-the-century Macedonia may also be consulted (Dakin 1966; Perry 1988), though the meanings of events in this period continue to be disputed. Several new treatments of the Macedonian Question, in both its historical and contemporary dimensions, have just been published as this book goes to press, and should prove useful (Pettifer 1999; Roudometof 2000; See also Gounaris *et al.* 1997; Roudometof 1996).

2. The self-designation of the new state is 'The Repubic of Macedonia'. However, as this book goes to press, its name remains disputed and under negotiation. The name by which it is officially recognised by the UN and other international organisations is 'The Former Yugoslav Republic of Macedonia'. A detailed, though flawed, account of events in the Republic between 1991 and 1995, based largely on daily news reports distributed via email, is provided by Shea (1997). Several more recent analyses, which document also the activities of NGOs in attempts to maintain peace, are provided by Ackermann (2000), Borden and Mehmeti (1998) and Petroska-Beshka (1996).

3. One of the more forceful statements of the temporal specificity of the name was made by Milcho Manchevski, the director of *Before the Rain*, when Greek lobbyists insisted that his film's country of origin be described at the Academy Awards as the Former Yugoslav Republic of Macedonia. He made the provocative suggestion that, if consistency were to be demanded, the United States should always be referred to as a former British colony (O'Steen 1995, in Brown 1998a).

4. The new government was based on a coalition between parties whose leaders and policies were identified as nationalist and extremist, as well as one party that campaigned on a platform of civil society. For more details, see Brown, this volume.

5. The Serbo-Croatian spelling of 'Kosovo' was standard usage until recently when, in the context of conflict between Serbs and Albanians in the region, the Albanian spelling of 'Kosova' began to appear in media reporting. We retain the (until recently) standard usage here, except for the self-designated term 'Kosova Liberation Army', but stress that this should not be taken to indicate any recommendation as to the future redrawing of political boundaries in the region.

6. The war was followed by the publication by different sides and agencies of claims and counterclaims regarding atrocities, and this has also prompted comparison, in particular, with the aftermath of fighting in Croatia and Bosnia. The titles clearly reveal the contrastive agendas. *Atrocités Grecques en Macédoine* (Miletich 1913) was followed by *The Crimes of Bulgaria in Macedonia* (Zaimis 1914). *Macedonia* (Georgevitch 1918) offers a coda, by detailing horrors inflicted on Serbs.

7. In this regard, debates over language are particularly significant, dealing as they do with a realm where different dimensions of human agency can be seen to be at work, while at the same time developments – mutations, impositions, accommodations – can be traced historically that are innocent of ideological intent, and reveal indisputable continuities.

8. Karakasidou (1997), while indisputably ground-breaking in relation to the Greek context, in this sense remains within the tradition of 'one at a time' accounts of nation-building set by earlier studies (for example, Handler 1988; Mosse 1985; Weber 1976; and subsequently Harp 1998). Danforth (1995), in contrast, innovatively deals with Greek and Macedonian nationalisms in tandem from the perspective of a third society, Australia. From neither account, though, do we get a clear sense of how Greek nation-building practices corresponded to those in neighbouring countries in the same eras, nor to the relation between this one state's internal policies in relation to cultural and linguistic difference and wider European discourses and practices concerning states, nations and minorities.

9.   An earnest and well thought-out variant of this view might be traced in Michael
     Ignatieff's work. He argues, in the case of Serbia and Croatia, that '... more than devel-
     opment, more than aid or emergency relief, more than peacekeepers, these societies
     need states, with professional armies under the command of trained leaders' (1998:
     160). He admits the apparent paradox of a liberal humanist calling for a strong state,
     but urges that the first imperative must be to address the fears of victimisation on all
     sides by creating some kind of honest broker.
10. These 'national' designations were not accepted by all state parties. Most controversy
     surrounded the designation 'Bulgarian minorities', which the Serbian state identified
     as 'Serbian' and the Greek state usually, though not always, as 'Slavic'. This posed
     major difficulties for the implementation of the minorities treaties (Cowan, work in
     progress in the League of Nations Archives, Geneva).
11. On the consequences of the various population exchanges for local Macedonian com-
     munities, see Agelopoulos 1997, and Karakasidou 1997; Hirschon's (1998 [1989])
     ground-breaking study of resettlement in Piraeus helps to delineate the larger picture
     within Greece. For a broader perspective on refugees in interwar Europe, see Skran 1995.

BIBLIOGRAPHY

Ackermann, Alice. 2000. *Preventing Violent Conflict in Macedonia.* Syracuse: Syracuse
    University Press.
Agelopoulos, Georgios. 1995. 'Perceptions, Construction and Definition of Greek National
    Identity in Late Nineteenth – Early Twentieth Century Macedonia'. *Balkan Studies* 36(2),
    247–63.
—— 1997. 'From Bulgarievo to Nea Krasia, from "Two Settlements" to "One Village":
    Community formation, collective identities and the role of the individual', in Peter
    Mackridge and Eleni Yannakakis (eds) *Ourselves and Others: The development of a Greek
    Macedonian cultural identity since 1912.* Oxford and New York: Berg.
Anderson, Benedict. 1983. *Imagined Communities: Reflections on the origin and spread of
    nationalism.* London: Verso.
Association of Macedonians in Poland. 1992. *What Europe Has Forgotten: The struggle of
    the Aegean Macedonians.* Five Dock, New South Wales: Politicon Publications.
Bivell, Victor (ed.). 1995. *Macedonian Agenda.* Five Dock, New South Wales: Politicon
    Publications.
Borden, Anthony and Ibrahim Mehmeti (eds). 1998. *Reporting Macedonia: The new accom-
    modation. A Cross-Community Reporting Project of the Institute for War and Peace Reporting
    and Search for Common Ground.* London: Institute for War and Peace Reporting.
Brown, K. S. 1995. 'Of Meanings and Memories: The national imagination in Macedonia'.
    Ph.D. dissertation for the Department of Anthropology, University of Chicago, Chicago.
    Ann Arbor, Michigan: UMI Microfilms.
—— 1998a. 'Macedonian Culture and its Audiences: An analysis of *Before the Rain*', in Felicia
    Hughes-Freeland (ed.) *Ritual, Performance, Media.* New York and London: Routledge.
—— 1998b. 'Whose Will Be Done? Nation and Generation in a Macedonian Family'. *Social
    Analysis* 42(1): 109–30.
—— 1999. 'Marginal Narratives and Shifty Natives: Ironic ethnography as anti-nation-
    alist discourse'. *Anthropology Today* 15(1), 13–16.
Burgess, Adam. 1996. 'National Minority Rights and the Civilizing of Eastern Europe'.
    Contention 5(2), 17–36.
Campbell, Alan Tormaid. 1995. *Getting to Know Wai Wai: An Amazonian Ethnography.*
    London and New York: Routledge.
Carabott, Philip. 1997. 'The Politics of Integration and Assimilation *vis-à-vis* the Slavo-
    Macedonian Minority of Inter-war Greece: From parliamentary inertia to Metaxist

repression', in Peter Mackridge and Eleni Yannakakis (eds) *Ourselves and Others: The development of a Greek Macedonian cultural identity since 1912.* Oxford and New York: Berg.

Carrithers, Michael. 1992. *Why Humans Have Cultures: Explaining anthropology and social diversity.* Oxford: Oxford University Press.

Chatterjee, Partha. 1986. *Nationalist Thought and the Colonial Word: A derivative discourse.* London: Zed Books.

Christides, Christ. 1949. *The Macedonian Camouflage in the Light of Facts and Figures.* Athens: Hellenic.

Cowan, Jane K. 1997a. 'Idioms of Belonging: Polyglot Articulations of Local Identity in a Greek Macedonian Town', in Peter Mackridge and Eleni Yannakakis (eds) *Ourselves and Others: The development of a Greek Macedonian cultural identity since 1912.* Oxford and New York: Berg.

—— 1997b. Review of Loring Danforth, *The Macedonian Conflict: Ethnic nationalism in a transnational world, Journal of Byzantine and Modern Greek Studies,* 21, 261–5.

—— forthcoming. 'Ambiguities of an Emancipatory Discourse: The making of a Macedonian minority in Greece', in Jane K.Cowan, Marie-Bénédicte Dembour and Richard A. Wilson (eds) *Culture and Rights: Anthropological perspectives.* Cambridge: Cambridge University Press.

Cowan, Jane K., Marie-Bénédicte Dembour and Richard A. Wilson (eds). forthcoming. *Culture and Rights: Anthropological perspectives.* Cambridge: Cambridge University Press.

Dakin, Douglas. 1966. *The Greek Struggle in Macedonia, 1897–1913.* Thessaloniki: Institute of Balkan Studies.

Danforth, Loring. 1995. *The Macedonian Conflict: Ethnic nationalism in a transnational world.* Princeton, New Jersey: Princeton University Press.

Dimen-Schein, Muriel. 1975. 'When is an Ethnic Group? Ecology and Class Structure in Northern Greece'. *Ethnography* 14, 83–97.

Friedman, Victor. 1975. 'Macedonian Language and Nationalism during the Nineteenth and Early Twentieth Centuries'. *Balkanistica* 2, 83–98.

Fuss, Diana. 1989. *Essentially Speaking: Feminism, nature and difference.* London: Routledge.

Georgevitch, T. R. (Dordevic, Tikhomir R.). 1918. *Macedonia.* London: G. Allen & Unwin Ltd.

Gounaris, Basil. 1996. 'Social Cleavages and National "Awakening" in Ottoman Macedonia', *East European Quarterly* 29(4), 409–26.

Gounaris, Vasilis. 1997. 'Anakyklondas tis Paradoseis: Ethnotikes Taftotities kai Meionotika Dikaiomata sti Makedonia', in Vasilis K. Gounaris, Iakovos D. Michailidis and Georgios V. Agelopoulos (eds) *Taftotites sti Makedonia.* Athens: Papazisis.

Gounaris, Vasilis K., Iakovos D. Mihailidis and Georgios V. Agelopoulos (eds). 1997. *Taftotites sti Makedonia.* Athens: Papazisis.

Gow, James. 1994. *Triumph of the Lack of Will: International diplomacy and the Yugoslav war.* London: C. Hurst and Co.

Greek Helsinki Monitor and Minority Rights Group – Greece. 1998. *Greece Against its Macedonian Minority: The 'Rainbow' trial.* Athens: ETEPE.

Hall, Stuart, Critcher, Chas, Jefferson, Tony Clarke, John and Brian Roberts (eds). 1978. *Policing the Crisis: Mugging, the state, and law and order.* London: Macmillan.

Handler, Richard. 1988. *Nationalism and the Politics of Culture in Quebec.* Madison: University of Wisconsin Press.

Harp, Stephen L. 1998. *Learning to Be Loyal: Primary schooling as nation building in Alsace and Lorraine, 1850–1940.* Dekalb: Northern Illinois University Press.

Herzfeld, Michael. 1997. *Cultural Intimacy: Social poetics in the nation-state.* New York and London: Routledge.

Hirschon, Renee. 1998 [1989]. *Heirs of the Greek Catastrophe: The social life of Asia Minor refugees in Piraeus.* Oxford and New York: Berghahn.

Ignatieff, Michael. 1998. *The Warrior's Honor: Ethnic war and the modern conscience.* London: Chatto & Windus.

Kaplan, Robert D. 1993. *Balkan Ghosts: A journey through history*. New York: St. Martin's Press.

Karakasidou, Anastasia. 1993. 'Politicizing Culture: Negating ethnic identity in Greek Macedonia'. *Journal of Modern Greek Studies* 11(1),: 1–28.

—— 1994. 'Sacred Scholars, Profane Advocates: Intellectuals molding national consciousness in Greece'. *Identities* 1(1), 35–62.

—— 1997. *Fields of Wheat, Hills of Blood: Passages to nationhood in Greek Macedonia, 1870–1990*. Chicago: University of Chicago Press.

Kennan, George. F. (ed.). 1993 [1914]. *The Other Balkan War: A Carnegie Endowment inquiry in retrospect with a new introduction and reflections on the present conflict*. Washington, DC: Carnegie Endowment for International Peace.

Kitromilides, Paschalis. 1989. '"Imagined Communities" and the Origins of the National Question in the Balkans'. *European History Quarterly* 19(2), 149–92.

—— 1996. 'Balkan Mentality: History, legend, imagination. *Nations and Nationalism* 2(2), 163–91.

Kofos, Evangelos. 1964. *Nationalism and Communism in Macedonia*. Thessaloniki: Institute for Balkan Studies.

Liakos, Andonis. 1993. 'Valkaniki Krisi kai Ethnikismos', in A. Liakos, A. Elefantis, A. Manitakis and D. Papadimitropoulos (eds). *O Ianos tou Ethnikismou kai I Elliniki Valkaniki Politiki*. Athens: Politis.

Lunt, Horace. 1984. 'Some Sociolinguistic Aspects of Macedonian and Bulgarian', in Benjamin Stolz, I.R. Titunik and Lubomir Dolezel (eds) *Language and Literary Theory*. Ann Arbor: Michigan Slavic Publications. pp. 83–132.

Mackridge, Peter and Eleni Yannakakis (eds). 1997. *Ourselves and Others: The development of a Greek Macedonian cultural identity since 1912*. New York and Oxford: Berg.

Mamet, David. 1991. *On Directing Film*. New York: Viking.

Martis, Nikolaos. 1983. *The Falsification of Macedonian History*. Athens: 'Graphic Arts' of Athanassiades Bros.

McNeil, J.R. 1992. *The Mountains of the Mediterranean World: An environmental history*. Cambridge: Cambridge University Press.

Miall, Hugh (ed.). 1994. *Minority Rights in Europe: The scope for a transnational regime*. London: Pinter Publishers.

Miletich, Liubomir. 1913. *Atrocités Grecques en Macédoine*. Sophia: Imprimerie de l'État.

Morgenthau, Hans. 1957. 'The Paradoxes of Nationalism'. *The Yale Review* 46(4), 481–96.

Mosse, George. 1985. *Nationalism and Sexuality: Respectability and abnormal sexuality in modern Europe*. New York: Howard Fertig.

Mouzelis, Nikos. 1994. *O Ethnikismos stin Isteri Anaptixi*. Athens: Themelio.

National Technical University of Athens. 1993. *On Scientific Truth about Macedonia*. Athens, Greece: National Technical University.

O'Steen, Kathleen. 1995. 'Macedonia flap hits Academy'. *Daily Variety*, 27 March, 1.

Perry, Duncan. 1988. *The Politics of Terror: The Macedonian revolutionary movements, 1893–1903*. Durham: Duke University Press.

Petroska-Beshka, Violeta. 1996. 'NGOs, Early Warning, and Preventive Action: Macedonia', in Robert I. Rotberg (ed.) *Vigilance and Vengeance: NGOs preventing ethnic conflict in divided societies*. Washington DC: Brookings Institute/World Peace Foundation.

Pettifer, James (ed.). 1999. *The New Macedonian Question*. Houndsmill, Basingstoke and London: Macmillan.

Pollis, Adamantia. 1993. 'Eastern Orthodoxy and Human Rights'. *Human Rights Quarterly* 15(2), 339–56.

Poulton, Hugh. 1995. *Who are the Macedonians?* Bloomington and Indianapolis: Indiana University Press.

Rosaldo, Renato. 1989. *Culture and Truth: The remaking of social analysis*. Boston: Beacon.

Rossos, Andrew. 1994. 'The British Foreign Office and Macedonian National Identity, 1918–1941'. *Slavic Review* 53, 369–94.

Roudometof, Victor. 1996. 'Nationalism and Identity Politics in the Balkans: Greece and the Macedonian Question'. *Journal of Modern Greek Studies* 14(2): 35–52.

Roudometof, Victor (ed). 2000. *The Macedonian Question: Culture, Historiography, Politics*. Boulder: East European Monographs.

Schwartz, Jonathan M. 1996. *Pieces of Mosaic: An essay on the making of Makedonija*. Aarhus: Intervention Press.

Shea, John. 1997. *Macedonia and Greece: The struggle to define a new Balkan nation*. Jefferson NC: McFarland.

Skran, Claudena. 1995. *Refugees in Inter-War Europe: The Emergence of a Regime*. Oxford: Clarendon Press.

Sorabji, Cornelia. 1993. 'Ethnic War in Bosnia?'. *Radical Philosophy* 63, 33–5.

Sutton, David. 1997. 'Local Names, Foreign Claims: Family inheritance and national heritage on a Greek island'. *American Ethnologist* 24(2), 415–37.

Todorova, Maria. 1997. *Imagining the Balkans*. New York and Oxford: Oxford University Press.

Vereni, Piero. 1996. 'Boundaries, Frontiers, Persons, Individuals: Questioning 'Identity' at National Borders'. *Europaea* 2(1), 77–89.

Vermeulen, Hans. 1984. 'Greek Cultural Dominance among the Orthodox Population of Macedonia during the Last Period of Ottoman Rule', in A. Blok and H. Driesser (eds) *Cultural Dominance in the Mediterranean Area*. Nijmegen: Katholieke Universiteit. pp. 225–55.

Weber, Eugen. 1976. *Peasants into Frenchmen: The modernization of rural France, 1870–1914*. Stanford: Stanford University Press.

West, Rebecca. 1941. *Black Lamb and Grey Falcon*. New York: Viking.

Wilkinson, H.R. 1951. *Maps and Politics: A review of the ethnographic cartography of Macedonia*. Liverpool: University Press of Liverpool.

Wolf, Eric. 1982. *Europe and the People without History*. Berkeley: University of California Press.

Woodward, Susan L. 1995. *Balkan Tragedy: Chaos and dissolution after the Cold War*. Washington DC: Brookings Institute.

Zaimis, Theodore. 1914. *The Crimes of Bulgaria in Macedonia, an authentic document based on facts and records, issued by the universities of Athens in the interest of truth and transmitted to the universities of the world*. Washington DC (Reprinted from the original Greek).

1 WHEN DIFFERENCE MATTERS: SOCIOPOLITICAL DIMENSIONS OF ETHNICITY IN THE DISTRICT OF FLORINA

Riki Van Boeschoten

A perceptive traveller heading north from Kozani to the border area of Florina will receive a number of signals indicating that he has crossed an invisible yet omnipresent boundary. Touring the villages, he may notice that apart from Greek, several other languages and dialects are used: Macedonian, Vlach, 'Arvanitika', the Pontic dialect and Rom. At village festivals in Slav-speaking villages, he may be surprised that none of the music is accompanied by song. At some weddings, he might perceive a muted tension or even open conflict between guests of different cultural backgrounds about the music performed by the orchestra. In some mixed villages, he might remark that the different ethnic groups live in separate neighbourhoods. After a more prolonged visit to the area, he would perceive this as a society highly stratified along ethnic lines. Local residents, all groups included, speak of a society divided into *ratses*.[1] Though the various ethnic groups live together, often even on friendly terms in spite of past conflicts, they perceive each other as 'different'.

This is also reflected in the pattern of marriage strategies. While no detailed study of marriage patterns in this area exists, in 1993 most of my respondents described ethnic mixing through marriage as a development of the last two decades. The discussion of this issue at village level is often accompanied by comments that point to a high degree of ethnic stratification. For example, informants spice their conversation with vivid ethnic stereotypes (Vlachs are cunning/intelligent and repress their women, refugees[2] are lazy/enterprising, Slav-speakers are sluggish/faithful, but their women are hard working, etc.). In other words, it does not take long to discover that people are actively engaged in maintaining ethnic boundaries and that a considerable amount of ethnic tension surrounds the process, especially between the Slav-speaking and the refugee groups.

Needless to say, in such a mixed but also highly institutionalised society, the opportunities for interethnic interaction are equally important: in the market place, in commercial activities, at village festivals and weddings and especially in the framework of national institutions (education, political parties, media). But even there ethnic divisions make their appearance and reinforce networks of intra-ethnic interaction: schoolchildren may be divided into 'Bulgarians' and 'Turkish-born' (that is, Greek refugees) and thus be inclined to stick to 'their own kind'. Ethnic divisions even appear within the local branches of national political parties, conflicts within the party often focusing on the interests of specific ethnic groups instead of on broader issues. Significantly, many of the leading Macedonian activists, now linked to the small 'Rainbow' party, had previously been active members of political parties of the broad left. In the early 1980s, they came into conflict with their respective parties over issues linked to their ethnic group (for example, over the use of the Macedonian language or the return of political refugees from eastern Europe). Likewise, during elections the ethnic origin of local candidates is duly taken into account, often seeming more important than the political programme of the party they run for. This process of 'ethnification' has been enhanced during the last few years and appears to be one of the 'unintended consequences' at the local level of the national media campaign around the 'Macedonian Issue'.

The question I wish to explore is why difference seems to matter in the Florina region and why it matters now. Why are ethnic boundaries not only maintained, but even strengthened, instead of being blurred in the process of globalisation? More specifically, how can we explain the prominent role of the ethnic factor in present-day social and political relations? During the first decade after the return to democracy in 1974, ethnic distinctions moved to the background, the rate of intermarriage was increasing and local debate focused more on national party politics. Why is it, then, that towards the end of the 1980s people who reached adulthood as Greek citizens and supporters of national parties 'discovered' their ethnic origin and started to interpret socio-economic problems of their area along ethnic lines?

APPROACHES

Since the publication of Fredrik Barth's seminal work, we have learned to see ethnicity as 'a form of social organization that results from the interaction of group and environment' (1969: 15), and not as the 'cultural stuff' it encloses. This approach emphasises the situations which 'control the dynamics of identity formation through which a group both chooses its own identity and, at the same time, has it imposed by the outside' (Morin 1982: 21). This implies that ethnicity can expand and contract according to the circumstances. In fact, ethnicity has no sense without social exchange, without the existence of 'the other'.

Yet, mere interaction with the other does not explain why difference matters, why it is perceived as socially relevant. An analysis at this level can show *how* boundaries are maintained but not *why* this happens. One way to explore this question is to look for the material bases of ethnicity, for example, by examining the differentiated access to wealth and power, or the relation between class and ethnicity. This is the so-called 'instrumentalist' approach, largely inspired by Max Weber. In this view, ethnic groups are seen as interest groups and their members as rational human actors, mobilised in reaction to their disadvantaged position in the social structure (Cohen 1974; Worseley 1984; Hechter 1975, 1978). Of course, class and ethnicity never exactly mirror each other. Explanations that simply reduce ethnicity to some aspect of the social structure, for example, class or colonial power, may be misleading, if only because they push under the carpet the obvious fact that ethnicity often cuts across such divisions.

The attempts to integrate a theory of ethnicity with class analysis seem more promising.[3] In order to achieve this, while avoiding any form of reductionism, we have to acknowledge that neither class nor ethnicity is a monovalent entity standing by itself. If social classes are not simple economic unities but are 'simultaneously economically, politically and ideologically shaped' (Wolpe, 1986: 122), in the same way ethnicity is not simply an ideological or cultural construct: it is affected by the same factors that favour class formation. If we understand that the relations of production are nothing but the framework in which both class and ethnicity are situated, it becomes easier to understand how, to paraphrase Stuart Hall *et al.*, ethnicity can become 'the modality in which class is lived' (1978: 394). At the level of subjectivity, this means that the same individual can have multiple identities, where the poles of reference can be class, ethnicity, religion, gender, community, regional origin or political affiliation. This image allows us to formulate the problem in slightly different terms: under what circumstances does ethnicity become the core of these identity feelings? And if it does, how does it relate to the other poles of reference?

Along similar lines, Michael Hechter has used the concept of a 'cultural division of labour' to examine the relative salience of class and ethnicity in complex industrialised societies. This occurs in stratified social systems, when culturally marked groups (in the event, ethnic groups) are unequally distributed over social classes and occupations (1978). An earlier version of this chapter was largely based on this concept of a cultural division of labour and I still believe that it offers important insights into the societal cleavages that divide the district of Florina along ethnic lines. Its explanatory force will be revealed, in fact, by a comparison of the Florina region with the township of Assiros in central Macedonia, where class formation has superseded ethnicity and Greek identity has taken the place of former ethnic allegiances.

However, the cultural division of labour model cannot explain everything and Hechter (1980) later recognised some of the flaws of his earlier analyses. For example, it does not fully take into account the fact that the cultural division of labour does not always affect all members of a particular ethnic group in the same way and consequently ignores intra-ethnic divisions. This has, of course, important implications for the dynamics of political mobilisation along ethnic lines. Secondly, the rational choice paradigm, on which Hechter's work is based, ignores the tension between choice and constraint, as well as the more subtle mechanisms by which identities are often negotiated on a daily basis. It seems important to see to what extent such hierarchical stratification systems may be the outcome of power relations with the national centre, and how people make sense of it in the light of present and past developments.

Finally, we should take into account the temporal factor. If we accept that the cultural division of labour is a stratification system which is developed at some point of history and may continue for decades, then why is ethnicity a more salient feature of group formation at certain times than at others? Or, to return to my initial question: why does difference seem to matter much more now than in the 1970s? In other words, it is necessary to integrate the material parameters of ethnicity and class into the global context in which identities are shaped. This means that the 'cultural stuff' evacuated by Barth in his earlier work has to be reintegrated differently (Barth 1994; Verdery 1994).

Along these lines, I will examine ethnic relations in the district of Florina, focusing on three aspects that seem to determine the social relevance of difference:

- access to resources
- state policies
- the impact of international developments since 1989.

The analysis is hampered by the lack of any in-depth studies on this area and therefore my remarks are largely based on observations made during relatively short periods of fieldwork in the region since 1988. Although new archival research, especially on the interwar period, has offered important insights compared to the complete blank I faced when I first visited this region, there are still too many gaps in our knowledge to draw a complete picture. My intent is therefore to outline an approach rather than to offer a fully elaborated analysis.

CULTURAL DIVISION OF LABOUR

The cultural division of labour is a topic of daily conversation at village level and forms part of the perceived boundaries between ethnic groups. It is not easy to determine whether these perceptions refer to a notion of status group in a Weberian sense or to measurable differences in the access to economic or cultural resources. Since 1951, official statistics do not recognise ethnic or linguistic groups as a parameter and therefore the position of each group in the socio-economic structure is rendered invisible. Although much more research is needed to obtain a full picture, the approximate data I gathered in a survey carried out in September 1993 (Van Boeschoten 1993) restored some visibility to what many local residents saw as a 'fact of life'. I, along with fellow anthropologist Helleen Van der Minne, visited more than half of the district's villages[4] and obtained our information mainly from local author-ities.[5] We used a questionnaire with detailed questions on demographic issues, the local economy, employment, education, cultural associations, the ethnic composition, the history of the village and the use of minority languages.

From this data we derived a picture of the ethnic composition of the district's rural area (Table 1.1). The town of Florina, not included in the table, has a mixed population of approximately 15,000 inhabitants; its only 'visible' group is the Gypsy community of about 3,000, settled in a neighbourhood at the town's outskirts.

Table 1.1 Ethnic composition of the rural population of Florina

	Number of Villages	Inhabitants	%	Total Ethnic groups	%
Slav speakers	43	15,228	42	23,189	64
Arvanites	3	2,114	6	2,213	6
Vlachs	6	789	2	1,386	4
Refugees	13	5,554	15	9,424	26
Mixed	29	12,557	35	-	-
TOTAL	94	36,212	100	36,212	100

Sources: 1981 census for the number of inhabitants. Information collected during the 1993 survey for the distribution of ethnic groups (see also note 4).

The survey revealed an important correlation between social and ethnic cleavages, and a clear pattern of social stratification along ethnic lines. At the bottom of this hierarchy were the Gypsies and the Slav-speakers, whereas the refugees were at the top.

The Gypsies were divided into three groups. The 'Tsingani' belong to the most prosperous group: they own trucks and sell chairs and vegetables all over northern Greece. The 'Yioufti' are musicians, whereas the 'Rom', the poorest group, work as a seasonal labour force in agriculture or sell scrap metal. Formerly nomads, today most Gypsies live in Florina town.

The Slav-speakers were predominantly engaged in small-scale agriculture and animal husbandry. On average, Slav-speakers owned less land and had higher numbers of unemployed and landless peasants than the other ethnic groups.[6] They were less well educated and, when employed outside agriculture, tended to work as unskilled labourers. The number of employees and civil servants was much lower than that of the refugees and Arvanites. Slav villages also showed the highest rates of emigration and the lowest numbers of town-dwellers.

The refugee group had fared the best. Better educated, they had greater access to state employment and better paid jobs, thus being less affected by unemployment. Refugee villages showed a low emigration rate, but high rates of urbanisation. Among the urbanised refugees many were state employees or practised liberal professions, whereas most urbanised Slav-speakers were employed in lower status jobs (as workers, in petty commerce and as primary school teachers). The refugees were also active in commerce and entrepreneurial activities and most of the industries in the Florina district are owned by members of this group.

The three Arvanite villages were less affected by this structure, as they were specialised in the building industry, with more than half of the active population working in it. However, due to the general crisis in the building sector, in 1993 these villages had high levels of unemployment, although lower than in the Slav villages. At present, this sector has recovered, but native Arvanites face increased competition from illegal immigrants from Albania. Their level of education was generally high and they had good access to state employment, but not to the same extent as the refugee group.

As for the Vlachs, we should distinguish between the 'Old Vlach' inhabitants of the villages of Pisoderi and Nimfeo, and the 'new Vlach' settlers. The 'Old Vlach' villages are now 'dead': most of their inhabitants have moved to Greek towns and only elderly people still live there, mainly shepherds and woodcutters. During the summer months, many urbanised Vlachs return to their native village on holiday. In general, these urbanised Vlachs are relatively prosperous: many have enjoyed higher education and practise liberal professions. The 'new Vlachs' came to the area in the period 1952–8 as part of a government resettlement programme. They were mainly settled in villages around Lake Prespa, a border region devastated by the Civil War (1946–9), most of its original inhabitants having fled across the border. The Greek government had confiscated their properties, some of which were distributed to the Vlach newcomers. In their area of origin (Epirus, especially Preveza and Igoumenitsa) most of these settlers had been nomadic shepherds, locally known as *skinites* (tent-dwellers). The people we spoke to in 1993 identified as Greeks of Vlach origin and, politically, they were supporters of the right. In economic and cultural terms, the 'new Vlachs' were at the lower scale of the social hierarchy: their landed property was small, most renting additional land at high prices. Their educational level was also low and very few continued their studies after secondary education. Yet until recently their income was well above that of many Slav villages: this was due to various factors, among which were the good prices for the area's main product (the famous Prespa beans), the supplementary income from employment in the fur trade in nearby Kastoria and from tourism and commerce. At present, all these sectors are in crisis due to increased competition from abroad, the Yugoslav conflict and the long-term effects of the economic blockade against the Republic of Macedonia.

The societal cleavages described above should be seen in the context of the overall economy of the district. The Florina region is one of the most isolated and less developed areas of Greece, with low levels of industrialisation and a high unemployment rate. The economic isolation of the area also has an important political dimension. Due to the centralised power structure of the

Greek state and the disproportionate participation of southern Greeks in the process of decision-making, most important decisions concerning the district are taken in Athens. Moreover, until very recently, high-level civil servants were largely recruited from other parts of the country. This hydrocephalous structure has caused resentment against the 'State of Athens' throughout northern Greece since the interwar period. In the Florina region, such feelings exist among all ethnic groups. Yet, because of the perceived boundaries dividing them, this resentment does not seem to function as a unifying factor. Rather, it is voiced in each group separately.

CLASS AND ETHNICITY

What is the correlation between class and ethnicity in this cultural division of labour? Could we say that ethnicity has become the 'modality in which class is lived' as Stuart Hall described race relations in South Africa? A number of anthropological studies have indeed shown a close relation between the two types of identity in societies where a hierarchical social stratification is largely patterned along ethnic lines. The highest correlation between class and ethnicity can be found in those sectors of society where the two overlap, for example, when factory owners belong to one ethnic group and the workers to another. Ethnicity can also cut across class or class can be segmented by ethnicity: for example, when an ethnic division of labour occurs within one and the same class (Worseley 1984: 240).

In the district of Florina, the relation between class and ethnicity is not as clear-cut as it is, for example, in South Africa. The notion of class may even seem problematic as this area, where the majority of the active population, made up of peasant smallholders, is distinguished by its low degree of 'classness'.[7] Since the sweeping land reform of the interwar period, large landowners or pastoralists have ceased to exist and dependent labour relations are not a structural phenomenon in the agricultural sector. And yet the tension between refugees and Slav-speakers was and is mainly centred on the access to the ownership of land. Obviously, this is a clear example where ethnicity cuts across class: all ethnic groups count peasants among their ranks, although Slav-speakers form the majority of the peasant class and seem more attached to the land. The difference in the average size of properties revealed by our survey may be of crucial importance to individual families and thus nurture feelings of 'groupness'. Yet, it is not a class distinction. What seems to be more important, in terms of the social relevance of difference, is the different trajectory of both groups in history. When the refugees were first established in the area, they were in a position similar to their Slav-speaking neighbours, or worse. The second and third refugee generation are clearly better off, as is shown by the high numbers of educated, urbanised and state-employed among their ranks. Although the reasons for this development are far from clear, I will discuss below some aspects of the process. For the moment, we will retain the importance of social mobility in the construction of boundaries.

In the small industrial sector, the relation between class and ethnicity is more clear-cut, where the two categories tend to overlap and class can be understood, in the Marxist sense, in relation to the means of production. As stated earlier, most of the small industries in the area belong to refugees, whereas the majority of the unskilled labourers are Slav-speakers. A matter that needs further research is whether the working class of these factories is segmented along ethnic lines. As the study of labour markets in Northern Greece by Vaiou and Chatzimichalis (1997) has shown, most companies employ a small number of privileged skilled labourers on a permanent basis, supplementing their labour force with unskilled labourers on temporary contracts, according to demand. This second group is usually recruited from unprivileged categories, such as women, members of ethnic minorities and immigrants. Unfortunately, this study did not include the area of Florina; it would have been interesting to see if ethnic networks in the industrial sector are at work for the recruitment of the permanent core of skilled labourers. Both the high correlation between class and ethnicity in this sector and the possible segmentation of the working class along ethnic lines are factors that would enhance the social relevance of ethnicity.

In the field of employment, the main bone of contention seems to be access to state employment, the main route to upward social mobility in Greece. Our survey revealed an important difference between ethnic groups, the refugees being the most favoured and Slav-speakers the less favoured group. Most of our respondents stressed that the latter gained access to state employment only in the 1980s and that the number of civil servants of Slav origin has been increasing only very recently. More detailed questions to our key informants also revealed a segmented access to state employment: Slav-speakers were better represented in lower status jobs, such as schoolmasters and field guards, whereas the most coveted job, employment at the electricity plant DEI, seemed to be more accessible to the refugee group.

Obviously, this matter is directly linked to the relationship between ethnic groups and the state. More information is needed to determine whether past state policies deliberately aimed at excluding the Slav-speaking group and, if so, on what grounds. Independently of its causes, however, the observed differential access to state employment along ethnic lines seems in itself a plausible explanation of why difference seems to matter. At the present stage of emancipation of young Slav-speakers from the peasant class to which they traditionally belonged, it seems socially even more relevant than access to landed property. Once again, concerns around upward social mobility are at the core of present tensions.

From the arguments developed above we could say that, to a certain extent, ethnicity has indeed become the modality in which class is lived, if we understand class not in a narrow sense as a relation to the means of production, but in a broader Weberian sense as the typical life chances of a social group (1980: 177). To this we should add two fundamental components introduced by Weber: the belief in a common political fate[8] and the concept of (ethnic, status group or simply social) 'honour', that is, 'the positive or negative social estimation of honour [which determines] every typical component of the life of men'.[9] These three parameters (typical life chances, common political fate and social honour) seem to play an important role in what I earlier called a sense of 'groupness'. Yet, they are not only determined by social interaction on the local scene, neither do they lead automatically to ethnicity or ethnic tension. They are linked to the process of nation-building and the policies developed by the state and its agents towards the politically and culturally 'other'. The state is not a neutral framework in which relations-in-interaction develop, but an active third party.

ETHNICITY AND STATE POLICIES

Anthropologists are paying increasing attention to the kind of state-making within which ethnic identities take shape (Verdery 1994). It is now commonly accepted that all nation-states were focused on the task of forming 'imagined communities' to assure national cohesion and overcome social, linguistic, cultural and religious cleavages, and thus to form homogeneity out of heterogeneity. The integration of Macedonia into the Greek nation-state in 1913 was the end of a long process, marking the most difficult phase of Greek nation-building, as this was the area of greatest cultural diversity. In a period of great social and political upheaval, aggravated by the influx of 1.5 million refugees from Asia Minor, the Greek authorities were under great pressure to adjust to the multiple problems involved. After a short intermezzo in the mid-1920s, when they tried to follow international standards in the field of minority rights (Carabott 1997), they opted for a policy of excluding culturally alien groups, rather than including them into an all-embracing notion of citizenship. Those who failed to conform to the prototype of the 'imagined community' were faced with the choice either to assimilate or to stick to their 'other' identity. In this context, the relations between the state and its cultural minorities, especially the Slav-speaking group, were characterised by mutual distrust.[10] In this sense, I would tend to agree with Katherine Verdery: ethnic identities develop from national identities and not the other way around, because the homogenising efforts of nation-building enhance the visibility of the non-conforming other (Verdery 1994: 47). Whether they assimilated or not, the alien 'others' faced the ethnic stigma attached to their group. Their past and present attitudes can be largely explained as a reaction to this stigma. This is the other face of the 'ethnic honour' noted by Weber.

Against this background, we can return to the socio-economic issues mentioned in the previous section and examine the role of the state, as a third actor, in the tension between refugees and Slav-speakers. The present animosity is nurtured by the memories of violent clashes, which took place in the 1920s between the indigenous population and the new settlers, over the distribution of former Muslim properties. Before the arrival of the refugees,

Slav-speaking peasants had formed the main labour force on the large Turkish estates on the plains or lived as smallholders in the free mountain villages. Since the end of the nineteenth-century, many had bought up Muslim property, under informal sale contracts, with money sent from abroad by family members. After the arrival of the refugees, however, the Greek state refused to recognise these contracts. In several instances, local state officials were unfair to Slav-speaking peasants, who consequently lost land (which they already cultivated or had bought from the Muslims) to the refugees.[11] Such instances explain why some Slav-speakers refer to the arrival of the refugees as the time in which '*the unbaptised Turks left and the baptised Turks came*'. They also explain why Slav-speakers felt discriminated against by the Greek state and treated as second-class citizens. The relations between refugees and Slav-speakers were further polarised by the intervention of the two main political forces of the interwar period, which exploited the conflict over land for their own political purposes. The Slav-speakers sided *en masse* with the royalists, whereas the refugees supported the Liberal Party of Venizelos (Mavrogordatos 1983; Gounaris 1994; Michailidis 1997). Apart from the general aim of national homogenisation, the Venizelist governments of the interwar period had their own agenda for supporting the rural refugees. By turning the destitute refugees into a class of peasant smallholders, they wanted to prevent them from joining a radical agrarian movement or becoming proletarians in the cities, thus closing ranks with the left-wing workers movement (Kontoyeoryiou, 1992: 57–8). In many parts of Macedonia, this policy was partially successful, but in the district of Florina, where fertile land was scarce and the competitors many, instead of creating a unitary peasant class, it created ethnicity.

The impact of state policies in the wake of the Civil War is also important to consider. The most visible effect of the Civil War was mass emigration.[12] Our survey data confirmed that most emigrants originated from Slav-speaking villages and emigrated mainly to Australia and Canada. Oral testimonies show that many families decided to emigrate not only on economic grounds, but also because of state repression (Danforth 1995: 185, 235).

The majority of Slav-speakers in the Florina region had sided with the left-wing Democratic Army. After its defeat in 1949, political stigma was thus added to ethnic stigma.[13] The division between winners and losers, between left and right, moved both class and ethnicity to the background, creating new cleavages across and within ethnic groups. And yet the ethnic factor continued to play an important role. Although state repression in the aftermath of the Civil War affected members of all ethnic groups, state policies singled out the Slav-speakers as a corporate group, independently of their past political affiliations. Secondly, whenever members of one ethnic group were able to take advantage of repressive state measures against another, this would strengthen the disadvantaged group's belief in a 'common political fate'. This occurred, for example, when the properties of political refugees, the majority of whom were Slav-speakers, were confiscated by the dictate of Law

2536/53. Although some were later returned to relatives of the former owners, many ended up in the hands of 'loyal' members of other ethnic groups. Paradoxically, the ethnic dimension of this issue acquired new social relevance after the restoration of democracy in 1974. Whereas until the 1980s political refugees of all ethnic groups were bound by a common fate, the PASOK laws of 1982 and 1985 concerning the return of political refugees singled out the Slav-speaking group by restricting this measure only to 'Greeks by descent' (*Ellines to yenos*).[14]

The combination of political and ethnic stigma seems to have had specific effects on employment outside the primary sector and hence on social mobility. The requirement of a 'national loyalty certificate' as a precondition for employment in the civil service – which in the rest of the country was mainly intended to exclude supporters of the left – acquired a specific dimension in areas with an important presence of ethnic minorities. Although this question needs documentation, it seems plausible to suggest that Slav-speakers, whose loyalty to the national cause had been contested ever since 1913, were disadvantaged with respect to the refugee group. By the end of the war, the refugees had ceased to be a stigmatised group (Michailidis 1997) and, for reasons I cannot develop here, many refugees had sided with the right in the Civil War (Michailidis 1997: 134; Margaritis 1989: 508–9; Kofos 1995: 286). This might partially explain the different trajectory of both groups after the war. At the same time, however, the focus on national loyalty opened up privileged channels of social mobility for those members of the Slav-speaking community who could prove their loyalty to the national cause. Yet, because of the double stigma attached to their group, in order to achieve access to those channels, they had to prove themselves 'more Catholics than the Pope'.

CLASS AND ETHNICITY IN CENTRAL MACEDONIA

If the salience of ethnicity in the district of Florina can be explained along the lines I have outlined above, this does not mean it applies to Macedonia as a whole. In other parts of this large area where people of different ethnic origin live together, the ethnic factor appears to have moved to the background and to be superseded by class. It seems therefore useful to draw some lines of comparison. I will focus my attention on Karakasidou's (1997) thorough study of the township of Assiros, located on the fertile plains east of Salonica. The historical depth of this study, along with the quality of the author's fieldwork, gives an extremely clear picture of social realignments over more than one century. From many points of view, this picture seems just the contrary of what happened in the district of Florina. But until we have a case-study of similar depth on the latter district, comparison can only be sketchy.

In Assiros, then, as in Florina, a cultural division of labour along ethnic lines existed at the end of the nineteenth century. But during the interwar period ethnic distinctions grew into class differences and the local poor Slav-speaking peasants were enculturated into the dominant Greek-speaking elite. In the process, the township of Assiros grew into a stronghold of Hellenism, a position that it maintains to this day. The main factors invoked by Karakasidou to explain this development form a striking contrast with the situation in Florina.

First, geographical location. Compared with the isolation of the latter and the low fertility of its land, Assiros was located in the midst of highly productive agricultural land and quickly developed into a major market town. By the mid-nineteenth century, this attracted an important number of Greek-speaking settlers from Southern Greece with a firm Greek identity. They developed into the dominant elite of the township, at first as merchants and money-lenders, later as large landowners, who exploited the labour of the mainly Slav-speaking peasants. Locally they were known as *tsorbatzides*.

Mainly through intermarriage, an established practice already in the 1920s, many Slav-speakers were integrated into this elite and 'hellenised'. Moreover, since the beginning of the century, the *tsorbatzides* had developed powerful links with the national administration in Athens, mainly through their involvement in the Macedonian struggle. Throughout the century, they exploited these political connections to their own advantage, thus increasing their wealth and power. For example, in the 1920s, when refugees were settled in the township, the *tsorbatzides* successfully resisted the distribution of Muslim properties to the newcomers and were able to buy or enclose a large proportion of these lands. They did so not as an ethnic group, as in Florina, but as a class, and from a position of power. During the whole interwar period, the labouring poor, either refugees or Slav-speakers, were dependent on the *tsorbatzides*, which increasingly polarised the class structure. Whereas in Florina the land reform gave rise to ethnicity, instead of creating a unitary peasant class, in Assiros it deepened divisions between the two opposing classes and thus made ethnicity seem less relevant.

The developments in the turbulent 1940s were also completely different in the two areas. Whereas in Florina the majority of the Slav-speakers sided with the left and the ethnic factor continued to play an important role, in Assiros most villagers followed the ruling class in siding with the right, with the few left-wing supporters coming mainly from refugee families. As pointed out by Karakasidou, the civil conflict divided social groups 'in terms of local political alliances and class identities rather than in terms of ethnicity', as was often the case in Florina, and 'socio-economic grievances were more important than ethnic or national injustices' (Karakasidou 1997: 204–5). In the aftermath of the Civil War the Assiros *tsorbatzides* belonged to the winners and were able to further consolidate and diversify the sources of their power.

From this comparison, three main elements should be retained. First, the question of social mobility. At the beginning of this century, the township of Assiros was very much an open society offering all groups opportunities for upward social mobility. Geographical location, the centrality of the market, the availability of fertile land and strong links between the local elite and the national centre all contributed to this development. In the district of Florina, meanwhile, such opportunities were scarce, apparently only available to a small portion of the local society (for example, Vlach merchants in the interwar period and urbanised refugees after the war). This contrast between an open and closed society seems to have had an immediate bearing on the social relevance of difference. Consequently, we might suggest the following hypothesis: when upward social mobility is open to all ethnic groups, it is more likely to give rise to class formation; when, on the contrary, such opportunities are more accessible to one ethnic group, while others are excluded, it enhances the relative salience of ethnicity.

Secondly, the importance of intermarriage. In Assiros, the early introduction of mixed marriages facilitated the hellenisation of Slav-speakers, especially through their women. This development was favoured by the fact that most of the Greek-speaking settlers came to the area as single males and married local women to set up a family. From the beginning of this century, marriage strategies were linked to the emergent class structure of the township: hypergamy was one of the main channels through which Slav-speaking families could move up the social hierarchy. In the district of Florina, this economic factor did not play an important role. The majority of both Slav-speaking and refugee peasants belonged to underprivileged groups and competed with each other over scarce resources, having little hope of changing their lot through intermarriage. For reasons which remain to be explored, mixed marriages have increased over the last 20 years, though this is still a rather marginal phenomenon. In both cases, the pattern of marriage strategies cannot explain the social relevance of difference: the rate of intermarriage is both cause and effect of existing perceptions of ethnic boundaries. We still have to ask why people start to intermarry and in what ways this process is linked to the social structure.

The third element is the crucial role played by local elites and their links to the national power centre. While available evidence for the district of Florina is scarce, it seems that a crucial role was played by pro-Greek oriented Slav-speakers, locally known as *Grecoman*, who had shown their loyalty to the Greek cause in the Macedonian Struggle. Many well-known 'heroes' of that bloody conflict, in which Greek and Bulgarian bands confronted each other at the beginning of the century, served as local party politicians in the interwar period. In Slav-speaking villages, the Greek faction often controlled the community council. It appears that two factors prevented the pro-Greek elite from contributing to the blurring of ethnic boundaries as happened in Assiros. In the first place, its power was based on political connections to the national power centre through a network of clientelist relations, but not on class. There is no equivalent of the Assiros *tsorbatzides*, who derived their dominant position from the combination of a strong class position and political influence. Moreover, in the Florina region the two ruling parties of the interwar period exploited existing tensions and thus deepened the division between ethnic groups. It seems plausible to suggest that during the 1940s, when this two-party system collapsed and the whole district shifted to the left,[15] these local elites lost a substantial part of their power base. In the second place, the quality of the relations with the national centre was not the same. In spite of their Greek identity, *Grecoman* leaders suffered from the same ethnic stigma as other Slav-speakers and were often treated with the same distrust by state authorities.[16]

PRESENT AND FUTURE PERSPECTIVES

I have left the most crucial question for the end. Why does difference matter more now than 20 years ago? Some writers have stressed the notion of perceived threat to explain the emergence of ethnicity (Eriksen, 1993: 68). In the case of Florina, this seems a useful notion, as the local society is living through rapid changes in the wake of the new national and international order, marked by the events of 1974 and 1989.

One factor that some local people may perceive as threatening is the increased upward social mobility of Slav-speakers. The restoration of democracy in 1974 reduced the privileged access to improved life chances that people linked to the authoritarian postwar regime had enjoyed. These people now face increased competition from those who were formerly excluded. Such fears have strengthened the identity feelings of previously, but no longer, privileged groups. This was evident, for example, for some refugees we spoke to, who stressed both their Greek and refugee identity. We remarked a similar trend among the Vlach settlers of the Prespa area. Although they do not belong to a privileged group, they profited from the consequences of the Civil War at the expense of the Slav-speaking former inhabitants. They moved up the social ladder from a position of propertyless, nomadic shepherds to one of sedentarised peasants. Members of this group not only stressed their Greek and/or Vlach identity, but also their allegiance to the political right.

For the Slav-speaking group, the political change had different effects: it initiated a period of rising expectations. They hoped to be granted full citizenship and equal treatment, just as in 1912 Slav-speakers had hoped to receive land after the departure of the Muslims. In both cases, when their expectations were disappointed, this strengthened their belief in a 'common political fate' and hence made their difference as Slav-speakers matter.

The concept of perceived threat received further emphasis in the context of the recent Yugoslav crisis and the renewed 'Macedonian Issue'. The emergence of nationalist movements in Yugoslavia, the violent break-up of the Yugoslav Confederation, the recognition of an independent Republic of Macedonia and, on the domestic scene, the emergence of a Macedonian Human Rights movement were perceived by many as a threat to national integrity. The new wave of Greek nationalism seems to be an immediate response to such threats. Government policies of the early 1990s and the virulent media campaign against 'the State of Skopje and its agents' had an immediate impact on the local society. The Greek trade embargo against the new republic had lasting negative effects on the local economy, and enhanced feelings of estrangement from and abandonment by the national centre. The nationalist overtones conveyed by the media further polarised ethnic relations, reversing the process towards a certain level of accommodation in the post-1974 period. The consequence of all this was that any new conflicts were interpreted along ethnic lines, in the light of political memories of the past.

One example is the recent conflict between the Slav-speaking village of Ayios Pandeleimonas and its neighbouring refugee village of Vegora over some 3000 stremmas of cultivable land, which were uncovered by the lake of Vegoritida. The drying-out of the lake had an immediate impact on the livelihood of Ayios Pandeleimonas. It has substantially reduced the traditional fishing activities of its inhabitants and the new land would solve the problems faced by a significant number of landless peasants (about 200). In the present context, the two villages, instead of joining hands to face the immanent ecological disaster, are set up against each other, engaging even in violent clashes. Again, the attitude of the official authorities further divided the two communities, instead of contributing to a peaceful settlement. The Prefect openly took the side of the refugees, couching his discourse in terms of the ongoing conflict between Athens and Skopje:

> If they take your land, so what? Even if they occupy your houses, I will not do anything. Because the inhabitants of Vegora are Pontians and Greeks, whereas you are Slav-speakers, and if you like you can ask for your rights in Sofia and Skopje![17]

A second example concerns the arrival of new immigrants. Following the break-up of former communist regimes, increasing numbers of Albanians and Pontic Greeks from the Soviet Union are crossing the Greek border, including to the Florina district. Although to date only a small number of new immigrants has settled in the district, Slav-speakers consider these groups as competitors on the seasonal labour market. They also fear a more permanent settlement of new immigrants of Greek origin and, in the light of past developments, believe that the latter might be granted a preferential treatment by the state authorities. In short, they fear a replay of 1924. Among the refugee population already established since the 1920s, the Yugoslav crisis has produced similar fears. As an 'uprooted people', they feel threatened by the climate of ethnic cleansing further north, fearing they might one day live through the same experiences as their grandparents and be uprooted again. Therefore, in daily conversations, they stress their role as 'guardians of the border'.

As these examples show, the present crisis has revitalised old conflicts or rephrased new tensions in terms of the past. The inter-ethnic competition for resources, state policies and party politics all play a role in this process, which determines the social meaning of difference. Yet in other realms of social life, a parallel process of accommodation has been set in motion, which in the long run might make difference less important or, at least, give it a different meaning. If the present increase in mixed marriages persists, and if the poorest strata of Slav-speaking peasants gain access to improved living standards, this might remove some of the present tensions.

There are also some signs pointing towards improved relations between the state and local society. Since 1994 Prefects are no longer appointed by Athens, but elected.[18] Together with the democratically elected village presidents, many of whom are young Slav-speakers, they are in a better position to convey the social climate in the area to the central authorities and have a certain degree of discretion in the application of state policies. In the socio-economic sector, some steps have been undertaken to tackle the problem of unemployment and underdevelopment. The establishment of a new electricity plant is well under way, and if all employees are recruited locally, this enterprise might absorb a great deal of the existing unemployment.

Of course, we are still some way from adopting the solutions found in other regions of Europe, which were destabilised by similar problems in the past. In South Tyrol, for example, where a similar cultural division of labour existed between German-speakers and Italian settlers, decentralisation, power-sharing techniques, transborder relations and institutionalised bilingualism have succeeded in defusing a situation potentially more explosive than that in the district of Florina (Markusse 1999). Moreover, the present volatile situation in the southern Balkans may at any moment tip the balance and jeopardise the process. In the meantime, as I hope to have shown in this chapter, the fact that difference seems to matter should be taken seriously.

ACKNOWLEDGEMENTS

This final version has profited from the comments of Hans Vermeulen, Cora Govers, Loring Danforth and Jane Cowan. I am grateful to all of them.

NOTES

1. This emic term of classification is used in various parts of Greece, often associated with a perceived notion of common descent. (Agelopoulos 1997: 135; Couroucli 1985: 48, Danforth 1989: 170–1).
2. The term 'refugee' refers to ethnic Greeks from Asia Minor, Thrace, the Black Sea and the Caucasus settled in this area in the 1920s following the Treaty of Lausanne (1923) for the exchange of population between Greece and Turkey.
3. See for example the articles by John Rex, John Solomos and Harold Wolpe in Rex and Mason (1986).
4. 51 out of 94 villages. The sample was representative for the distribution of ethnic groups in the district. We visited 23 out of 43 Slav-speaking villages, 15 out of 29 mixed villages, five out of 13 refugee villages, all three Arvanite villages and five out of six Vlach villages.
5. Official interviews with the Prefect, the Statistical Service and the Director of the Employment Office. In each village interview with the mayor, secretary or other members of the Community Council, as well as more informal interviews with local inhabitants or 'neutral outsiders'.

6. The average land tenure in the homogeneous refugee villages included in the survey amounted to 49 stremmas, as against 32 for homogeneous Slav-speaking villages. In mixed villages, the average was 40 stremmas. Our survey also showed 1555 unemployed and 1121 landless, of whom 90 per cent and 88 per cent respectively lived in Slav-speaking villages or in mixed villages with a Slav-speaking majority. The number of (mainly unskilled) workers in homogeneous Slav-speaking villages was 666 as against only nine in homogeneous refugee villages, whereas the number of employees was only 245 in the former and 428 in the latter.

7. In the sense that the peasantry is a class in itself, but with a 'vague peasant consciousness', see Hobsbawm (1973).

8. *'Gemeinsame politische Schicksale'* in the original, which in the English translation is sometimes simply rendered as 'political memories'. This term is not used in a deterministic sense, but rather refers to the collective interpretation of common political experiences. For example, Weber explains that the German-speaking Alsatians at the time did not have a sense of a German national identity but were pro-French oriented, because of the memories of the French revolution, which freed them from feudalism (1980: 242–3).

9. Weber (1978: 932), where the author refers to status honour, but elsewhere he explains that the same kind of honour is also an aspect of ethnicity or class formation. For the German text, see Weber (1980: 534).

10. The Greek authorities saw the Slav-speaking group as the 'soft underbelly of the nation' because they feared Slav-speakers might be attracted to Bulgarian propaganda, and therefore considered them unreliable guardians of the northern border.

11. Karavidas (1931: 211–32, 298–305, 307–18), Malouchos (1924). On the tension between refugees and Slav-speakers in general see Pelagidis (1994: 187–90), Gounaris (1990: 324; 1994: 232, 235), Koliopoulos (1999: 41–4), Michailidis (1997).

12. Between 1951 and 1971, the rural area of the district lost 14,000 of its inhabitants, that is, 27 per cent in real population (Chouliarakis, 1988: 111).

13. They were labelled as 'EAMo-Bulgarians', indiscriminately, a theory which equated ethnic origin with participation in the left-wing resistance movement EAM.

14. Decision no. 106841, 29.12.1982, Official Journal, Vol 2, No. 1 and Law 1540/85, Official Journal Vol. 1, No. 67. On this issue see Karakasidou (1993: 12–13), Danforth (1995: 122–4).

15. This shift marked all ethnic groups, but the right maintained strongholds in certain villages and in the town of Florina. As elsewhere in northern Greece, Turkish-speaking refugees generally sided with the right and Caucasian refugees with the left. For voting patterns after the war, see Michailidis (1997).

16. See Varda (1993) for archival documents on this subject. For the position of *Grecomans* see also Gounaris (1994), Carabott (1997).

17. See parliamentary question 1314 of 9.8.93 put by the Greek Communist Party (GCP).

18. This decentralisation effort is, however, offset by the fact that many administrative powers have been transferred to the regions, which continue to be controlled by the central government.

BIBLIOGRAPHY

Agelopoulos, Georgios. 1997. 'From Bulgarevo to Nea Krasia, from "Two Settlements" to "One Village": Community formation, collective identities and the role of the individual', in Peter Mackridge and Eleni Yannakakis (eds) *Ourselves and Other: The development of a Greek Macedonian cultural identity since 1912*. Oxford: Berg.

Barth, Fredrik (ed.). 1969. *Ethnic Groups and Boundaries: The social organisation of cultural difference*. Oslo and London: Allen and Unwin.

—— 1994. 'Enduring and Emerging Issues in the Analysis of Ethnicity', in Hans Vermeulen and Cora Govers (eds) *The Anthropology of Ethnicity*. Amsterdam: Het Spinhuis.

Carabott, Phillip. 1997. 'Slavomakedones kai Kratos stin Ellada tou Mesopolemou'. *Istor* 10, 235–78.

Chouliarakis, Michail. 1988. *Oi Exelixeis tou Plythismou ton Agrotikon Periochon tis Ellados, 1920–1981*. Athens: EKKE.

Cohen, Abner. 1974. 'Introduction: The Lesson of Ethnicity', in Abner Cohen (ed.) *Urban Ethnicity*. London: Tavistock.

Couroucli, Maria. 1985. *Les Oliviers du Lignage*. Paris: Maisonneuve et Larose.

Danforth, Loring M. 1989. *Firewalking and Religious Healing: The Anastenaria of Greece and the American firewalking movement*. Princeton: Princeton University Press.

—— 1995. *The Macedonian Conflict: Ethnic nationalism in a transnational world*. Princeton: Princeton University Press.

Eriksen, Thomas Hylland. 1993. *Ethnicity and Nationalism: Anthropological perspectives*. London: Pluto Press.

Gounaris, Vasilis. 1990. 'Vouleftes kai Kapetanii: Pelateiakes Scheseis sti Mesopolemiki Makedonia'. *Ellinika* 41, 313–35.

—— 1994. 'Oi Slavofonoi tis Makedonias. I Poreia tis Ensomatosis sto Elliniko Kratos, 1870–1940'. *Makedonika* 29, 209–37.

Hall, Stuart, Critcher, Chas, Jefferson, Tony Clarke, John and Brian Roberts (eds). 1978. *Policing the Crisis: Mugging, the state, and law and order*. London: Macmillan.

Hechter, Michael. 1975. *Internal Colonialism: The Celtic Fringe in British national development, 1536–1966*. Berkeley: University of California Press.

—— 1978. 'Group Formation and the Cultural Division of Labour'. *American Journal of Sociology* 84(2), 293–317.

—— 1980. 'Internal Colonialism Revisited'. Paper presented to the 1980 Conference of Europeanists, Washington DC. 24 October 1980.

Hobsbawm, Eric. 1973. 'Peasants and Politics'. *Journal of Peasant Studies* 1(1), 3–22.

Karakasidou, Anastasia. 1993. 'Politicizing Culture: Negating ethnic identity in Greek Macedonia'. *Journal of Modern Greek Studies* 11(1), 1–28.

—— 1997. *Fields of Wheat, Hills of Blood: Passages to nationhood in Greek Macedonia, 1870–1990*. Chicago: The University of Chicago Press.

Karavidas, Kostas. 1931. *Agrotika*. Athens: Papazis.

Kofos, Evangelos. 1995. 'The Impact of the Macedonian Question on Civil Conflict in Greece, 1943–1949', in John O. Iatrides and Linda Wrigley (eds) *Greece at the Crossroads: The Civil War and its legacy*. Pennsylvania: Pennsylvania State University Press.

Koliopoulos, John. 1999. *Plundered Loyalties. World War II and Civil War in Greek West Macedonia*. New York: New York University Press.

Kontoyeoryiou, Elisabeth. 1992. 'Agrotikes Prosfygikes Egkatastaseis sti Makedonia, 1923–1930'. *Deltio Kentrou Mikrasiatikon Spoudon* 9, 47–59.

Malouchos, Dinos. 1924. 'Ta Ktimatika Zitimata tis Makedonias: I Antallagi kai i Egkatastasi ton Prosfygon'. *Koinotis* 3, 3–6; 4, 4–6; 6, 11–13.

Margaritis, Yorgos. 1989. 'Emfylies Diamaches stin Katochi (1941–1944): Analogies kai Diafores', in H. Fleischer and Nikos Svorono (eds) *I Ellada 1936–1944: Diktatoria, Katochi, Andistasi*. Athens: Morfotiko Idryma ATE.

Markusse, J. 1999. 'Relaxation of tensions in the multi-ethnic border province of South Tyrol: the importance of cross border relations', in Hans Knippenberg and Jan Markusse (eds) *Nationalising and Denationalising European Border Regions, 1800–2000. Views from geography and history*. Dordrecht/Boston/London: Kluwer Academic Press.

Mavrogordatos, George. 1983. *Stillborn Republic: Social coalitions and party strategies in Greece, 1922–1936*. Berkeley: University of California Press.

Michailidis, Iakovos. 1997. 'Slavofonoi kai Prosfyges: Politikes Synistoseis Mias Oikonomikis Diamachis', in Vasilis Gounaris, Iakovos Michailidis and Georgios Agelopoulos (eds) *Taftotites sti Makedonia*. Athens: Papazisis.

Morin, Francoise. 1982. 'Anthropological Praxis and Life History'. *International Journal of Oral History* 3(1), 20–30.

Pelagidis, Efstathios. 1994. *I Apokatastasi ton Prosfygon sti Dytiki Makedonia (1923–1930).* Thessaloniki: Adelfoi Kyriakidi.

Rex, John and David Mason (eds). 1986. *Theories of Race and Ethnic Relations.* Cambridge: Cambridge University Press.

Van Boeschoten, Riki. 1993. 'Report to the European Commission: Minority languages in Northern Greece. Study visit to the districts of Florina and Aridea' [unpublished].

Vaiou, Dina and Kostas Chatzimichalis. 1997. *Me ti Raptomichani stin Kouzina kai tous Polonous stous Agrous.* Athens: Exantas.

Varda, Christina. 1993. 'Opseis tis Politikis Afomoiosis sti Dytiki Makedonia sto Mesopolemo'. *Ta Istorika* 18–19, 151–70.

Verdery, Katherine. 1994. 'Ethnicity, nationalism and state-making', in Hans Vermeulen and Cora Govers (eds) *The Anthropology of Ethnicity.* Amsterdam: Het Spinhuis.

Weber, Max. 1978. *Economy and Society: An outline of interpretive sociology.* Vol 2. Berkeley: University of California Press.

—— 1980. *Wirtschaft und Gesellschaft: Grundriss der verstehenden Soziologie.* 5th ed. Tübingen: J.C.B. Mohr (Paul Siebeck).

Wolpe, H. 1986. 'Class Concepts, Class Struggle and Racism', in John Rex and David Mason (eds) *Theories of Race and Ethnic Relations.* Cambridge: Cambridge University Press.

Worseley, Peter. 1984. *The Three Worlds: Culture and world development.* London: Weidenfeldt and Nicholson.

2   OS ELLIN MAKEDONAS: AUTOBIOGRAPHY, MEMORY AND NATIONAL IDENTITY IN WESTERN GREEK MACEDONIA

Piero Vereni

How does one become?
How do men become when bound up in tragic machines in which the calculation of probabilities offers no salvation? Who survives the game? (Clemente 1994: 19)

The main character in a story by Isak Dinesen leaves his house one night to repair the banks of a flooded river. He moves in darkness under heavy rain, falling down and getting up again, losing his way and finding it again. At dawn, his task over, he makes his way home and turns back to look towards the river. He realises that his frenetic and partly random movements, his work of the night before, have produced the outline of a stork in the muddy ground. The Western idea of identity is in some ways comparable to this man's glance towards the mud impressions: the unequal marks produced by actions only partly intentional are interpreted as a design endowed with semantic unity, with a meaning that binds identity. That unity is represented by the coherence of the design, a coherence linked indissolubly with memory, and dependent on the capacity of the mind to ponder the traces left by life. This bond between memory and identity – which Western modernity has rendered as inescapable in its public dimension (Gillis 1994) as in its personal one (Hacking 1995) – may be expressed in the telling of a story that becomes itself the privileged dimension of individuality:

What does the unity of an individual consist in? The answer is that this unity is the unity of a narrative embodied within a single life ... any attempt to elucidate the concept of personal identity independently and separately from those of narrative intelligibility and responsibility is doomed to failure. All such attempts have, in fact, been unsuccessful. (MacIntyre 1981: 261).

The appeal of collective, imagined communities lies in their capacity to provide each person an assurance that a design exists, that a stork has been traced for each one of us. The paradox for communities as minutely imagined as the national one is the requirement that the traces are solely to be retraced. Whether looking to the future (let us build a new stork together) or the past (let us retrace the stork of our forefathers), the national project remains irreparably paradoxical in the way it treats the relation between identity

47

and memory collectively: it strengthens the hope for meaning yet mortifies the hope for a *single* meaning unique to each person (Cavarero 1997).

Several incompatible versions of history have fought it out for decades in Macedonia. Their continuous confrontation has reinforced, rather than undermined, a conviction that there is a 'true' history, and that rival versions can be dismissed as false. The prestige with which History has been endowed in Macedonia makes it a reference point for any discourse connected to memory, and for the constitution of personal identity.

The curious autobiography with which these pages are concerned is the clearest case I encountered of this ambiguous and complex relation between the 'authority' of history, the definition of collective identity, and the constitution of personal identity through the workings of memory. By inscribing his story within that of the nation, Leonidas, the author, seeks from the nation a justification of a life whose difficulties otherwise seem insurmountable. He inserts his personal narrative within a natural model in the hope of guaranteeing that this life has not been wasted, that, back there, at the very bottom, lies a stork. He retraces the death of his mother, his misfortunes and fortunes as so many steps toward Greekness, as the compliance to a model that, he has been assured, is important. Within the confines of the national discourse, the life of Leonidas stops being that of a blind, solitary man wandering in the darkness and mud, and becomes instead a meaningful story with a recognisable design. Yet this is where the contradiction of the national discourse emerges. It proposes a collective identity which each person is to embody on an individual level. Each person's narrative, however, by unfolding events that may be contradictory, destroys (even if involuntarily) the rigid notion of identity proposed by the nation – thus frustrating the definition of collective identity and messing up the scheme of the national model.

This chapter is based on the textual analysis of five notebooks written in Greek by Leonidas Khristopoulos between 1992 and 1995. The notebooks treat various subjects but revolve essentially around four central themes: the history of Macedonia, autobiographical reminiscences, the fortunes of his family, and political issues. Leonidas, a Macedonian of Greece, is a farmer born in 1927 at Petres in the district of Florina (western Greek Macedonia), where he still lives.[1] The notebooks in question were given to me directly by Leonidas, who allowed me to photocopy them (they will henceforth be referred to as N1, N2, etc.). After translating them I discussed them at length with him to clarify several obscure points, and the information gathered in this way contributes considerably to this work. This paper draws largely on the contents of N1 and N2 but material from the other notebooks has also been taken into consideration.

THE FRAMEWORK: IDEOLOGY OF THE TEXT

The narration of a person's life, even when set in the context of the history of his/her country, involves sophisticated inclusion and exclusion mechanisms dictated by requirements which, though occasionally documentary, are normally in the nature of personal vindication and apologetics. The person addressed, or interlocutor, plays a decisive role in the selection of memory precisely because of the collaborative effort that every text requires of its reader (Eco 1979). Should the nature of the interlocutor remain completely indefinite, as is the case with the present notebooks, becoming therefore a 'disinterested' representative of humanity, the text (at least in scope) assumes the function of 'monument' more than document. On questioning Leonidas as to whom the notebooks are addressed, he replied without hesitation: 'To my grandchildren, so that they do not forget who we are.' What emerges clearly from the style of the text, however, is that Leonidas is addressing a reader located far beyond the restricted circle of his family. Leonidas constitutes himself in these notebooks, which means that he not only tells us what happened but, more importantly, why he is what he is. More than the style, it is the means adopted that reveals the foundational value placed by Leonidas on writing. Educated within the Greek national system, Leonidas has learnt to attribute the written word with far more weight than the spoken one, an authoritativeness that is itself part of nation-building.

The diffusion of a national model of belonging is a crucial step in the construction of a nation. It is often a model of decontextualised belonging, which bestows univocal, unalienable traits – a single national language, a single alphabet, a common past and single religion – along with a single national corpus of popular traditions. The trade-off proposed by the Greek national discourse and either forced upon or voluntarily accepted by the people, was a simple one. To citizens like Leonidas, with an 'impure' and culturally heterogeneous heritage, the architects of the nation argued as follows: in exchange for your history you will receive a new one, a greater, more fascinating history that goes further back in time and whose geographical span corresponds to the area covered by the borders of the state.

Learning to read and write was essential for such a barter to take place. The nation imposed its language on citizens, who thereby discovered how remembrance could acquire, through writing, a quality of permanence, stability, 'truth'. But if this enabled the citizen to assimilate the new memories belonging to the collective past of the nation, the act of writing also allowed him/her to give permanent expression – and therefore the stamp of truth – to his/her own personal reminiscences and impressions, even when divergent from the collective truths imposed by the national discourse. In the context of a border area like western Greek Macedonia, writing has become, for some, a means of 'non-antagonistic resistance' to the process of nation-building. It is a form of resistance inasmuch as autobiography institutes narrative routes that question the very concept of 'identity' proposed by the nation, that is, the sameness of a nation at all times and under all circumstances. It is non-antagonistic, however, in the sense that it does not contest, rather, it makes use of the national discourse's devices and intent to persuade heteroglot members of their Greekness. As in the case examined here, it expresses the author's will to inscribe himself within Greekness, even if filtered through his personal 'ideology'.

What, then, is the 'ideology' of the text below? I have glossed the emergent three core-concepts that stand at the centre of Leonidas' writings and our conversations together, as:

1. the twofold Macedonia and twofold history
2. authoriality (the right to authorship)
3. belonging (being an *Ellinas Makedonas*).

1. History, Histories. Macedonia, Macedoniae

Telling one's own story is generally hard; doing so 'in Macedonia' is probably more so than usual. This is, in part, because every personal history appears, from the viewpoint of the narrator, always ridiculous in its partiality, belittled by its banality by Greater History.[2] Should nothing be 'forgotten', Macedonia acquires a geographical, historical and mythological amplitude in which, in the space of 2500 years, all that is conceivable as a 'historic event' accumulates: heroes and traitors, leaders and slaves, rulers and ruled, vanquishers and vanquished. In the face of this crowded stage of leading actors how can one ordinary person make his own voice heard? How can he narrate the personal event that made him who he is when this event did not take place in Greater History (and thus did not happen at all), however crucial it may be to his own Lesser History? Coming to terms with Greater History is a complex operation, constantly undermined by that very discrepancy between the differential significance of the events narrated, that is, the death of one's mother compared to that of Alexander the Great. In the notebooks, however, the symbolic intensity with which such parallel events are normally charged is rhetorically inverted. The death of Alexander is thus attributed to indigestion (reducing the event to the level of a common misfortune), while the death of Leonidas' mother becomes the symbol of the defeat of a collective identity: 'They did not kill my mother who had so suffered under the Bulgarians, they killed our Nation, Greece' (N1: 18–19).

This historical chiasmus – the domestication of a grand event and the apotheosis of a personal tragedy – is also enacted on a geographical level. While Macedonia is by no means an indefinable or even unreal location, as many Westerners have portrayed it (see Brown 1995: 45–56), its definition is both contextual and personal. It can express a larger 'imagined community' or a smaller, specific 'locality', depending on the perspective adopted, that of Greater or Lesser History respectively. I am thus not so concerned with defining Macedonia rigorously, either via geography or history (Wilkinson 1951: 2–6; Aarbakke 1992: 4–5). Rather, I want to stress Macedonia's 'twofold' nature: it is both the collective *space* of an imagined or 'primordial' community (Geertz 1963) and the domestic *place* of a personal life that recognises and remembers.[3] This semantic duality is always evident in Leonidas' notebooks.

2. Authoriality, Authority

At the beginning of N1 Leonidas cites the key fact that gives him the authority to write a history of Macedonia and of his mother:

As a Macedonian Greek (*os Ellin*[4] *Makedonas*), which I am, I know this history. Some of it I know through the study of our history books, but most of what I know comes from the stories of my ancestors. (N1: 1)

Leonidas contrasts his direct access to historical knowledge as a native to the indirect access gained by reading: 'From father to son, these things were told me at home by my great-grandparents, but especially by my mother' (N1: 1). To make explicit the weight of these initial statements and their role in the construction of the identity of Leonidas as an *Ellinas Makedonas*, I must recount an incident from my fieldwork. Once, when I was walking with Leonidas through the market of Amindeo, a man of around forty, selling eggs, approached him. Also a Macedonian of Greece, this man had recently returned to Greece after a few years in Canada, and had undoubtedly received a higher level of formal education than Leonidas. To my astonishment they embarked on a lively and well-informed conversation on the history of Macedonia, on Slav invasions and the 'Tatar' origins of the Bulgarian peoples. Leonidas' knowledge of certain subjects being clearly less precise, he was gracefully but firmly corrected by his interlocutor as to certain 'errors'.

　I was somewhat embarrassed by this as I always showed great confidence in him as a source of historical information, and I did not want him to believe I was disappointed. When this man left us Leonidas indeed tested my trust in him: 'He certainly knows a lot about history, doesn't he? Even more than me ... I am old, and am beginning to mix up names and dates.' I pointed out that it was simply a question of different kinds of knowledge, constructed in different ways. Leonidas grasped my meaning at once and brightened up: 'Yes, of course, he has studied and learnt these things in America, in books, while I have lived them in my life.' This key idea, of history lived in life, is given concrete expression by Leonidas at the end of another notebook: 'These are the correct historical events, written in the life which we lived' (N4: 20). The authority to write thus derives from his twofold status as an eyewitness and 'native' (*dopios*). He is entitled to write about the Civil War because he has experienced it first-hand, and about the Macedonians of antiquity because he considers himself their descendant. In strictly anthropological terms, Leonidas' move is typically 'ethnicist':[5] when a 'native' decides to tell his story in order to found himself as such, he justifies his authority to do so with the very argument that forms the object of his demonstration: I will demonstrate that I am a native, and I can do so because I am a native.[6] The key factors are therefore first-hand experience and sources that are reliable inasmuch as they are 'continuous' (from father to son ...) and emotionally close to the narrator. History becomes memory thanks to two persons, the only ones explicitly mentioned by Leonidas as repositories of knowledge: his mother, Stavroula Gatsou, and his father's maternal grandfather, Stefanos Tsiotsios.

Anthropological literature has underlined the importance of the mother figure in the transmission of knowledge and in the process of enculturation, which makes the role of Stavroula Gatsou foreseeable to some extent.[7] The agency of Stefanos Tsiotsios is, at first, rather surprising – especially if we consider the following statement:

I was just in time to know my great-grandfather. When he died in 1935 I was 8 years old. I remember ever so well all that my great-grandfather Stefanos Tsiotsios told me. He had a daughter, Stavroula Tsiotsiou, who married Khristos Khristopoulos. And this is why *our surname* changed from Tsiotsios to Khristopoulos. (N2: 2, italics added)

Until the end of the war, Leonidas lived in a house that included his paternal grandparents Stavroula Tsiotsiou and Khristos Khristopoulos, his own nuclear family and that of Georgos, his father's brother, in what is termed a *zadruga*, an extended family group of the agnatic kind.

3. Choosing One's Belonging

The fact that Leonidas recalls in such warm terms a man whose name he does not carry, actually claiming a 'direct' descent in contravention of the patri-lineal descent ideology, should not surprise us unduly. This great-grandfather, after all, headed the *zadruga* within which Leonidas grew up. Leonidas' attitude can therefore be partly explained as a response to the *zadruga* as a corporate *local* group. When more than one patriline cohabited together, the *zadruga*'s indentity was defined by the patriline originally in residence, even if the surname had changed.

This was the case with Khristos Khristopoulos, when he married Stavroula Tsiotsios without taking her back to his *zadruga* (of the Khristopoulos family), going instead to live with his in-laws, the Tsiotsios. The groom was, in these unusual cases, called *domazet* (in Greek *spitogambros*), which meant 'married into the house' (that is, of his wife's parents). Had the bride no brothers – as in the present case – the next generation brought with it a change of the *zadruga*'s name, which became that of the *domazet*; the latter passed it onto his children, who became heirs, even in the local sense, to the *zadruga*.

That his great-grandfather was still alive when Leonidas was a child con-tributed additionally to the boy's affective bond with the Tsiotsios branch. The great-grandfather's stature was later kept alive by Leonidas' mother, thus playing a significant role in the construction of Leonidas' personal and national identity. Although in the notebooks Leonidas exploits the contra-dictions between descent and residence epitomised by Khristos Khristopoulos, other evidence demonstrates that Leonidas chose *anyway* not to belong, emotionally at least, to the Khristopoulos family branch whose name he carried.

This latter fact was made apparent at our first encounter when I knew nothing about his notebooks. He introduced himself as Leonidas Gatsos (his mother's surname, another choice about belonging), and it was only later that he told me his 'official' name. I saw him introduce himself as Leonidas Gatsos on at least one other occasion, and it is notable that in both cases the subject of conversation was the 'history of Macedonia'.

This may merely corroborate the views of those who consider claims about the rigid agnatic structure of the *zadruga* as essentially 'mythical' and who object to the Western representation of this institution as a form of projection (Todorova, 1990). Or it may be taken as supporting evidence for those who see the *zadruga*'s homogeneity as an essential factor in its structural tenacity (Rihtman-Auguštin, 1988). In the present context, however, it is essential to emphasise the apparently extraordinary flexibility of Leonidas in 'manipulating' his own descent. Independently of what his identity card proclaims, Leonidas 'feels' (and 'declares' himself, as we saw above) more a Gatsos or a Tsiotsios than a Khristopoulos. If Leonidas' choice of belonging to the Tsiotsios group can be explained by privileging the dimension of the *zadruga* as household over the *zadruga* as descent group, his identification as a Gatsos is a manifest violation of the patrilineal principle of descent. This choice entails a decision of the utmost gravity which, as will become clear, concerns his belonging to one national community rather than another. The reasons for this choice lie in the personal history of Leonidas and in the way he has decided to recount it to *himself* (even before recounting it to us).

THE PICTURE: THE FOUNDATION OF ONESELF

In his notebooks Leonidas intertwines the principal 'events' of Greater History and his own Lesser History. This twofold story results in a personal and collective identity which Leonidas defines as Macedonian-Greek, opposing it to 'Bulgarian' (and more generically 'Slav' in his vocabulary) and 'simply Greek'. In defining himself as an *Ellinas Makedonas*, Leonidas also constantly plays on the opposition between his identity and that of the refugees settled in the region after the compulsory exchange of population between Greece and Turkey in 1923–6. This latter opposition takes place on a different 'ideological' plane, however, referring to cultural differences that have taken on political connotations for economic reasons.

Greater History and Greater Geography

Leonidas writes with an urgency dictated by a pressing need: to re-establish the truth. The dispute with FYROM, as the Former Yugoslav Republic of

Macedonia is called in Greece, over the use of the name 'Macedonia' and that nation's claims of descent from the Macedonians of antiquity, deeply disturbed Greek Macedonians, who found themselves in an untenable psychological and political position. While politicians of FYROM laid claim to a minority in Greece, Greek politicians preoccupied themselves with history, treating ancient Macedonia exclusively as a region of Greece. Aware that the claims of FYROM ran the risk of baring old wounds, and that the categorical pronouncements of certain Greek politicians ran the risk of depriving the wounds of all meaning, Leonidas accepts the challenge and undertakes to come to terms with both.

His starting point is the Macedonian State of antiquity, the existence of which cannot be doubted: 'And he dares to say that a Macedonian State never existed! To Pontians perhaps the Macedonian State never existed. But to *Makedones Ellines* it certainly did' (N1: 2–3). As Leonidas drove home to me, this state is the most ancient in the world, along with the Kurdish and Indian ones. It was a state politically autonomous from Greece, Alexander first having united the Thracians and then having 'descended towards southern Greece for union' (N1: 3). Leonidas employs the term 'union' (*enosis*), which alludes to the project for reconstructing the modern Greek state on the scale of the Byzantine empire. This project kindled irredentism:

Greece included considerably fewer than half of those who regarded themselves as Greeks ... It was easy to stir up agitation in favour of enlarging Greece's frontiers by a progressive extension of *enosis* (union). (Woodhouse, 1986: 163)

Leonidas, significantly, employs a term usually associated with modern Greek history to indicate the conquest of Greek land by Alexander the Great:

The most important thing for every *Ellinas Makedonas* to know is this: At that time Alexander created the Macedonian-Greek State from top to bottom. Now in 1821 and 1912–13 the Greek State rose from bottom to top. (N1: 4–5)

This historical symmetry (according to which Greece returns a favour received more than 2200 years previously) is the most valid proof of Macedonia's status *vis-à-vis* Greece: 'It is very painful to me, as it must be to many others, to hear it said that a Macedonian State never existed. Yes! It did exist!' (N1: 4). Leonidas immediately specifies however: 'But it was not Slav! Because the Slavs appeared for the first time in the Balkans in the seventh and eighth centuries.'

The next crucial phase in History for Leonidas coincides with the presence of the Slavs in Macedonia, who settled there and subjugated the local population, the Macedonians. The Turks then took over where the Slavs left off:

And so [we], subjugated by the Roman Empire. Subjugated by Byzantium. Subjugated ever so much by the Slavs and then subjugated by the Turks, weren't able to organise ourselves to become a State. (N1: 4)

This uninterrupted history of subjugation (even during Byzantium) comes to a close for the *Ellines Makedones* only with the liberation of 1913. This explains why the Macedonians of Greece don't speak Greek as a mother tongue:

This Language we speak is a mixture of dialects. Among the words we speak some of them are Slav, a few are Vlach, some are Albanian and many are Turkish. This language sprang up because there were no schools in Macedonia, since there were many Turks here. So words were stolen, one here, one there, having been subjugated all these years. But they do not correspond either with Bulgarian or Serbian. (N1: 7)

A further quote says:

We Macedonians speak a dialect that has no grammar. The vast number of whose words are Turkish. And many resemble Slav ones ... But this inasmuch as we were subject to the Slavs from the seventh and eighth centuries. Up until 1200 after Christ ... It's obvious that Slav words have remained. In the same way as Turkish words have remained. Since we were subjected another 400 years to the Turks. Neither the Slavs, nor the Turks, but not even the Pontians can make us change our loyalty. And our patriotism. (N2: 3–4)[8]

History continues, in fact, with the liberation from the 'Turkish yoke' or, in the words of Leonidas: 'And now the struggle of the Macedonian People against the Turks and Bulgarians. From the year 1870 up until 1912, its liberation' (N1: 15). It is at precisely this point that the Greater History of the Macedonian People encounters the Lesser History of Leonidas Khristopoulos, impersonal 'competence' of the past becoming affective 'memory'. This crucial passage is achieved through the mediation of the mother of Leonidas, Stavroula Gatsou, witness, protagonist and veritable agent of memory.

In 1907, towards the end of the period known in Greek history as the 'Macedonian Struggle', the father and paternal grandfather of Stavroula Gatsou were killed by a band of Bulgarian *komitadjides* (members of an armed band; see Michailidis, this volume, note 1): 'This is why my mother knew so many things about the Struggle of the Macedonian People' (N1: 15). Leonidas' mother takes on the leading role at this stage, on the margins of history and memory. The names of captain Gatsos (father of Stavroula and grandfather of Leonidas) and Khristos Tsikas, betrothed to Donka Gatsou, Stavroula's elder sister, make their appearance next to the heroic names of the Macedonian Struggle (Pavlos Melas, Ionas Dragoumis, Kotas). The following is the complete account of this episode:

They would gather and organise themselves and head for the mountains, *Andartes* against the Turks. But also against the Bulgarian State and the *Komitadjides*. Who had been founded by the Bulgarian State to take away Macedonia from us to the advantage of Bulgaria. On the Bulgarian side in the village of Keli were Tane Klianchov. In that of Vevi, Tzole Gergin. These two killed the father of my mother and her grandfather. But the death of the Bulgarian *Komitadjides* came from my mother. Because as my mother was taking bread and food to her brother Nikolas ... it was there she saw the band of the *Voivode* Tane, six men with their horses. She went home to the village of Tsegani and told her sister Donka, who was older and was betrothed to Khristos Tsikas. And my aunt Donka told the *Andartis* Khristos Tsikas. And he galloped with his horse to the summit of mount Kaimaktsalan, to the huts of Farmaki. Giannis Karavitis was there, with the Greek Forces of the *Andartes*. He sent a band of around ten men to the cottage of Zervi, where the Bulgarian *Komitadjis* with his band were. It was there that the battle began. But there was no way they could bring them out. And so one of the Greeks secretly went behind the cottage, set fire to it, and so they were forced to come out of it. And then not even one of them remained, they were all killed. And it was in this way that my mother took back the blood of her father and grandfather. (N1: 16–17)

Leonidas invests this event with epic dimensions, a status sanctioned by its collective commemoration by members of his mother's village. Leonidas tells how, at the death of the *voivode* Tane, the inhabitants of this village composed a song about this event, a few verses of which I relate below:

Where are you, Tane, darling of your granny?
I am here, granny, and am making bombs
for my liberation
...
The blood of her grandparents
little Stavroula of the clan Gatsos wanted back
and to her brother-in-law gave she information ...[9]

A family event is therefore retranslated into history through the form of an epic narrative, removed from individual memory to become collective heritage. Having claimed a 'descent' from Gatsos, Leonidas can, by hereditary right, style himself as belonging to that history of the 'Macedonian State' as declared in the title of N1: 'History of the Macedonian State. Philip – Alexander King of Macedonians. And Story of My Mother'.

This history is not only glorious, but ambiguous, as it sees only part of Macedonia being liberated during the Struggle in question:

But always the great European States have wronged us. Even then, in the First World War, France supported Serbia [and] gave her 8 prefectures of Macedonia. Italy gave Albania the prefecture of Koritsa with 29 villages and Germany [and] Russia gave Bulgaria Philipopolis that is today's Plovdiv with 5 prefectures of Macedonia. (N1: 5)

Leonidas' historical Macedonia coincides exactly with the maximum extension claimable and claimed by the various irredentist movements, past and present; it also coincides fairly precisely with what is indicated or mapped as 'geographical Macedonia' (see Barker 1950: 9; Perry 1988: 13; Karakasidou 1993: 2; Agelopoulos 1996: n.2; Gounaris 1996: n.3), even though there is no 'geographical' – 'natural' – reason for such a definition, making it a matter of political interpretation (Wilkinson 1951: 2). If this is the Macedonia that history hands down to Leonidas, memory supplies him with a different Macedonia.

Lesser Geography and Lesser History

The map referred to above, traced with the aseptic cartographic precision of numbers, is not Leonidas' 'knowledge' of his land. The Macedonia known by

Leonidas consists of local names and particulars, an area familiar to him like the back of his hand: in conversation he often indicates with his arm the direction of a place under discussion. His Macedonia, therefore, coincides with the borders of his own familiarity. Hence, when he explains, 'as my mother told me, their grandparents came from Naoussa', that 'coming' is conceived as an arrival from distant places – though Naoussa is geographically in Macedonia. When he talks about the people who fled beyond the border during the Civil War, it is about people who went 'abroad', even when they remained in the geographic Macedonia. Similarly, Leonidas has no sympathy for FYROM or for its name, continuing to refer to it as 'Serbia'.

Above all, for Leonidas the 'Macedonian Struggle' – at which time 'History' fades into 'history' and remembrance – takes place and is fought out in familiar villages: Prespa, Pisoderi, Agios Germanos, Keli, Agios Athanasios, Vevi. The resistance against 'the Turk and the Bulgarian State' was fought by men who came from these villages, with one qualification: 'And from many other parts, other villages, but I don't know these men' (N1: 9). Leonidas never knew either Ionas Dragoumis or Captain Kotas in real life, that much is clear. He knows, however, of their local adventures, and can imagine these characters of history within 'his' Macedonia, by placing them within a context that is not imaginary at all, but lived in daily life. It is the familiarity of the horizon that renders men familiar, as it is likewise the strangeness of the background that makes them 'unimaginable'. And it is in this context of locality, in these reduced and familiar spaces, that Leonidas also inscribes his own life.

Born in 1927, the first event of importance in his life takes place a decade later, when his father puts a stop to his education:

I was doing very well at the public school. I finished school in 1939. My teacher, I.K. of Cyprus, had great affection for me. He came four times to plead with my father so that he would send me to high school. Unfortunately, however, my father did not agree with the ideas of my school teacher. We had cows and sheep, he wanted me to graze them so that he could be elsewhere. This was the worst thing that happened to me. And it was my father who did it to me, because he did not send me to the high school of Amindeo. It was as if he clipped the wings of my future life. (N3: 2; also recounted in N5: 1)

This longing for an education appropriate to his potential is a recurring theme of my conversations with Leonidas. It must be understood within the linguistic and political climate of his childhood. Macedonian was not only considered a mere 'dialect' or 'idiom' lacking grammar. It was also in that era, during the Metaxas regime, banned by law. One could be severely fined for using it in private conversations, and Leonidas tells of several such occasions. Despite the Grecophile affiliations of a large part of the local population, it was only when they learned the Greek language that the state recognised them as truly Greek. Most inhabitants of the district of Florina learned Greek through going to school.

The school/language link is given concrete expression by Leonidas when he explains the very existence of Macedonian, in the context of his 'decision' to belong to the branch of Stefanos Tsiotsios (the great-grandfather who effected the 'change of surname' by giving his daughter Stavroula in marriage to Khristos Khristopoulos):

Since we have been subjugated by the Turks for 400 years, how could we possibly have a grammar without Schools? Since the Turks did not allow Greek schools. It was only at the Fanari in Constantinople that there was a Greek school in 1785 ... It was to this school that my great-grandfather Stefanos Tsiotsios went, in 1862, to the 'FANARI' school of Constantinople. And there he learnt a few Greek letters, but wrote them with the pronunciation of Local speech. (N2: 1–2)

There is no grammar without school, no Greekness without grammar; the great-grandfather Stefanos lived long enough to provide Leonidas with a living proof of this.

The second critical event of Leonidas' life occurs during the early phases of the civil war, when an explosion in a mine field close to where he was grazing sheep caused severe permanent physical damage (he lost his left hand). This episode is narrated in three notebooks (N2: 21–2; N3: 5–7; N5: 9), yet N3 (dedicated exclusively to his autobiography) provides more specific details. Gravely wounded, Leonidas made his way home on a donkey with the aid of a fellow villager: 'As my mother told me, my father had taken out his knife to kill me because he saw me wounded. And then he was stopped by Methodios D' (N3: 7).

I have not questioned Leonidas as to when his mother told him this episode, but it cannot have been long after the actual event, since she died two years later. What is certain is that relations between father and son were further strained.[10]

The third major event in Leonidas' life occurs two months after his return from the Florina hospital where he recovered from his accident. Witness rather than protagonist of the tormented episode in question, Leonidas has obvious difficulty in explaining it to himself, embarking four times on its narration (N2: 22–8; N3: 8–15; N4: 9–12; N5: 9–10). On each occasion, he uses different forms and tones. The attempt of certain villagers to murder his father, Periklis Khristopoulos, along with two of his friends, is the object of detailed treatment in N2 and N3 and of a rather scanty one in N4 and above all N5. A gang of *rufianofrones*[11] lays an ambush for Leonidas' father as he and his son are irrigating their field. A friend of his father becomes victim to a brutal beating while the father escapes. Leonidas acts as an involuntary bait in a second similar attempt when he is found in the fields by the gang: to attract the father's attention they pretend to beat him, but the father intervenes with a shotgun and the assailants flee. N2 ends abruptly on this note. In N3 the father, following these attempts on his life, leaves as an *andartis* for the mountains. N4 ends in a likewise laconic fashion, while N5 focuses on the departure of the father with other individuals from the village, rather than on the attempted murder.

Leonidas generally writes in a lively manner, with a sense of both humour and tragedy, and he knows how to alternate styles. The exceptional difficulty the reader encounters in comprehending this episode corresponds to the difficulty Leonidas has in writing it. On this occasion Leonidas seems unable to 'get to the point'. He circles round events and persons, and lingers on thoroughly irrelevant details. No reasons are given for the attempts on the life of his father. But what is even more surprising is that he attaches no moral value to the incident whatsoever, depriving it of that 'ideological' context in which he usually places every episode of Greater or Lesser History. Ever master of his literary means (pathetic in his account of interrupted education, tragic in that of his accident, dramatic or epic in the event of the death of his mother), Leonidas cannot morally 'place' this event which he nevertheless considers central to his life. Our conversations have rarely touched on this episode, and those few times have been at my instigation. It is only recently that Leonidas told me his father's fate: he had escaped to Serbia, lived several years in Czechoslovakia, and finally settled in the Federal Yugoslav Republic of Macedonia where he died in the 1970s. Leonidas says he went to find him on five occasions, although there is no trace of these visits in his notebooks. They do, however, make reference to Greek citizens who had escaped during the Civil War and whom he met when in the Yugoslav Republic of Macedonia. The father went to stay for a while with his other sons who had emigrated to Australia, but never came back to Greece.

Reticent on the subject of his father in his notebooks as in life, Leonidas is disposed to linger at length on the last great incident of his life: the death of his mother. It takes place during the difficult years of the Civil War, when Leonidas' fellow villagers are confronted by both right-wing government militia and the left-wing Greek People's Liberation Army (*ELAS*). Having taken refuge in a village held by *ELAS andartes*, the house in which the mother was staying with her children is bombarded. Leonidas emerges practically unhurt, but his brothers and especially his mother are gravely wounded. The hospital of Amindeo, considering them *andartes*, refuses them entry twice. They are left in the village square until the intervention of Khristos Tsikas (the mother's brother-in-law and leader of the revenge against the Bulgarian *komitadjides* who had killed her father and grandfather), who finally manages to have her admitted to hospital. It is too late, however, and she dies a few days later. The event is recounted four times (N1: 18–19; N3: 22–9; N4: 13–14; N5: 15–18), although N5 only speaks of the wounding, and not of the mother's actual death.

The reasons for this narrative iteration are symmetrical and opposed to those of the previous episode concerning the father. Leonidas repeats himself because this tragic incident is the final key that closes the circle of his identity. N3 (26) tells how Leonidas goes to his uncle for help after having been rejected at the hospital:

When he saw me with my clothes all bloody he took fright. And my uncle got up from the bed where he was sleeping to find a doctor. But the authorities of the place don't let him do this. And they say to him: 'They are fine where they are, stretched out on the ground. Let them die, for those are "Bulgars".'

Leonidas is keen to reveal the contradictions of such an accusation (N3: 26–7):

And so I ask at this point. The son of my grandfather was killed as a sergeant, on the Albanian Front. And his father they turned out as a Bulgarian. That is, our grandfather. The father and grandfather of my mother were killed by Bulgarian *Komitadjides* in the year 1907. Because they were Greek. Well, then! Who are the real Greeks?

A few remarks are necessary on the parental relations referred to in this passage. We know who the father and grandfather of his mother were; but which grandfather is he talking about, and who is the son? The grandfather in question is Leonidas' paternal grandfather, Khristos Khristopoulos, father of Periklis Khristopoulos (Leonidas' own father). All we knew up to now was that Khristos Khristopoulos was responsible for the 'change' of Leonidas' family's surname from Tsiotsios (the branch of Stefanos, the great-grandfather educated in Constantinople) to Khristopoulos, when he married Stavroula, the paternal grandmother of Leonidas. The son referred to is Georgos Khristopoulos, son of Khristos and Stavroula and paternal uncle of Leonidas, killed during the Greek resistance against the Italian invasion of Albania. Leonidas only refers to his paternal uncle on this occasion, and adds nothing more on his paternal grandfather. He deliberately avoids all mention of Khristos Khristopoulos, telling us only that he was 'sent away as a Bulgarian'. The same summary of Leonidas' national pedigree is in another notebook, also after an account of the his mother's death:

So! My Grandfather was sent away as a Bulgarian. While his son Georgos was killed in Albania, during the war, with the rank of sergeant. The father of my mother and the grandfather were killed by the Bulgarians of *Vojvoda* Tane in the year 1906, because they were with the Greeks. My mother instead was killed by Greek cannon-balls. (N4: 14)

I first heard this 'formula' at the very beginning of my acquaintance with Leonidas. He told it to me at the Florina train station, where we casually met and he offered me some of his home-made brandy (*tsipouro*). I heard the same condensed version of the national fortunes of his family on at least another three occasions, and am convinced (as much as he is) that it is essential to an understanding of 'who' Leonidas is.

Os Ellin Makedonas

The formula of Leonidas' identity can be easily conceived in the form of a diagram. Figure 2.1 shows Leonidas' descent from the Khristopoulos and the Gatsos family lines. In the eyes of the world, these two lines of descent are symmetrical: both present the inadmissible scandal of a switch from one national identity to another at the point of generational shift. I have placed a question-mark next to the two nationalities of Leonidas, to highlight the impossibility of a single resolution. The formula is therefore a sharp criticism of 'nationalist naturalness' and of any doctrine of identity that considers descent – one's blood and the inescapable necessity of 'nature' – as the determining factors of one's national identity.

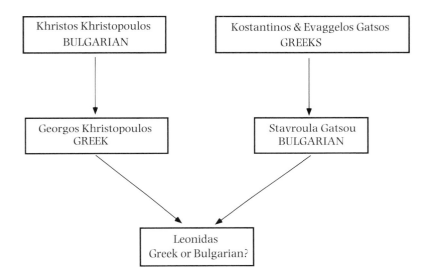

Figure 2.1 Khristopoulos and Gatsos family lines of descent

Leonidas is not a man to be easily discouraged, however, in the face of such a setback of non-existent 'natural' national identity. Instead of giving up, he chooses his own descent. Neither Bulgarian, nor simply Greek, Leonidas is an *Ellinas Makedonas*. Greekness derives from the culture he has accepted, from the adherence to a civilisation transmitted to him by Lesser History (his mother, his grandfather, Stefanos, who learned Greek at school); his Macedonianness, on the other hand, furnishes him with a solid foothold in Greater History. In refusing to be 'Slav' or 'Bulgarian', Leonidas seeks and finds those deeper roots which he requires in the Macedonians of antiquity. This interpretation clearly provides no explanation of why Leonidas chose this direction rather than another; yet my work takes as its starting point the difficulty of giving strictly causal elucidation in the matter of national identity. What would have become of his 'family tree' if his accident had not stopped him from following his father up the mountains, as he claims he was willing to do? And who would Leonidas be today if his mother had not died, accused of being Bulgarian? Confronted by what Goffman has termed 'fatal events'

(Goffman 1983) in the construction of his national identity, Leonidas certainly cannot be described as a pawn in a nationalist game greater than himself; he *acted* and was the agent of choices. I was able to verify with a small experiment this selection of identity, by showing Leonidas the diagram I had created of his kindred (see Figure 2.2).

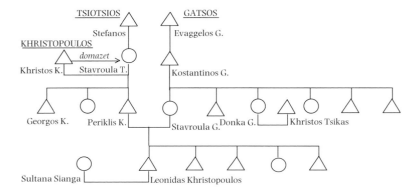

Figure 2.2 Author's graphic representation of Leonidas' family tree

He immediately protested that this family tree was 'wrong' because the chronological succession of generations unfolded from top to bottom ('do the roots of a tree wave in the air, I'd like to know?'); and on my asking him to 'complete' the diagram (prevailing upon him as little as possible and merely writing on the sheet where he indicated), what resulted was Figure 2.3. The relatives he added are designated by a thicker line, while for the sake of simplicity only the founder of the Tsiotsios line, Iannis, is given a name here – although Leonidas gave me the names of all these 'new' relatives.

I had been expecting the extension of the Tsiotsios branch but I could not have guessed in which direction and, above all, on which level of generation (G) this would have taken place. Instead of indicating the siblings of his paternal grandmother (G+2) – that is, two generations removed from 'ego' – Leonidas ascends directly to his great-great-grandfather (G+4) and from there on to his great-grandfather's brothers (G+3). His final descent, down to G+1, illustrates a familiarity with the Tsiotsios branch that can only be attributed to a deeply grounded affective alliance. This explains Leonidas' statement that it was his grandfather Khristos Khristopoulos who was responsible for their change of surname: it is only 'one' marriage (that of Stavroula Tsiotsiou, the 'necessary' woman in this agnatic grid) that keeps Leonidas and the Tsiotsios family branch apart. The 'underestimation' of the father's branch of the family was also to some extent foreseeable, due to the twofold effect of Leonidas' orientation towards the *zadruga*, and his father's branch's national choice to be 'Bulgarian', later 'Macedonian'. Leonidas not surpris-

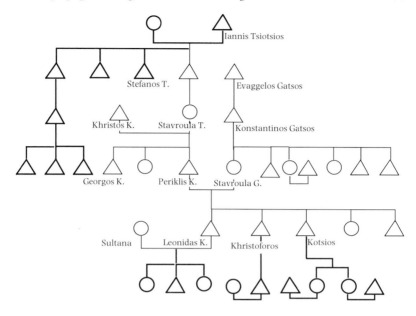

Figure 2.3 Leonidas' further elaboration of family tree

ingly underplays his relationship with a man who chose a nationality other than Greek. Yet a complete silence from this quarter was unexpected.

Whereas the extension towards the 'upper left' of the family tree thus confirmed my suppositions beyond my expectations, the extension towards the 'lower right' was at first incomprehensible. Leonidas' brothers all emigrated to Australia between 1955 and 1964; he hardly hears from them. Light began to dawn on me when he described the partners of his nephews and nieces: they were all 'foreign' (*kseni*) and included an 'Italian', an 'Australian English' and a 'South African English'. With the word *kseni* Leonidas designates Australian citizens of non-Greek descent. Searching once more through my notes, I found what had until that moment appeared of little interest. Leonidas had talked to me about these nephews and nieces at our first encounter, emphasising the cosmopolitan and inter-national (in the etymological sense of the word) character of his family. His 'Italian' and 'South African' relatives further confirm the unsustainability of the natural principle of national descent. Leonidas has chosen another way of representing himself: in time through history and memory, and in space through the integration of the Greater Macedonia of maps with the Lesser Macedonia of daily experience.[12] Leonidas continues to inhabit this Macedonia of his own without forgetting the other one, that of History.

Within his 'local Macedonia', Leonidas appears to know everyone and everyone seems to know him. Going around with Leonidas is always a mine of information for an anthropologist. Yet he, too, is beginning to think that the *historically deep locality*, of which he is a spokesman when he declares himself to be an *Ellinas Makedonas*, runs the risk of disappearing under conditions of globalisation that disperse people across the planet. Nevertheless, his family tree remains a hopeful metaphor of connectivity, and the onerous task of taking leave is therefore handed over to Leonidas (N6: 29):

'Our Kin. Our Roots'

A big tree was planted.
It grew to be very large.
And its roots spread beyond the confines of the field.
But also beyond the confines of the village.
'What does this mean?'
This means our large kin.
In Constantinople we have kin
In Serbia we have kin
In Australia we have kin
In Greece we have kin.
And at home, at our roots, what remains?
Only two elderly people: Leonidas and his wife Sultana.

ACKNOWLEDGEMENTS

For constructive criticism and help on this chapter, and for many other kindnesses, I am deeply grateful to Fikret Adanir, Georgios Agelopoulos, Maria Couroucli, Pietro Clemente, Jane Cowan, Hastings Donnan, Effi Gazi, Vasilis Gounaris, Sarah Green, Adam Kuper, Gilles de Rapper, Eugenio Testa, Bjørn Thomassen and Stuart Woolf. Very special thanks to Rea Alexandratos for having made this chapter possible through her help and love. *Ston barba Leonida, me agapi kai timi.*

NOTES

1. I use the term 'Macedonian of Greece' to indicate Greek citizens whose mother tongue is Macedonian, irrespective of their political, ethnic or national affiliations.
2. The opposition between Greater and Lesser History, implicit in Leonidas' narratives and analytically distinguished by me, partially echoes the familiar distinction between High Culture and Low Culture (Gellner, 1983). However, it owes more to Cirese's (1973) exploration of the dynamic and dialectical relationship between hegemonic and subaltern cultures. Thus, I am concerned with the ways an identity 'determined' by nationalism is not just passively accepted but may be 'transformed' by national subjects.

3. The Greek word *patridha* and the Italian word *paese* pointedly share the same ambiguity, being able to indicate either one's nation-state or one's specific and 'very local' place of origin.
4. Leonidas uses this archaic variant *Ellin* only on this occasion, to commence the notebook on the 'History of the Macedonian State'. It indicates his search for a 'continuity' with the past.
5. I subscribe here to Cohen's (1994: 119) definition of ethnicity as 'the politicisation of culture'.
6. On 'ethnic' autobiography and the circularity of the foundation of oneself and the authority to write, see Fischer (1986). On the paradoxical consequences brought when anthropologists take these 'ethnicist' criteria as self-evident, see Kuper (1994) and Gefou-Madianou (1993).
7. For Macedonia, see Agelopoulos (1993) and Karakasidou (1996).
8. The rather derogatory judgement of their mother tongue is widely diffused among the Macedonians of Greece, a consequence of repressive policies and negative attitudes towards Macedonians by the Greek state and the Patriarchist Orthodox church over many years. See Cowan (1997) for a similar (but only partially overlapping) attitude towards Macedonians in Sohos, a town of central Greek Macedonia.
9. These verses, one of the two examples of written Macedonian in the notebooks, are written in Greek characters.
10. This incident, which evokes both the 'sacrifice of Isaac' and the Oedipus complex, probably had moral legitimacy in this community. Sarah Green (personal communication) remarks that 'amongst *Sarakatsani* in Epirus ... [i]n the interests of both the victim and family, a badly wounded relative was to be put out of their misery.'
11. Leonidas coined this neologism to indicate 'informers' and 'intriguers'. It means literally 'loyal to informing' and it models itself on terms like *ethnikofrones* ('loyal to the nation') and *vasilofrones* ('loyal to the king'), employed during the Civil War. The term *Rufianos* can also mean 'pimp' or 'procurer'; *rufianofronos* carries these connotations of immorality.
12. That the coexistence of experienced locality with envisaged nation is not exclusive to Leonidas – even if rarely acknowledged by specialists of Macedonia – is clearly corroborated by the report of Captain Patrick H. Evans, parachuted into the Florina district of 'western Greek Macedonia' in 1944: 'The Macedonians are actuated by strong but mixed feelings of patriotism. In Greece this seems to be of three kinds, usually coexisting in the same person. There is a certain loyalty to the Greek State; and a thriving and at same time fervent local patriotism and a feeling, hard to assess because rarely uttered before strangers, and because it fluctuates with the turn of events and of propaganda, for Macedonia as such, regardless of present frontier-lines, which are looked upon as usurpation. ... But what is far stronger than the Macedonian's feeling for Greece is his local patriotism, not so much his love of country as of his own bit of country, his *patridha* – in this he resembles the population of Greece generally.' How ironic that this text, so attentive to the local and personal (and therefore variegated) dimension of Macedonia, should have been cited by a scholar (Rossos 1991: 294–5) who appears not to share this idea at all, preferring the Macedonia of maps and 'purity': 'a natural economic, and, in the main, an ethno-cultural unity' (1991: 282).

BIBLIOGRAPHY

Aarbakke, Vemund. 1992. 'Ethnic Rivalry and the Quest for Macedonia 1870–1913'. Unpublished MA thesis, Institute for East European Studies, University of Copenhagen.
Agelopoulos, Georgios. 1993. '"Mother of the Nation": Gender and ethnicity in rural Greek Macedonia'. Paper presented in the conference 'The Anthropology of Ethnicity', University of Amsterdam, 15–18 December 1993.

——— 1996. 'Perceptions, Construction, and Definition of Greek National Identity in Late Nineteenth–Early Twentieth Century Macedonia'. *Balkan Studies* 36(2), 247–63.

Barker, Elisabeth. 1950. *Macedonia: Its place in Balkan power politics.* London and New York: Royal Institute of International Affairs.

Brown, K.S. 1995. 'Of Meaning and Memories: The national imagination in Macedonia'. Unpublished Ph.D. dissertation, Department of Anthropology, University of Chicago.

Cavarero, Adriana. 1997. *Tu che mi guardi, tu che mi racconti: Filosofia della narrazione.* Milano: Feltrinelli.

Cirese, Alberto M. 1973. *Cultura egemonica e culture subalterne.* Palermo: Palumbo.

Clemente, Pietro. 1994. 'Epifanie di perdenti', in S. Bertelli & P. Clemente (eds) *Tracce dei vinti.* Firenze: Ponte alle Grazie.

——— 1997. 'Paese/paesi', in M. Isenghi (ed.) *I luoghi della memoria: Strutture ed eventi dell'Italia unita.* Roma-Bari: Laterza.

Cohen, Anthony P. 1994. *Self Consciousness: An alternative anthropology of identity.* London and New York: Routledge.

Cowan, Jane K. 1997. 'Idioms of Belonging: Polyglot articulations of local identity in a Greek Macedonian town', in P. Mackridge and E. Yannakakis (eds) *Ourselves and Others: The development of a Greek Macedonian cultural identity since 1912.* Oxford/New York: Berg.

Eco, Umberto. 1979. *Lector in fabula: La cooperazione interpretativa nei testi narrativi.* Milano: Bompiani.

Fischer, Michael M. J. 1986. 'Ethnicity and the Post-Modern Arts of Memory', in J. Clifford and G. E. Marcus (eds) *Writing Cultures: The poetics and politics of ethnography.* Berkeley: University of California Press.

Geertz, Clifford. 1963. 'The Integrative Revolution: Primordial sentiments and civil politics in the new states', in *The Interpretation of Cultures.* New York: Basic Books, 1973.

Gefou-Madianou, Dimitra. 1993. 'Mirroring Ourselves through Western Texts: The limits of an indigenous anthropology', in H. Driessen (ed.) *The Politics of Ethnographic Reading and Writing: Confrontations of western and indigenous views.* Saarbrücken – Fort Lauderdale: Verlag Breitenbach Publishers.

Gellner, Ernest. 1983. *Nations and Nationalism.* Oxford: Blackwell.

Gillis, John R. (ed.). 1994. *Commemorations: The politics of national identity.* Princeton: Princeton University Press.

Goffman, Erwin. 1983. *Where the Action Is: Three essays.* London: Lane.

Gounaris, Basil C. 1996. 'Riciclando le tradizioni. Identità etniche e diritti delle minoranze in Macedonia'. *Il Mondo 3. Rivista di teoria delle scienze umane e sociali* 1–2, 94–109.

Gramsci, Antonio. 1929. 'Osservazioni sul folclore', in *Letteratura e vita nazionale.* Torino: Einaudi, 1950.

Hacking, Ian. 1995. *Rewriting the Soul: Multiple personality and the sciences of memory.* Princeton: Princeton University Press.

Karakasidou, Anastasia. 1993. 'Politicizing Culture: Negating ethnic identity in Greek Macedonia'. *Journal of Modern Greek Studies* 11(1), 1–28.

——— 1996. 'Women of the Family, Women of the Nation. National enculturation among Slavic speakers in northwestern Greece'. *Women's Studies International Forum* 19(1–2), 99–109.

Kuper, Adam. 1994. 'Culture, Identity, and the Project of a Cosmopolitan Anthropology'. *Man* (n.s.) 29(3), 537–54.

MacIntyre, Alasdair. 1981. *After Virtue: A Study in Moral Theory.* Indiana: University of Notre Dame Press.

Perry, Duncan. 1988. *The Politics of Terror: The Macedonian revolutionary movements, 1893–1903.* Durham: Duke University Press.

Rihtman-Auguštin, Dunja. 1988. 'The Communal Family between Real and Imagined Order'. *Narodna Umjetnost,* Special Issue 2: 209–19.

Rossos, Andrew. 1991. Document. 'The Macedonians of Aegean Macedonia: A British officer's report, 1944'. *The Slavonic and East European Review* 69(2), 282–309.

Todorova, Maria. 1990. 'Myth-Making in European Family History: The Zadruga revisited'. *East European Politics and Societies* 4(1), 30–76.

Wilkinson, H.R. 1951. *Maps and Politics: A review of the ethnographic cartography of Macedonia.* Liverpool: The University Press.

Woodhouse, C.M. 1986. *Modern Greece: A short history.* London and Boston: Faber and Faber.

3 ON THE OTHER SIDE OF THE RIVER: THE DEFEATED SLAVOPHONES AND GREEK HISTORY

Iakovos D. Michailidis

Yet there may be a counter-history, which we should also know, and which runs parallel to the history of the victors, the Church, or the state. This history, which cannot rest on the same foundations, sometimes cannot survive other than orally or in some other way. (Ferro 1996: 19)

HISTORICAL ACRIMONY

The Voice of the Ancestors

On 6 April 1904, Turkish soldiers entered the home of the Orthodox notable, Nikolaos Vannis, in the village of Aetos, Florina prefecture, and arrested the famous *voivode*[1] Alexi Turundjiev from Xyno Nero. The arrest, which was part of the Ottomans' mass persecution of Exarchists after the Ilinden uprising in the summer of 1903, was the result of a well-laid trap. It had been set for this legendary *komitadjis* by Vannis himself, along with the village priest, Papa Alexis, and in collaboration with the Turkish authorities.[2] The news of the arrest of 'Alexi from Exi Sou' was received with profound relief by the Patriarchists in the area, who had suffered hell on earth from Turundjiev's activities (Krustevski-Koska, 1993: 166). He was incarcerated at Monastir and hanged in the marketplace a year and a half later, on 12 September 1905.[3]

Thirty years later, in November 1943, another Turundjiev (Giorgos Touroundzias) from Xyno Nero was appointed head of the Florina branch of the Slavo-Macedonian People's Liberation Front (*SNOF*), the resistance organisation of the Slavo-Macedonians of Greece (Panovska, 1995: 104). But Giorgos Touroundzias was not the only, nor even the most eminent, figure in his family involved in the resistance against Axis occupation. Ilias Turundjiev, probably a relative of Giorgos, played a leading role in the events of the 1940s. A well-known communist, he was arrested by the Metaxas dictatorship regime in 1938, but released after he had recanted and renounced communism. The Occupation and the Civil War found him and a number of

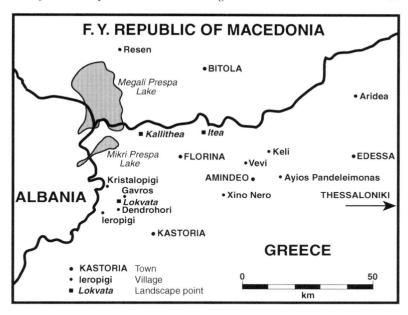

Map 3. The West Central corner of Geographical Macedonia

other Slavo-Macedonians courting Tito's partisans, and it was not long before he had become a separatist[4] and was engaging in anti-Greek activities. Thus, in April 1944 he set up the 'Kastoria and Florina Regiment', whose members were Slavo-Macedonian separatists, formerly (in many cases) pro-Bulgarian. He quickly won the sympathy and trust of his partisan comrades (Koliopoulos, 1994: 168–9). At the conference of Macedonian refugees from Aegean Macedonia, which was held at Monastir on 3 December 1944, he and 29 others were elected to the central committee (Mamurovski 1992: 48–9).

Ilias Turundjiev probably never knew Alexi; but he would certainly have heard about him through the family traditions, where legend and fact frequently meet and enmesh. He would undoubtedly have been proud of his illustrious grandfather, who had managed to break free of the oppressive mediocrity of the locality and link his name with the fortunes of the region. It is also very likely that he would have inherited, through the 'secret channels' of family tradition, something of his forebear's enmity towards Greek nationalism. It seems that these memories, in which old, unfulfilled desires were kept concealed from an intrusive environment, eventually began to weigh on his mind. Within him grew a passion for vengeance, which propelled him onto the path of lawlessness and then of exile.

Turundjiev's case is by no means the only one of its kind, nor the most important. But it does show us that the capitulation of Turundjiev's community to Greek forces produced only temporary truces. Different allegiances continued to develop in such places, long after Greek rule was established. This is, in part, because powerful local pro-Bulgarian forces – *voivodes*, teachers, and clergy – active in the Bulgarian campaign in Macedonia during the period 1870–1912 had been mythified by their communities, and bequeathed their descendants a heavy burden.

This chapter is an attempt to prove what should be self-evident but is often denied: that sometimes at a local and a personal level, memories and meanings of historical events do not exactly tally with official views of national history. Personal memories (especially memories of glory), the whole tradition of one's family and one's birthplace, and the way one perceives and perhaps converses with one's past, may prove more powerful than even the strongest efforts to incorporate and assimilate those persons, and cultivate in them a national heritage. The field of investigation will be twentieth-century Macedonia, and the object of study those Slavophones[5] who oppose Greek nationalism and the Greek national ideology. It will be shown that the Ilinden bloodbath was the first of two periods that produced Slavophone heroes, whose legacies have endured to the present day and whose national allegiances are claimed retrospectively by two different states: Bulgaria and FYROM. The second heroic period in these Slavophones' history was undoubtedly the 1940s. The experiences of the Occupation and the Civil War created a new generation of Slavo-Macedonian heroes (as they identified themselves then), many of whom were descendants of the first Ilinden heroes and who had grown up during the interwar period. Both these periods bear the bitter stamp of failure. But whereas Ilinden was an epic but failed uprising, just one defeat in the Slavophones' struggle against the powers that be, the end of the Civil War was probably their swan-song. It marked the crushing of all their aspirations, and their utter defeat, since they were then forced to leave Greece and seek refuge outside their homelands. Both these periods, 'the first and the second Ilinden', as they have been termed (Kofos 1996), have something else in common, too. They were periods of armed attempts to win liberation from, respectively, Ottoman and Greek rule. At the same time they were the continuation of family and local traditions on the field of battle.

By contrast, the third period, which is how I regard the interval between the establishment of the People's Republic of Macedonia (PRM) in 1945 and the present day, has not been characterised by armed defence of family and local heritage. Rather, it has taken the form of, on the one hand, official historiography about the 'unredeemed homelands' and, on the other, political action in the diaspora (for example, Canada, Australia and Eastern Europe) and through the various refugee associations established by Slavophones. The modern historical literature produced in FYROM, relating to the geographical area of Greek Macedonia, comes primarily from historians and history researchers whose origins lie in Greek Macedonia, most of whom were members of the Democratic Army[6] during the Greek Civil War. Given such personal backgrounds, the history written contains a particular political bias. While political bias is not unknown among Greek historians either, the danger here is that these works of FYROM historians could encourage the perpetuation, in some form, of the family tradition initiated by the first Ilinden generation.

The Greek historical corpus on Macedonia groans under the mass of monographs, collective works, and other studies relating both to the Greek-speaking heroes and to the Slavophones who joined the Greek side. Rhapsodic accounts and epic hagiographies adorn the canvas of Greek history.[7] In recent years, however, as the diplomatic dispute (an oxymoron, admittedly, yet offering comfort and hope) between Athens and Skopje has come to a head, a number of special studies and articles by Greek scholars have taken a distance on their monotonously triumphalist fifty-year-plus historiographical heritage,[8] most of which had included Macedonia and its history merely to justify, and thus to safeguard, the northern boundaries. They have retrained the spotlight on the great absentee, the Macedonia of the start of the century, where local people's ever-changing convictions were simply a faithful reflection of the uncertainty of the everyday situation and cannot, therefore, be considered reprehensible today.

The initiative taken by some Greek scholars, using historical and anthropological perspectives, has encouraged a dialogue between scholars from Greece, Bulgaria and FYROM. In a recent article, K.S. Brown (2000) reveals the ways in which some Slavo-Macedonian historians have started to revise the 'pantheon of national heroes'. Yet any revision of 'the whole interpretative and chronological frame on which their profession was so solidly based' is still, he claims, doubtful.[9] The Bulgarian, and particularly the Slavo-Macedonian, historians are in an exceptionally difficult position. This, as we shall see, is directly connected with the 'unredeemed territories' syndrome, a widespread malaise in the Balkans. Clearly, the ability of Greek historians to take a more critical stance is partly due to the security afforded by their country's military and diplomatic victories on the battlefields. Only a few decades ago, particularly in the 1940s, when Greek ascendancy in Macedonia was being challenged, Greek history researchers would refer to the anti-Greek Slavophones in extremely negative terms, ascribing very pejorative connotations to the words 'Slav' and 'Bulgarian'.[10]

Within Greek historiography, the Greek victors of the struggle for Macedonia cast their shadow over the 'others', especially those whom fate identified initially with the Bulgarian side and later with the PRM. These people have been left on the sidelines of history, disinherited by the historical past, fugitives from the pantheon of heroes created by official Greek historiography. They have nonetheless stitched together their own tradition, steeped in failures and denials, unfulfilled aspirations and historical insecurities. Paradoxically, the history written by the victors often sides, if indirectly, with the losers. For by condemning any memory of their struggles against Greek nationalism, it justifies the losers' cause: their quest for their own nation. Their classification as villains has the understandable effect of making them heroes to many of their own people, the 'others'. The space–time continuum of Greek Macedonia offers countless illustrations of this.

This chapter takes a step towards reconciliation with those many Slavophones whose memories have never been acknowledged in Greek historiography.[11] Responding to those who have discerned a general 'nationalistic paranoia' in Greece and who have accused Greek historians, mainly, but also other scholars, of indulging in 'nationalistic ravings', it attempts a more critical approach to the nationalism of all sides. The chapter was prompted by having seen, through my researches, the bitter consequences of this exclusion. Although I am aware that, given the available historical evidence, both written and oral, my own analysis is far from neutral, I have tried to depict sympathetically the grievances of some Macedonian peasant communities. The epic tone of my account matches their own stories, and was judged most suitable to describe their pain and humiliation. Acknowledging their suffering, and understanding the ways this motivates their vision of Macedonian history, I do not, however, justify all their past actions. Furthermore, I worry that a history of unfulfilled longings, as much as a history of national triumph, undermines efforts toward peaceful coexistence.

The discipline of history is all the poorer, and the quest for truth all the more difficult, because the Slavophones of Greece rarely left memoirs of the interwar period for specialists to consult. It is therefore difficult to investigate Slavophones' own views: how they perceived their present and envisaged their future. Inadequate – indeed usually non-existent – education owing to almost total dependence on the land, fear due to unfavourable external circumstances, and the acrimony born of constant disappointments disarmed the few who might have written down their personal history. They thus deprived posterity of any opportunity to learn the inside story or to chart its microhistory.

The Rolis family from Itea, in the Florina prefecture, falls into the same category as the Turundjievs. Stefanos Rolis went underground around 1900, after he had murdered the local Muslim landlord, Ali Tcherkez. He soon joined the *chet*[12] of the legendary Giorgi Ivanov (also known as Marko Lerinski), who was training aspiring *voivodes* in 1901, and later the *chet* of the teacher Giorgi Pop Hristov, who was active in the Florina area in the same period. He later fled to Skopje, where he wrote his memoirs at an advanced age in 1968 (Krustevski-Koska 1993: 159–62).

His grandson, Stefanos, was a typical case of a Slavo-Macedonian who vacillated during the harsh 1940s before finally coming down on the anti-Greek side. The Bulgarian occupation of Macedonia flung him into the embrace of Anton Kalchev, the Bulgarian officer who set up the secret pro-Bulgarian organisation known as the Ohrana. He fled his village in April 1945, evidently because the Bulgarian army had withdrawn from Greece, though it remains unclear whether he went to Monastir or to Bulgaria.[13]

The Terpovski and Chalev families from Dendrohori followed a similar course. Kiro Chalev was the grandson of a teacher named Kiriak Terpovski, who had been one of the most prominent local cadres of the Internal

Macedonian Revolutionary Organisation (IMRO) at the beginning of the twentieth century. Kiro came into contact with communist ideas while still a youth, and in 1934 joined the Young Communists of Greece. In 1939, at the height of the Metaxas dictatorship, he paid for his communist views with four months in prison. A year later, in the winter of 1940–1, he served in the Greek army and fought against the Italians. His subsequent career was brilliant. The founding conference of the Kastoria branch of *SNOF* was held at his home on 20 October 1943 (Mamurovski 1995: 13). Shortly afterwards, he joined the Goche Delchev *chet*, which had been set up by the Slavo-Macedonian guerrillas of the Greek Communist Party (GCP). He soon became one of the leading lights of the Slavo-Macedonian *Nofites* and in May 1945 he became a guerrilla fighter following the instructions of the Central Committee of the People's Liberation Front (*NOF*). His guerrilla activities eventually cost him his life, for he was killed in a bombardment on 17 March 1949 in the village of Kallithea, near Prespa (Pop-Janevski 1996: 277–8).

The Terpovskis were one of the eminent Slavo-Macedonian families who played a leading part in the dramatic events of the 1940s. The renowned Lazo Terpovski and his brothers Kosta and Hristo were first cousins of Kiro Chalev. Like many of his Slavo-Macedonian compatriots, Lazo was a member of the GCP. Very active and something of a firebrand, he was soon indicted by the Metaxas dictatorship regime and incarcerated with a number of comrades at Akronafplia. He was released in June 1941, following the intervention of the Bulgarians,[14] and continued to work for the GCP. Terpovski supported the GCP's views on the Macedonian Question and regarded the Slavo-Macedonians as one of the peoples of Macedonia. He also played a leading part in effecting a rapprochement between the GCP and the Slavo-Macedonian members of the Ohrana. These activities took him into the eye of the storm, and he was executed in April 1943 in the village of Imera, Kozani prefecture, by a group of armed Greek Pontians[15] who had sided with the Germans (Koliopoulos 1994: 162–3).

All the aforementioned individuals, examples of just one segment of the Slavophone population, were called upon at various times to cross the line and approach the Greek side. But even in cases where they themselves wished it, the social circumstances prevented them from doing so. And so they remained true to the 'other side of the river', hearkening grimly to the memories of their ancestors. They were the Don Quixotes of Bulgarianism to begin with and of Macedonianism later on, the people whom the current of life always cast up with the losers. And they were, thus, from the perspective of the Greek historiography, always the people on the other side.

Our Country Calls Us

Family tradition was unquestionably the primary factor that led various Slavophones to take sides. Almost as important, however, was the tradition of their place of origin. Many Slavophone villages that had sided with the Exarchate[16] during the Macedonian Struggle unreservedly supported *SNOF* and later the People's Liberation Front (*NOF*) in the 1940s. Dendrohori of the Kastoria region was a typical example.

Dendrohori was an ordinary Macedonian village. According to the available archival evidence, the vast majority of its 250 or so families sided firmly with the Exarchate at the beginning of the twentieth century.[17] It was one of the first Slavophone villages to revolt during the Ilinden uprising in the summer of 1903, and it paid a heavy price. The Turkish army entered the village, killed a number of inhabitants (Georgieff and Trifonoff 1995: 280–1) and burnt it almost down to the ground (Pelayidis 1987: 357).

One landmark event in the history of Dendrohori took place shortly before the Ilinden uprising, on 31 May 1903. Bulgarian guerrillas clashed with Turkish troops at Lokvata on Viniari, one of the peaks of Mount Mali-madi. It was an unequal battle: the Turkish soldiers numbered in the hundreds, the *chets* were a few dozen. The rebellious Dendrohorians were accompanied by some of the most important *komitadjides* in the area: Pando Kljashev, Vasil Chakalarov, and Laki Popovski from Krystallopiyi, Mitro Vlaho from Makrohori, and Ditso Antonov from Ayios Dimitrios, Kastoria prefecture. The battle, fast and furious, went on for eleven hours. The Turks prevailed, but there were heavy losses on both sides: more than a hundred Turks were killed, while the *komitadjides* lost 14 men, including Chakalarov's 29-year-old brother Foti, the two *voivodes* Antonov and Popovski, and nine guerrillas from Dendrohori (Pop-Janevski 1996: 53; Silianoff 1983: 272). This decimation of Dendrohori left an indelible mark on the historical memory of the village. A few weeks later, on 21 June, Lazar Poptrajkov, an ideologist and *komitadjis* from Dendrohori and a founding member of the Kastoria branch of IMRO, composed a moving ode at Berik to his comrades who had fallen at Lokvata, entitled 'Lokvata and Viniari'.[18]

The legendary Battle of Lokvata and Poptrajkov's poem had a tremendous impact.[19] In the years that followed, the Slavophone villagers gave that tragic experience a mythical and heroic dimension. Dendrohori's commitment to the Exarchate remained virtually unchanged throughout the interwar period. Both during the Balkan Wars and during the First World War, a number of the villagers identified with Bulgaria and then emigrated there. In the 1930s, communist ideas, which were closely bound up at the time with the slogans calling for an 'independent' and 'autonomous' Macedonia, had a great impact in the village.

The 1940s revived the memories from the beginning of the century. In May 1941, the villagers, together with a number of Slavo-Macedonians from other villages – Krystallopiyi, Ieropiyi, Ayios Dimitrios, Kraniona, and Vatohori – organised a celebration at Lokvata. During this, speeches were made in Bulgarian and wreaths were laid in memory of the *komitadjides* who had fallen at the epic battle in 1903 (Pop-Janevski 1996: 102–4). In the years which followed, the general state of flux and the hopes of achieving a communist regime guaranteeing equal rights for the ethnic minorities prompted many Dendrohorians to rebel. Thirty-three villagers joined the 'Macedonian Brigade' (Pop-Janevski 1996: 127–8), including prominent Slavo-Macedonian separatists like Kosta Zurkov, Dono Chalev, and Evdokia-Vera Nikola Baleva. Dendrohori's active involvement in the Civil War and its adherence to the communist and separatist cause ultimately led to its total destruction. The Slavophone villagers were forced into exile and the village became inhabited by Vlachs from Epirus.

The Dendrohorians are now dispersed all over the world. Most of them, some 204 families, live in FYROM. Four families are in Serbia, one in Slovenia, 53 in Australia, 53 in Canada, 64 in America, twelve in former Czechoslovakia, 15 in Bulgaria, four in Romania, five in the former Soviet Union, two in Albania, and 32 families remaining in Greece. Those in Greece are scattered in Kastoria, Florina, Thessaloniki, Athens, Piraeus, Volos, Xanthi, and Lamia (Pop-Janevski 1996: 314–27). However, scattered as they are to all four corners of the globe, they have still managed to remain closely in touch and seem to feel a remarkable nostalgia for their birthplace. The Battle of Lokvata in particular still holds an intense poignancy for them. So it is not surprising that Poptrajkov's poem has been translated recently into the official language of FYROM from standard literary Bulgarian and, recently, into Greek (Karadza 1993).

A number of other villages in Greek Macedonia are in the same category as Dendrohori. These include Xyno Nero, Vevi, Keli, Ayios Pandeleimonas and Gavros. All of them played a leading part both in the events of 1903 (when all were torched by the Turkish army) and in the Occupation and the Civil War (when their adherence to the separatist camp brought reprisals from those supporting the Greek side). Such prominent Slavophones as Vasil Chakalarov from Krystallopiyi, a former member of the rural police force and active *Snofite*, Mihail Keramidjiev from Gavros, and the important separatist and head of the armed Slavo-Macedonian band known as the *Grupa Lazo Terpovski*, Naum Pejos, linked the names of these villages both with the Exarchate at the beginning of the century and with activities against Greece in the 1940s.

The generation of the second Ilinden continued along the trail that their predecessors had blazed in 1903. The goals, the visions and the aspirations had scarcely changed at all. Indeed, the summer of 1903 was a source of inspiration for all the Slavo-Macedonians in *SNOF* and *NOF*. This is clearly demonstrated by the fact that, during the Civil War, many of the leading cadres of *SNOF* adopted *noms de guerre* that had been used originally by heroes of the Ilinden uprising. Pavle Rakovski, for instance, a member of the Central Council of *NOF*, went by the name of Goche (Delchev). He evidently wished to underline the similarities he shared with the renowned *komitadjides* from Kilkis and Inspector General of the *chets* in 1901–2. Naum Pejos used the name of the famous Kastorian *komitadjis*, Vasil Chakalarov, the propagandist of the Slavo-Macedonian *Nofites* in the Edessa area. Vangel Sapardanov rose to prominence as Ilindenski. Giorgi Kostov appropriated the name of Janne Sandanski, the extreme left-wing IMRO hardliner (Kirjazovski 1982: 115).

THE MOMENT OF VINDICATION

Historians and History Researchers

The 'third Ilinden' – the survival of the family tradition of the anti-Greek Slavophones to the present day – has abandoned its armed aspect. It has transmuted chiefly into historiography and political activity among the diaspora and through the various refugee associations.

As far as historiography is concerned, all the drive and vigour of the Slavo-Macedonians was channelled towards their new homeland, the PRM. It is significant that almost the entire historical output regarding Greek Macedonia has been, and still is, in the hands of Slavo-Macedonian political fugitives from Greece. They, in their turn, have understandably filled tens of thousands of pages, giving vent to the irredentist longings and the tribulations of their generation. What was peripheral in Greece is, in this context, in the spotlight; what was reprehensible has been vindicated. Their history, and the history of their comrades of the first and the second Ilinden, has become a heroic, national affair.

Risto Kirjazovski, an eminent historian, was born on 6 January 1927 at Ayia Anna, Kastoria prefecture. A guerrilla fighter with *ELAS* and the Democratic Army from 1943 to 1949, he was one of the defeated who left Greek Macedonia; and his new homeland, the PRM, gave him unstintingly all that his birthplace had denied him. In 1959, he was offered a post in the Archive of Macedonia and in June 1974 he joined the National History Institute in Skopje. His scholarly career culminated in 1981, when he received his doctorate from the School of History in the Faculty of Philosophy of Skopje University (Mladenovski 1987: 7–12). His prolific output has focused on Greek Macedonia, and he has written more than a hundred books, articles, reviews and critiques, all of which reveal his nostalgia for his lost homeland and the unassuaged longing and irredentism of his generation (Jiovanovits 1987: 13–20).

Kruste Bitoski is a similar case. Born in 1926 at Gavros, Kastoria prefecture, he too left Greece for the PRM and quickly established himself there. In 1965, he completed his doctoral thesis in history, and worked in the National History Institute, Skopje, from 1967 onwards (Ivanovski 1986: 7–11). His scholarly output, over seventy articles, books and book reviews, focuses on Greek Macedonia (Tsfetkovska 1986: 13–18).

In the same category we must also include Hristo Antonovski, who developed the dominant theoretical approach on the existence of a 'Macedonian minority' in Greek Macedonia. Born in 1923 in the village of Hryssa, Pella prefecture, he was a former column leader of the National Youth Organisation and in charge of the local communist cell in Edessa (Valden 1991: 62). Now a veteran historian in his new homeland, he enjoys the privileges accruing from the part he has played in constructing a national myth.

Another notable link in this chain of Slavo-Macedonian historians was Todor Simovski from the village of Piyi, Kilkis prefecture. Originally a member of the Greek police force, he later joined both *SNOF* and *NOF* (Kirjazovski and Simovski 1976: 299). He followed the example of most of his comrades at the end of the 1940s and fled to the PRM, where he embarked upon a systematic record of the history of Greek Macedonia. His most important work is dedicated 'to my father, Hristo P. Simovski, to my brother, Apostolos H. Simovski, and to the tens of thousands of my compatriots who gave their lives for national and social freedom' (Simovski 1978).

Antonovski, Kirjazovski, Bitoski, and Simovski are not the only cases, however. I venture to assert that the historical output, both official and unofficial, published in FYROM and relating to Greek Macedonia, has been entrusted almost exclusively to people who originate from there. Indeed, bearing in mind that the national ideology of the PRM draws elements of its myth from Greek Macedonia, it would be no exaggeration to say that its historiography has incorporated strong nationalistic elements.

Refugee Organisations and Emigrés

However, as has already been pointed out, the writing of history is only one way in which the Slavo-Macedonian fugitives from Aegean Macedonia have established themselves. The other means has been through their commanding presence in the diaspora. Both in the interwar period and after the Civil War, thousands of Slavo-Macedonians emigrated from Greek Macedonia to the New World, to Australia, America and Canada, taking with them all the tensions and, frequently, the confrontations and discord of their birthplace.

John Bitov is a successful businessman now living in Toronto. Of Slavo-Macedonian origin, he hails from the village of Gavros, Kastoria prefecture. His business activities and financial prosperity have not deterred him from taking part in the activities of his co-national emigrants. He is now president of the World Macedonian Congress and is known for his vehement criticism of the Greek government. This is illustrated by the lively exchange he had in September 1992 with the then Foreign Minister of Greece, Mihalis Papakonstandinou, who had called on him to hear his views. Bitov (Papakonstandinou does not mention him by name) reacted strongly when the Minister introduced himself as a Greek Macedonian, retorting that the only Macedonian present was himself. He informed the rather stunned Minister that he, Papakonstandinou, had enslaved his, Bitov's, village, the place where the bones of his fathers and his grandfathers lay buried (Papakonstandinou 1994: 160–1).

Many other Slavo-Macedonian immigrants from Greek Macedonia fall into the same category as Bitov. The economist Mihail Gramadikovski from Kallithea, Florina prefecture, is president of the Association of Macedonians in Poland.[20] Stefo Pljakov from Sklithro, Florina prefecture, is president of the 'Macedonian Union' in Toronto.[21] Soker Mitrev from Sitaria, Florina prefecture, is president of the Council of Macedonians from Aegean Macedonia in Melbourne[22] and the mechanical engineer Don Rakovski from Kratero, Florina prefecture, was president of the Union of Child Refugees from Aegean Macedonia.[23]

A special case is Kole Magov, who left Greece at an early age in 1945. He now lives in Skopje and is president of an organisation named Dignity. He is author of a number of books and articles (Magov 1995). He has several times complained to international organisations that the Greek authorities have prevented him from visiting his village and defending his property.[24] His brother Stavros Magos was one of the many Slavophones who wavered between Greek and various other identities. Stavros Magos leased the lignite mine at Vevi for years and was a close political associate of Filippos Dragoumis[25] during the 1920s. However, a succession of disappointments and probable frustration with official Greek policy soon propelled him 'across the river'. In July 1936, he was jailed by decision of the Public Security Board of Florina prefecture, accused of engaging in separatist activities (Varda 1993: 168). On his release, he forged close ties with the Bulgarians, joining the Bulgarian propagandist committee organised by Kalchev in Florina. Magos travelled frequently to Sofia to obtain Bulgarian books and to request the appointment of Bulgarian priests and teachers (Chrysochoou 1950: 70). When the Germans withdrew and his life was in danger, he fled to Bulgaria.[26]

For all the above-mentioned individuals, their tenacious adherence to 'Macedonianism' is not simply a historical imperative dictated by personal memories. It is also vital to their political survival in the game of party politics that is being played out in FYROM, especially to win the votes of the *Egejci* (Aegean Macedonians). This is confirmed in the way that politicians of every stripe flock to the events staged by the refugee organisations.[27]

WHAT THE FUTURE HOLDS

These two interested constituencies – Aegean refugees from whose ranks come many historians of FYROM on the one hand and, on the other, the immigrants in the Australian and American diaspora who provide the bulk of funds for the political parties – are, and will continue to be, the fundamental parameters that perpetuate the Macedonian Question. Political ambitions mainly, revanchism often, the need for self-determination, and a nostalgia at least as strong as that felt by the first-generation Greek refugees from Asia Minor for several decades after the Asia Minor Disaster – these are the source of the present irredentist claims. These claims for the union of all Macedonian lands into one state are coming from the Aegean Refugee Associations, not from the government of FYROM. The Greek audience has not yet realised how serious these parameters are. It is lost homelands, lost youth, acrimony and unfulfilled longings that pull the strings of the thorny Macedonian Question.

We are obviously living in the generation of the 'third Ilinden', in an age in which the politics of arms has been supplanted by the power of the pen and of money. However, the radical upheavals in the Balkans make it absolutely imperative that the Balkan peoples smooth out their historical differences and effect a rapprochement. I believe, in fact, that the Greek and the Slavo-Macedonian historians, and indeed all their Balkan colleagues, bear an enormous responsibility in this respect, perhaps greater than all the rest. What historiography needs is a radical change of approach, to unhitch itself completely from the wagon of nationalism. Bigotry and excesses – such as the use by Greeks of the terms 'Bulgarian' and 'Slav' as insults, and the references by the Slavo-Macedonians to the 'genocide of hundreds of thousands of Macedonians by the Greek authorities' – certainly do not help. What I am proposing is not merely a gesture of good will; it is the *sine qua non* for a meaningful rapprochement. Otherwise, I fear that the strife between neighbours over the historical past of greater Macedonia will never be confined to a narrow historical, academic context, but will remain forever a profoundly politicised and nationalistic issue, making any mutual rapprochement that much more difficult.

ACKNOWLEDGEMENTS

This chapter has benefited a great deal from comments by Georgios Agelopoulos, Jane Cowan, Basil Gounaris and Riki Van Boeschoten.

ACRONYMS

ELAS: (*Ellinikos Laikos Apeleftherotikos Stratos* = Greek People's Liberation Army). Pro-communist military organisation, by far the most popular resistance group in Greece during the German Occupation.

IMRO: (Internal Macedonian Revolutionary Organisation). Political and military organisation established by activist Bulgarians in 1893 seeking independence for the Bulgarians in Macedonia.

NOF: (*Narodno Osloboditelen Front* = People's Liberation Front). Political and military organisation established by communist Slavo-Macedonians from Greek Macedonia during the Greek Civil War. A member of the organisation is referred to as a *Nofite* (plural: *Nofites*).

PRM: (People's Republic of Macedonia). One of the federal states of the People's Republic of Yugoslavia established on 2 August 1944.

SNOF: (*Slavianomakedonski Narodno Osloboditelen Front* = Slavo-Macedonian
People's Liberation Front). Political and military organisation established
by communist Slavo-Macedonians from Greek Macedonia during the
German Occupation.

NOTES

1. *Voivode* (plural: *voivodes*) refers to the chieftain of a Bulgarian armed band (*chet*)
   involved in resistance against Ottoman rule in Macedonia. A member of such a band
   was called a *komitadjis* (plural: *komitadjides*), 'committee member', in reference to the
   Central Committee of the Internal Macedonian Revolutionary Organisation. The
   Exarchate refers to the Bulgarian Orthodox Church, which the Ottoman government
   allowed Bulgaria to establish in 1870 and which operated as an organ of Bulgarian
   national propaganda. Its supporters were called 'Exarchists'. The Patriarchate refers
   to the established Orthodox church, based in Constantinople, which operated as an
   organ of Greek national propaganda, and whose supporters were known as 'Patriarchists'.
   The Ilinden uprising, so-called because it was launched on the feast day of St Elijah
   (20th July by the 'old' Julian calendar, 2 August by the 'new' Gregorian calendar, in
   1903), was a peasant uprising against Ottoman rule carried out in numerous locations
   in Macedonia.
2. Archive of the Greek Foreign Ministry 1904/AAK/A, 'Monastir', Kalergis to Foreign
   Minister, Monastir, 14 April 1904, Reg. No. 418.
3. Public Record Office/Foreign Office (hereafter PRO/FO) 195/2208, microfilmed in
   the Research Centre of the Museum of the Macedonian Struggle (MMS) and indexed
   as MMA6/b/39, Pierre K.D. Pissurica to the Consul General, Monastir, 12 September
   1905, No.K5, f.K62, Haus-, Hof- & Staatsarchiv/Politisches Archiv XXXVIIII, 'Konsulat
   Monastir', Vol. 394, Prochaska to Goluchowski, Monastir, 12 September 1905, Reg.
   No. 39.
4. During the Greek Civil War some Slavo-Macedonians supported the unification of Greek
   Macedonia with the newly established PRM and within a Yugoslav or a Balkan
   federation.
5. The term 'Slavophones' is used to denote the Slav-speakers of Macedonia in general
   without any reference to their actual ethnic or national allegiance. The term 'Slavo-
   Macedonians' stands for those who openly challenged Greek and Bulgarian nationalism
   during the 1940s.
6. The military branch of the GCP during the Greek Civil War (1946–9).
7. Examples are the monographs by Koemtzopoulos (1968); Vakalopoulos (1987); and
   Fitzios (1988); and the articles by Pallas (1961), Notaris (1964), Tzimopoulos (1982)
   and Sakellaropoulos (1992).
8. Examples include Gounaris (1990, 1993, 1994); Koliopoulos (1994, 1995); Vouri
   (1992); Michailidis (1996a, 1996b). The most representative example, however, is
   the edited collection by Gounaris, Michailidis and Agelopoulos (1997).
9. I am grateful to Keith Brown for letting me consult his unpublished paper.
10. Nikoulakos (1944); Grigoriou (1947); *Makedonia*, 16 January 1949. Basil Gounaris
    discusses the subject in an unpublished article titled 'Egnosmenon koinonikon
    fronimaton: Koinonikes kai alles opseis tou antikommounismou sti Makedonia tou
    Emfiliou Polemou' ('Of Well-Established Social Convictions: Social and other aspects
    of anticommunism in Macedonia during the Civil War (1945–1949)').
11. In a talk he gave at the Aristotle University of Thessaloniki, Professor Ioannis
    Koliopoulos said:

I hope this brief analysis of the Greek position on the Macedonian Question has clarified certain facets and aspects of the history of this region that have hitherto been clouded by various subsequent developments and expediencies, both national and international. This clarification, in which the university has played a prominent part in the past few years, together with a reconciliation with this country's historical past, will give us a better understanding of ourselves, and also help us to adapt to a new world that is taking shape. We must adapt cautiously, but without angst; gradually freeing ourselves from the oppressive allure of the historiography of 'lost homelands' ... forging our national unity, which will henceforth be founded on the modern perception of what constitutes a nation, namely a cultural community of all the peoples and groups that have settled in, or passed through, this blessed land over the centuries, with the linguistic and other cultural survivals helping to compose one of the richest cultural heritages and testifying to both the acquisitional capacity and the incomparable vigour of this nation of ours. (Koliopoulos 1992: 17–18).

12. An irregular band of armed men. See note 1.
13. PRO/FO 371/48185.
14. On 29 June 1941, 27 members of the Greek Communist Party, among them many Slavo-Macedonians, were released from the prison of Akronafplia having declared themselves, upon instructions by the Bulgarian Embassy, Bulgarian nationals.
15. Greek refugees originating in the interwar period from the Pontus, Black Sea region of Turkey.
16. Bulgarian Orthodox Church established in 1870. See note 1.
17. The information is taken from the electronic data base of the Research Centre for Macedonian History and Documentation of the Museum of the Macedonian Struggle in Thessaloniki.
18. The first two verses are as follows:

> A longing brings me to you,
> O proud mountain peaks,
> To see your rocks stained
> With the blood of untamed young men.
> The heavy memories will live forever
> Of the *voivode*'s heroic death,
> Since the comrades have scattered in all directions
> The heartbeat of freedom.

> Kosturskoto Blagotvoritelno Bratstvo, Sofia (1940).

19. This is illustrated by the fact that on the monument erected at Krushevo to commemorate the Ilinden Uprising, the list of 58 names of heroes and places includes '*Lokvata i Vinjari 1903*' (Brown 1995: 284).
20. Radio broadcast, PRM, 7 April 1993.
21. *Zora*, 2 (1994), p. 6.
22. Radio broadcast, PRM, 24 November 1994.
23. Radio broadcast, PRM, 5 December 1989.
24. Human Rights Watch, *Eleftheros Typos*, 23 March 1992.
25. A prominent member of the Greek parliament in the interwar period well known for his Macedonian clientele and sensitivity.
26. PRO/FO 371/48185.
27. It is telling that President Gligorov delivered the opening address at the Second World Congress of Child Refugees, held in Skopje in the summer of 1998.

BIBLIOGRAPHY

Brown, K.S. 1995. Of Meanings and Memories: The national imagination in Macedonia. Vol. 1. Unpublished doctoral dissertation, Department of Anthropology, University of Chicago.

—— 2000. 'A Rising to Count on: Ilinden between politics and history in post Yugoslav Macedonia', in Victor Roudometof. (ed.) *The Macedonian Question: Culture, historiography, politics.* New York: East European Monographs.

Chrysochoou, Athanasios. 1950. *I Katochi en Makedonia, Vol.2, I Drasis tis Voulgarikis Propagandas, teux.1, 1941 kai 1942.* (*The Occupation in Macedonia, Vol. 2. The Effect of Bulgarian Propaganda, Part 1: 1941 and 1942*). Thessaloniki: Society for Macedonian Studies.

Ferro, Marc. September 1996. 'Goiteia kai Fovos tis Istorias' ('The Appeal and Fear of History'), *Manière de Voir/Le Monde Diplomatique* 9, (Greek edition). Athens.

Fitzios, Harilaos. 1988. *Pavlos Melas o Protomartis.* (*Pavlos Melas, First Martyr*). Athens: Nea Thesis.

Georgieff, Velitsko and Staiko Trifonoff. 1995. *Makedonija i Trakija v Borba za Svoboda (Krajat na XIX – Natsaloto na XX vek).* (*Macedonia and Thrace in the Struggle for Liberty*) (*From the end of the 19th to the beginning of the 20th century*). Sofia: Macedonian Scientific Institute.

Gounaris, Vasilis K. 1990. 'Vouleftes kai Kapetanioi: Pelateiakes Skeseis sti Mesopolemiki Makedonia'. ('Parliamentary Ministers and Captains: Clientelistic Relations in Interwar Macedonia'). *Ellinika* 41, 313–35.

—— 1993. 'Ethnotikes Omades kai Kommatikes Paratakseis sti Makedonia ton Valkanikon Polemon'. ('Ethnic Groups and Party Factions in Macedonia during the Balkan Wars'), in *Ellada ton Valkanikon Polemon 1910–1914.* Athens: Etaireia Logotechnikou kai Istorikou Archeiou. pp. 189–202.

—— 1994. 'Oi Slavophonoi tis Makedonias. I Poreia tis Ensomatosis sto Elliniko Ethniko Kratos, 1870–1940'. ('The Slavophones of Macedonia: The process of integration into the Greek nation state', 1870–1940). *Makedonia* 29, 209–36.

Gounaris, Vasilis K., Iakovos D. Michailidis and Georgios V. Agelopoulos (eds). 1997. *Taftotites sti Makedonia.* (*Identities in Macedonia*). Athens: Papazisis.

Grigoriou, E. 1947. *To Voulgarikon Orgion Aimatos eis tin Ditikin Makedonia, 1941–1944.* (*The Bulgarian Bloodbath in Western Macedonia, 1941–1944*). Athens: Pirsos.

Ivanovski, Orde. 1986. 'Dr Kruste Bitoski'. *Glasnik* 30(1–2), 7–11.

Jiovanovits, Niki. 1987. 'Bibliografija na Objioveni Trudovi na Dr Risto Kirjazovski'. ('Published articles of Dr Risto Kirjazovski'). *Glasnik* 30(1), 13–20.

Karadza, Vasko. 1993. '"Lazar Poptrajkov. I Lokvata kai to Viniari": Odi gia tin iroiki machi tis 31 Maiou 1903'. ('"Lazar Potrajkov: Lokvata and Viniari": An Ode on the Heroic Battle of 31 May 1903'). Unpublished manuscript. Skopje.

Kirjazovski, Risto. 1982. 'Ilindenskite Revolucionerni Tradicii vo NOV na Makedoncite od Egejska Makedonija vo Tekot na Graganskata Voina vo Grcija (1945–1949)'. ('Traditions from the Ilinden Revolution, from the War of National Liberation Waged by the Macedonians of Aegean Macedonia to the Civil War in Greece, 1945–1949'). *Prilozi za Ilinden* 9, Krushevo: Kiro Ntandaro: 111–21.

Kirjazovski, Risto and Todor Simovski. 1976. *Dokumenti za Utsestvoto na Makedonskiot Narod ot Egejskiot del na Makedonija vo Gragjanskata Voina vo Grcija 1946.* (*Documents on the Participation of the Macedonian People of Aegean Macedonia in the Civil War in Greece in 1946*). Vol. 3. Skopje: Archive of Macedonia.

Koemtzopoulos, N. 1968. *Kapetan Kottas o Protos Makedonomachos.* (*Captain Kottas, the First Macedonian Freedom Fighter*). Athens.

Kofos, Evangelos. 1996. 'Makedoniko: Apotimisi Politikis kai Prooptikes'. ('The Macedonian Question: An assessment of policy and prospects'). Lecture at the Hellenic Centre. London.

Koliopoulos, Ioannis S. 1992. *I Makedonia kai i Diamorfosi tis Ethnikis Ideologias Politikis tis Neoteras Ellados*. (*Macedonia and the Shaping of the National Ideology and Policy of Modern Greece*). Thessaloniki: Aristotle University.

—— 1994. *Leilasia Fronimaton: To Makedoniko Zitima stin Katechomeni Ditiki Makedonia, 1941–1944*. ('*The Pillaging of Convictions: The Macedonian Question in occupied Western Macedonia, 1941–1944*'). Vol. 1. Thessaloniki: Vanias.

—— 1995. *Leilasia fronimaton: To Makedoniko Zitima stin Periodo tou Emfiliou Polemou (1945–1949) sti Ditiki Makedonia*. (*The Pillaging of Convictions: The Macedonian Question during the Civil War, 1945–1949*). Vol. 2. Thessaloniki: Vanias.

Kosturskoto Blagotvoritelno Bratstvo, Sofia. 1940. *Lokvata i Viniari ot Lazar Poptraikoff*. (*Lokvata and Viniari by Lazar Potraikoff*). Sofia: Nova Kambana.

Krustevski-Koska, Aleksandar (ed.). 1993. *Spomeni i Biografii na Ilindenci*. (*Memoirs and Biographies of the Ilinden Fighters*). Bitola: Archive of Macedonia.

Magov, Kole. 1995. *Za Makedonskite Tsovetski*. (*For Macedonian Human Rights*). Skopje: Makedonsko Radio.

Mamurovski, Tasko. 1992. *Paskal Mitrevski i Negovoto Vreme (1912–1978)*. (*Paskhalis Mitropoulos and His Times, (1912–1978)*). Skopje: Institute for National History.

—— 1995. *Makedoncite vo Egeiska Makedonija (1945–1946)*. (*The Macedonians in Aegean Macedonia*). Skopje: Institute for National History.

Michailidis, Iakovos D. 1996a. 'Slavofonoi Metanastes kai Prosfiges apo ti Makedonia kai ti Ditiki Thraki (1912–1930)'. ('Slavophone Emigrants and Refugees from Macedonia and Western Thrace'). Unpublished Ph.D. thesis. Department of History, Aristotle University of Thessaloniki.

—— 1996b. 'Minority Rights and Educational Problems in Greek Interwar Macedonia: The case of the primer "Abecedar"'. *Journal of Modern Greek Studies* 14(2), 329–43.

Mladenovski, Simo. 1987. 'Dr Risto Kirjazovski'. *Glasnik* 30(1), 7–12.

Nikoulakos, P. 1944. *Voulgaroi, oi Aimovoroteroi Anthropoi, oi Aspondoteroi Echthroi mas*. (*Bulgarians: The most bloodthirsty people, our most implacable enemies*). Alexandria.

Notaris, I. 1964. 'O Kapetan Vangelis (Captain Vangelis)'. *Aristotelis* 43, Florina: 9–14.

Pallas, G. 1961. 'Ethnomartires Makedonomachoi Kapetan Tellos Agras kai Ant. Migkas' ('National Martyrs and Macedonian Freedom Fighters: Captain Tellos Agras and Andonios Migas'), *Aristotelis* 25, Florina: 17–21.

Panovska, Liljana 1995. *Terorot vo Egejskiot del na Makedonija 1941–1944*. (*Terror in Aegean Macedonia 1941–1944*). Skopje: Institute for National History.

Papakonstandinou, Mihalis. 1994. *To Imerologio Enos Politikou. I Emploki ton Skopion*. (*The Diary of a Politician: The embroglio with Skopje*). Athens: Estia.

Pelayidis, Stathis. 1987. 'Ligo Meta to Ilinden (20 Iouliou 1903) stis Perioches Kastorias kai Florinas'. ('Shortly after Ilinden (20 July 1903) in the Kastoria and Florina Areas'), in *O Makedonikos Agonas. Simposio*. (*The Macedonian Struggle: A Symposium*). Thessaloniki: Institute for Balkan Studies and Museum of the Macedonian Struggle.

Pop-Janevski, Lazo. 1996. *Kosturskoto Selo Dimbeni*. (*The village of Dimbeni, Kastoria Prefecture*). Skopje: Ayrora.

Sakellaropoulos, G. 1992. 'Ioan. D. Sakellaropoulos. O Flogeros Patriotis (Ioannis D. Sakellaropoulos. The Ardent Patriot'). *Makedoniki Zoi* 27(315), Thessaloniki: 44–5.

Silianoff, Christo. 1983. *Osvoboditelnite Borbi na Makedonija*. (*Liberation Struggles in Macedonia*). Vol. 1. Sofia: Georgi Dimitrov.

Simovski, Todor. 1978. *Ta Katokimena Meri tis Makedonias tou Aigaiou. Geographikoi, Ethnikoi kai Oikonomikoi Charaktirismoi*. (*The Inhabited Parts of Aegean Macedonia: Geographical, ethnic and economic characteristics*). Vol. 1 (Greek translation). Skopje: Institute for National History.

Tsfetkovska, Nadezda. 1986. 'Bibliografija na Objioveni Trudovi na Dr Kruste Bitoski'. ('Published articles of Dr Kruste Bitoski'). *Glasnik* 30(1–2), 13–18.

Tzimopoulos, G. 1982. 'O Giorgos Dikonimos Makris, Enas Kritikos Machitis tis Lefterias'. ('Yorgos Dikonymos Makris: A Cretan Freedom Fighter'). *Makedoniki Zoi* 17 (190), Thessaloniki: 36–8.

Vakalopoulos, Konstantinos. 1987. *Ion Dragoumis – Pavlos Yiparis, Korifaies Morfes tou Makedonikou Agona. (Ion Dragoumis and Pavlos Yiparis: Leading lights of the Macedonian Struggle).* Thessaloniki: Barbounakis.

Valden, S. 1991. *Ellada – Yugoslavia. Yennisi kai Ekseliksi Mias Krisis kai oi Anakatatakseis sta Valkania, 1961–62. (Greece and Yugoslavia: The birth and development of a crisis and the upheavals in the Balkans, 1961–62).* Athens: Themelio.

Varda, Christina. 1993. 'Opseis tis Politikis Afomoiosis sti Ditiki Makedonia sto Mesopolemo'. ('Aspects of Political Assimilation in Western Macedonia between the Wars'). *Istorika* 10(18–19), 151–70.

Vouri, S. 1992. *Ekpaideusi kai Ethnikismos sta Valkania. I Periptosi tis Voreioditikis Makedonias, 1870–1904. (Education and Nationalism in the Balkans: The Case of North-Western Macedonia, 1870–1904).* Athens: Paraskinio.

4 'HOW CAN A WOMAN GIVE BIRTH TO ONE GREEK AND ONE MACEDONIAN?' THE CONSTRUCTION OF NATIONAL IDENTITY AMONG IMMIGRANTS TO AUSTRALIA FROM NORTHERN GREECE

Loring M. Danforth

Most scholarly work on ethnic nationalism has focused on the construction of national identity as a large-scale collective phenomenon and as a long-term historical process. It has not paid sufficient attention to the construction of national identity as a short-term biographical process that takes place over the course of the lifetime of specific individuals. For this reason, as Eric Hobsbawm has pointed out, far too little is known about people's 'thoughts and feelings towards the nationalities and nation-states which claim their loyalties' (1990: 78).

Many important questions are raised by focusing attention on the construction of national identity at the individual level. How do people develop a sense of national identity? How do they choose a national identity when more than one possibility is available to them? How is this identity transmitted from one generation to the next? How and why do people change their national identity? Finally, how is it possible for residents of the same village and even members of the same family to adopt different national identities?

In this chapter I explore these questions through an analysis of the indigenous theories of identity used by people from the region of Florina in northern Greece who have emigrated to Melbourne, Australia, when they argue about whether they are Greeks or Macedonians. These people, the majority of whom speak both Greek and Macedonian, share a common ethnic identity: they are 'local Macedonians'.[1] However, as a result of the recent intensification of the nationalist conflict between Greeks and Macedonians over which group has the right to identify itself as Macedonians, immigrants from Greek Macedonia to Australia have been forced to make a difficult decision and adopt one of two mutually exclusive national identities: they must choose whether to be Greeks or Macedonians. What is more, they must do so in Australia, an explicitly multicultural society where ethnic and national identity is more freely and self-consciously constructed than it is in the nation-states of the Balkans, with their claims of national purity and homogeneity.

THE CONSTRUCTION OF NATIONAL IDENTITY

In nationalist ideologies the national identity of a person is usually regarded as something permanent, innate and immutable. It is often thought to consist of some natural or spiritual essence which is identified with a person's blood or soul. While generally avoiding such overtly biological or spiritual metaphors, much anthropological writing has held that people share a particular ethnic or national identity because they possess certain cultural traits in common, because they share a common culture. People are Greek, in other words, because they speak Greek, have Greek names, and attend the Greek church.

It was the work of Fredrik Barth (1969) that was largely responsible for the rejection by many anthropologists of this essentialist notion of ethnic and, by extension, national identity. Instead of defining ethnic groups as 'culture bearing units', groups whose members share a common culture which distinguishes them from members of other groups, Barth defined them as 'categories of ascription and identification'. According to this approach, the crucial feature of ethnic identity is 'the characteristic of self ascription and ascription by others' (1969: 10–13). Barth's insights make it possible to understand how the boundaries between ethnic and national groups are able to persist despite the fact that people are constantly flowing across them; how ethnic and national categories are maintained despite the fact that membership in these categories is always changing.

Once the assertion of ethnic or national identity is no longer equated with 'belonging to' a particular culture or exhibiting certain cultural traits, once it is understood as a form of political consciousness, as an often explicit and self-conscious political choice, then we are in a position to understand how separate groups with distinctly different identities can exist even when there are no 'objective' cultural differences that distinguish between them. Because the existence of these two groups and of the boundary between them depends exclusively on the 'subjective experience of difference' (Sahlins 1989: 270), it is possible for people who share a common culture to adopt different ethnic or national identities. Once we abandon the notion that adopting a particular identity is necessarily the result of being a member of a certain culture, we can consider the reverse: that being or becoming a member of a certain culture is rather the result of adopting a particular identity. In other words, people may not in fact be Greek because they speak Greek, have Greek names, and attend the Greek church. On the contrary, they may speak Greek (and not one of the other languages they know), use the Greek (and not the Slavic) form of their names, and attend the Greek (and not the Macedonian) church because they are Greek, that is, because they have chosen to identify themselves as Greek.

Barth's work also emphasises the active role individuals play in what are often highly contested struggles involving the creation and distribution of new identities. While states with their powerful military, educational, and ecclesiastical bureaucracies often attempt to impose national identities from above, it is ultimately the individual who chooses what national identity to adopt, or in some cases whether to adopt any national identity at all. Such a situational approach to identity not only avoids the problems associated with a reified and essentialist approach, in which the assertion of a particular identity is equated with the possession of some natural or spiritual essence, or even the possession of certain cultural traits. It also draws attention to the fact that identity 'is a socially constructed, variable definition of self or other, whose existence and meaning is continuously negotiated, revised and revitalized' (Nagel 1993: 2).

In a study entitled *Ethnic Options: Choosing Identities in America*, Mary Waters (1990) documents the fact that identities often change through time, both over the life cycle and across generations. Parents may try to hide or deny a particular identity that their children 'rediscover' as they approach adulthood themselves. An identity may be adopted if world political events give it enhanced prestige, or conversely it may be shed if it becomes stigmatised. Often these changes in identity are not perceived by the actors themselves as changes, but are seen as the correction of an error or the achievement of a new insight that is accurate, in contrast to the earlier perception that was in error.

Given the common nationalist view of the immutability of identity, conversion from one identity to another is bound to raise serious questions of authenticity and legitimacy, for if national identity is a fact of nature, something determined by blood or by birth, then it is 'unnatural', if not impossible, to change it. As Handler puts it, from a nationalist perspective people 'cannot *choose* what they naturally *are*' (1988: 51). The new identities people ascribe to themselves, therefore, are often challenged or even rejected by others. This is particularly true when national identity is manipulated in an obvious way to serve personal self-interest (Sahlins 1989: 223). When the construction of identity is contested in this manner, the criteria people use to define their identity and assess its legitimacy are often explicitly cited. Such arguments over the relevance of various criteria for the determination of group membership make the process of identity formation unusually accessible to anthropological analysis.

A situational approach to identity, while taking into consideration the role of personal choice in the process of identity formation, must also remain sensitive to the role played by external factors that limit or constrain the choices individuals face as they construct the identities that shape their lives. For identity formation is not entirely a matter of self-ascription; it is a matter of ascription by others as well. Identities are shaped or structured by powerful political, economic, social and cultural forces, the most important of which inevitably involve the hegemonic power of the state. State policies, the ideologies that legitimate them, and the institutions and organisations that realise them, all influence the process of identity formation as individuals are socialised and become citizens of particular states. To a great extent states have the power and the resources to determine what choices are available to people and what the rewards or the sanctions will be when they exercise these choices and adopt specific identities.

The degree to which state hegemony constrains individual choice in the construction of national identities varies tremendously. At one end of the spectrum stand nation-states whose ideologies of national homogeneity and ethnic purity lead them to limit quite narrowly the choices available to their citizens. Despite the best efforts of a nation-state to ensure that all its citizens develop one and the same national identity, however, the hegemonic power of the state is never absolute. Some individuals are always willing to endure severe persecution by asserting an identity that defines them as members of an ethnic or national minority. At the other end of the spectrum stand countries like the United States, Canada and Australia, whose democratic and pluralist ideologies place significantly fewer constraints on the identities their citizens may adopt. In the case of third- or fourth-generation immigrants from Europe, the choice of identity may become sufficiently fluid and free from stigma that one can begin to speak of ethnicity as a 'lifestyle choice' or a 'matter of taste', something to be adopted one day and discarded the next (Jusdanis 1995: 27).

The construction of identity among immigrants from nation-states in the Balkans who have settled in large pluralist democracies is a particularly complex process because it is influenced by hegemonic constructions that have their origins in both the countries where they were born and the countries where they have settled. These immigrants bring with them identities constructed in their homelands and face the challenge of reconstructing them in the diaspora. From the perspective of these immigrants themselves, particularly those who now identify themselves as Macedonians in a national sense and feel that this identity was denied in their homeland, the most salient feature of the politics of identity in the diaspora is the fact that they now enjoy the freedom to express an identity which they were unable to express freely before.

For the purpose of understanding the role of diaspora communities in the transnational conflict between Greeks and Macedonians, it is precisely this point that is most relevant. While many groups experience serious discrimination in the United States, Canada and Australia, for white immigrants from Europe full enjoyment of the rights of citizenship in these countries is compatible with a fairly wide range of ethnic identities. Immigrants who are members of national minorities in the Balkans, for example, experience considerably more freedom to assert their identities in the United States, Canada and Australia than they do in their countries of origin. More specifically, it is much easier to be a Macedonian in Australia than it is in northern Greece. Macedonians in Australia acknowledge this with their frequent expressions

of gratitude and appreciation for the fact that in Australia they enjoy the right
to express freely their identity as Macedonians. They often add with bitter irony
that Macedonians in Greece, the 'birthplace of democracy', do not enjoy
these same rights.

From an anthropological perspective, however, it is clear that while
Macedonians in Australia do enjoy a degree of freedom with respect to the
expression of their ethnic identity that is not available to them in Greece, the
choices facing them in Australia are certainly not unlimited. They are con-
strained by a complex set of hegemonic forces that have to do with both
multicultural politics in Australia and nationalist politics in the Balkans.
From the perspective of the English-speaking majority that dominates
Australian society at all levels, it makes very little difference whether
immigrants from northern Greece identify themselves as Greeks or
Macedonians. Regardless of their choice of identity at this level, however,
immigrants from northern Greece remain 'Europeans', 'ethnics' or 'people
of non-English speaking background', as opposed to 'real Australians'.

Immigrants from northern Greece to Australia, like immigrants to Australia
from anywhere else in the world, encounter constraints in the process of constructing new identities for themselves in another sense as well. Their choices
are limited by the ethnic categories that exist in the official discourse of
Australian multiculturalism and that dominate government bureaucracies,
social service agencies and the educational system. Immigrants choose from
among the many 'ethnic communities' which together constitute Australian
society; they become members of the 'Italian community', the 'Polish
community' or the 'Turkish community'.

It should be immediately apparent that the ethnic categories of Australian
multicultural discourse replicate or reproduce almost precisely the national
categories of nationalist discourses throughout the world. Immigrants from
the Balkans to Australia have more freedom to choose an identity than their
fellow villagers they left behind, but the choices they face are essentially the
same. Whether they live in Australia or the Balkans, they must be Serbs or
Croats, Greeks or Macedonians.

The truth of Pellizzi's observation that 'in exile nations become ethnicities'
(1988: 155) is confirmed by the parallels that exist between the construction of national identities in the Balkans and the construction of ethnic
identities in Australia. The disintegration of Yugoslavia and the emergence
of Croatian, Serbian and Macedonian national identities in the Balkans is part
of the same transnational chain of events that has led to the demise of the
Yugoslav community in Australia and the development there of Croatian,
Serbian and Macedonian communities. The hegemony of national categories
of identity is such that even in multicultural Australia they cannot be escaped.
In Australia, as in northern Greece, it is difficult for people to preserve or
construct regional or ethnic identities that have no counterpart at the national
level. It is difficult for them to resist becoming either Greek or Macedonian
and to remain simply 'local Macedonians'.

Any analysis of the process by which ethnic and national identities are constructed at the individual level must also take into consideration the fact that such identities are not only situational, but also multiple. People have many collective identities, each of which may be relevant in different ways and at different times. While national identity may be one of the broadest and most all-inclusive identities a person has, it certainly does not exclude or even transcend in importance other identities which define individuals as social beings (Hobsbawm, 1990: 11). Local, regional, ethnic, national and even transnational identities may all coexist and together constitute important aspects of an individual's overall identity, not to mention other forms of collective identity based on religion, class, gender or age. The precise nature of the relationships among these different identities – whether they coexist without conflict or whether they are mutually exclusive – varies greatly. For example, while it may be possible to be both Greek and Australian, it may not be possible to be both Greek and Turkish.

One aspect of the construction of collective identities that is central to the study of ethnic nationalism is the process by which individuals who previously defined themselves primarily in terms of regional or ethnic identities often associated with rural villages, local dialects and oral cultures, come to acquire a sense of national identity associated with 'a literate high culture which is co-extensive with an entire political unit and its total population' (Gellner 1983: 95). Cultivating a sense of national identity in people who previously did not have one – turning 'peasants into Frenchmen' (Weber 1976) – not to mention instilling the 'proper' national identity in people who have somehow managed to acquire the 'wrong' one, is the ultimate goal of all national movements. Needless to say, it is a long, complex process that may take place peacefully or violently, and that may destroy as many identities as it creates.

This is particularly true in the case of an ethnic group that inhabits a frontier zone on the border between two nation-states, each of which attempts to impose a different national identity on members of the contested group. With the nationalisation of ethnic identities and the politicisation of local cultures, a national identity develops like a thin veneer on top of pre-existing regional or ethnic identities. Gradually the ethnic group whose territory is divided by a national boundary splits as its members develop two different and mutually exclusive national identities.

For the local Macedonians from the region of Florina in northern Greece this process, which had its beginnings in the late nineteenth and early twentieth centuries, is still continuing in the 1990s, both in northern Greece as well as in diaspora communities in Canada and Australia. Inhabitants of the same villages, members of the same families, who have adopted different national identities, continue to argue about whether they are Greeks or Macedonians. They continue to argue about what nationality they really are.

GREEKS AND MACEDONIANS IN MULTICULTURAL AUSTRALIA

Since the end of the Second World War, immigration has dramatically transformed the nature of Australian society. In 1947, Australia's population stood at just under 7 million people, 90 per cent of whom were English-speaking and Australian-born. With the arrival of over 4 million immigrants during the next 40 years, Australian society became one of the most ethnically diverse in the world. By 1988, the year it celebrated its bicentenary, Australia had a population of over 16 million people who came from more than 100 different ethnic groups. Over 20 per cent of its population were immigrants and 20 per cent more were Australian-born children of at least one immigrant parent.

The rise of multiculturalism in the 1970s as the dominant ideology governing many aspects of Australian society was motivated in part by the increasing assertiveness of second- and third-generation 'ethnic Australians'. This new attitude led to the growth of ethnic community organisations and migrant groups that in turn made significant demands on the Australian government to provide 'new Australians' with improved social services, particularly in the areas of education and welfare. As a result, the principle that interest groups which were based on the ethnic identity of their members were legitimate elements in the formulation and administration of government policies gained widespread acceptance.

According to the 1986 census, 337,000 people in Australia stated that they were of Greek ancestry, and 148,000 of them (44 per cent) lived in Victoria. Of the 138,000 people in Australia who listed Greece as their birthplace, 66,000 lived in Melbourne. According to the same census, of the 277,000 who stated that they spoke Greek at home, 113,000 lived in Melbourne.[2] Greek is spoken by more Australians than all other languages except English and Italian.

In the 1970s the Greek population of Melbourne was concentrated in inner-city neighbourhoods such as Northcote, South Melbourne and Richmond. By the late 1980s, however, many Greeks had moved to middle-distance and outer metropolitan suburbs such as Preston, Thomastown and Lalor. While Greeks in general remained employed in low-skilled jobs in manufacturing and in the retail trades, many second-generation Greeks have experienced a significant degree of upward social mobility.

According to the estimate of the ethnic composition of the Australian population prepared for the Bicentenary in 1988 (Jupp 1988: 124), there are 75,000 people of Macedonian ethnic origin in Australia, 46,000 of whom are thought to have come from the Republic of Macedonia in the former Yugoslavia, 28,000 to have come from Greece and 1,000 from Bulgaria. In an essay on the Macedonians prepared for the Jupp volume, Peter Hill estimates that there may actually be as many as 100,000 people of Macedonian ancestry in Australia (1988: 691).

Census data on the Macedonian community of Australia are extremely unreliable for several reasons. Until recently Australian census forms asked people simply to list 'country of origin' for themselves and their parents. People who identified themselves as Macedonians, therefore, appeared in the Australian census data as 'Bulgarian-born', 'Yugoslav-born' or 'Greek-born'. In the 1986 census, people were asked for the first time to state their 'ancestry', defined in an information booklet accompanying the census forms as 'the ethnic or national group from which you are descended'. At this time, 42,000 people in Australia listed their ancestry as Macedonian; 21,000 of them were born in Yugoslavia and 4000 of them were born in Greece, while the rest of them were born in Australia. Almost half of the people of Macedonian ancestry in Australia lived in Victoria, the vast majority of them in Melbourne. According to the 1986 census, there were 46,000 people in Australia who spoke Macedonian at home, 21,000 of whom lived in Melbourne.[3]

This description of the Greek and the Macedonian communities of Australia has been presented as an account of two dichotomous and mutually exclusive national groups – Greeks and Macedonians. Such an account, however, replicates and perpetuates the hegemonic constructions of both Australian multicultural discourse and Balkan nationalist discourse. In doing so, it obscures the fact that there exists a group of people from the region of Florina and other areas of northern Greece who speak both Greek and Macedonian, who share one common regional or ethnic identity – that of 'local Macedonians' – but who have been divided into two hostile factions, each of which has adopted a different national identity. These are the people whose lives have been most dramatically affected by the recent politicisation of the Macedonian Question. Individual villages and families have been split, with one villager, one brother, identifying as a Greek, the other as a Macedonian.

In many cases the choices made and the positions taken in the present have parallels in the past. There are also, of course, many cases where new choices are made and new identities constructed. Some migrants to Melbourne who identify themselves as Greeks have seen their children grow up and come to identify themselves as Macedonians.

There are many factors that influence the process of identity formation as it takes place among immigrants from Florina to Australia. Balkan history, village politics, family situation and individual biography all play important parts in this complex process. People may identify themselves as Greeks for a variety of reasons. They may come from a village that supported the Patriarch in the early twentieth century or a family that supported the Greek government during the Civil War. They may come from a wealthy family or have grown up in the city of Florina itself, or they may simply have been the youngest child in the family and grown up speaking Greek in the home because their older brothers and sisters had already started school. They may have left Greece as adults, having been fully socialised into Greek national society as a result of completing high school or serving in the military. Alternatively they may be involved in a profession that can be practised more readily in the Greek community of Melbourne with its large, private educational system and its well-established professional and business elite. They may also have married into a family with a strong sense of Greek national identity. Finally, they may fear that if they publicly identify themselves as Macedonians, they may not be able to return to Greece, or that their relatives still living in Greece may be harassed by Greek government officials. One person, for example, refused to discuss the Macedonian issue with me, saying: 'It's too political, too dangerous. I don't want to talk. The people in the Pan-Macedonian Association might find out what I said, and I'd get in trouble.'

People from Florina may identify as Macedonians for a variety of reasons as well. They may come from a village that supported the Exarch in the early twentieth century or a family that supported the communists during the Civil War. They may have been born in a small, poor village inhabited exclusively by local Macedonians, or they may have been the oldest child in the family and grown up speaking Macedonian with their parents and grandparents. Alternatively, they may have left Greece for Australia at a very young age and may not have been fully socialised into Greek national society, but only into the 'local' society of their family and village. People who left Greece after the Civil War, settled in Yugoslavia or some other eastern European country and then emigrated to Australia from there are almost certain to have adopted a Macedonian national identity. People who remained in Greece, but who experienced harassment and persecution at the hands of the Greek government in the years following the Civil War, may also have developed a Macedonian identity. Finally, people who marry into a family with a strong Macedonian identity or who have no relatives still living in Greece are likely to develop a Macedonian identity as well.

Some local Macedonians from Florina living in Australia have adopted a third stance with regard to the question of national identity. They attempt to maintain a neutral stance in the conflict between Greeks and Macedonians by refusing to identify themselves publicly with either one of the two mutually exclusive national groups. In many cases they want to preserve the unity of their village organisations, which provide them with their primary sense of identity; in some cases, they may value both national cultures and not want to restrict themselves by identifying themselves exclusively with either one. Finally, they may be genuinely unable to choose either one of the two mutually exclusive national categories to identify themselves with. On several occasions, people who had adopted this third position refused to discuss the Macedonian issue with me. When I asked a man I met at a village picnic if he was a Greek or a Macedonian, he said: 'I can't talk. I can't say anything.' Then he gestured to the people dancing a 'local' dance on the cricket field in front of us and said: 'These are my people; this is my village. That's all I can say.'

The institutions founded by the early local Macedonian immigrants from Florina to Melbourne testify to the divisions in their community that have been created in large part by the different national ideologies that have competed for their loyalty over the past century. This is particularly true in the case of the Church, the institution that lies at the centre of many southern and eastern European diaspora communities. In 1950 a group of immigrants from Florina, who identified themselves as Macedonians and who opposed communism, founded the 'Macedonian Church of Saints Cyril and Methodius in affiliation with the Bulgarian Orthodox Church of North and South America and Australia (which at that time was independent of the Holy Synod in Sofia). Years later, however, after the reconciliation of the diaspora church and the Holy Synod in Sofia, a priest from Bulgaria was sent to Melbourne who insisted that the Church of Saints Cyril and Methodius was a Bulgarian church and that its members were all Bulgarians. In 1985 the trustees of the church, who identified themselves as Macedonians, renounced the jurisdiction of the Bulgarian Orthodox Church and attempted to gain control of the church. The Supreme Court of Victoria, however, ruled against them and the Macedonian community soon abandoned what had now become a Bulgarian church.

Another group of immigrants from Florina who also identified themselves as Macedonians, but who supported communism, founded the Macedonian Orthodox Church of St George in 1959, which eventually became affiliated with the Macedonian Orthodox Church in the Republic of Macedonia, in the former Yugoslavia. This Church is now one of the most powerful institutions in the Macedonian community of Melbourne and in all of Australia. Finally, in 1967, a third group of immigrants from Florina, a group who identified themselves as Greeks, established the Greek Orthodox Church of Saints Cyril and Methodius. Thus the tripartite division of Macedonia among Bulgaria, Yugoslavia and Greece is replicated in the different affiliations of the churches founded by immigrants from Florina who settled in Melbourne.

Rough estimates suggest that there may be 27,000 people from the district of Florina who are now living in Australia. According to a survey conducted by Hill (1989: 125), there are over 10,000 people in Melbourne whose families come from a group of 14 villages in the Florina area and who have large and active village associations in Melbourne. In addition, immigrants from the city of Florina itself and from about ten other villages in the region have also settled in Melbourne. It is quite possible, therefore, that there are as many as 15,000 people from the Florina area who are living in Melbourne, heavily concentrated in the northern suburbs of the city.

INDIGENOUS THEORIES OF IDENTITY

In the early 1990s, the attention of the Greek and Macedonian communities in Australia was focused on the Macedonian conflict. The most burning issues confronting the two communities were the struggle of the Republic of Macedonia to gain international recognition under its constitutional name and the parallel, but somewhat less immediate, struggle of Aegean Macedonians to gain recognition from the Greek government as an ethnic or national minority. During this time, conversations among Greeks and Macedonians in Melbourne inevitably turned to questions of identity. At weddings, soccer games, village dances and picnics they argued passionately and endlessly about whether they were Greeks or Macedonians, about what makes a person Greek or Macedonian, and about how people could ever know what a person's nationality really was.

Peter Savramis is a Macedonian, not a Greek.[4] He left his village near Florina and came to Melbourne in the early 1970s. Peter takes great delight in arguing with people in Greek, Macedonian and English about the Macedonian question. He prides himself on being able to present his position articulately, convincingly and without getting in a fight. Peter often talks about the Macedonian conflict at construction sites around the city, where he works installing heating and air conditioning systems.

One day in the autumn of 1991 an Italian contractor introduced Peter to Kostas, a Greek carpenter who would be working with him on a new house.

'This is my friend Peter', the contractor said. 'He's Macedonian, but he speaks Greek.'

With a look of suspicion Kostas asked Peter in heavily accented English: 'What kind of Macedonian are you? Are you one of those ones who makes trouble?'

'No', Peter replied. 'We're just trying to protect our culture from the Greek government.'

'What do you mean?' asked Kostas.

Peter suggested they speak in Greek.

'Where are you from?' asked Kostas in Greek. 'Are you one of the ones who wants to take our land?'

'Wait a minute', Peter said. 'I'm a Macedonian. What land are you talking about? I'm from Macedonia, Macedonia of the Aegean.'

'You speak good Greek!' said Kostas, somewhat surprised.

'Yes', said Peter. 'I speak pure Greek. I learned it in school.'

'You're a Greek-Macedonian', said Kostas.

'No! I'm a Macedonian', replied Peter.

Kostas was starting to get angry. 'But you can't understand those Yugoslavs who want to take our land.'

'When it comes to language,' Peter explained, 'a Macedonian from Greece and a Macedonian from Yugoslavia can understand each other perfectly. They speak the same language. Why does it bother you if I'm Macedonian? Are you Greek?'

'Yes.'

'If I said that you weren't Greek, wouldn't you tell me to get stuffed?'

'Yes.'

'It's the same for me. If you say I'm not a Macedonian, I'll tell you to go get stuffed.'

'But you're a Greek-Macedonian', insisted Kostas again.

'I'm a Greek citizen,' said Peter, 'but I'm a Macedonian by birth. You could have an Australian passport, but by birth what are you?'

'A Greek', replied Kostas.

'It's the same with me', said Peter. 'I'm Macedonian by birth. If a hundred years ago they divided up Greece, and Italy and Bulgaria and Turkey each took a part, what would you be?'

'I'd still be a Greek', replied Kostas.

'That's right', said Peter, shaking Kostas' hand. 'And I'm still a Macedonian. I am what I am, and you are what you are. If you say I'm not a Macedonian, then I'll say you're not a Greek.'

An analysis of the indigenous theories of identity that underlie arguments like this confirms the value of David Schneider's (1968, 1969 and 1984) discussion of blood and law as two of the most powerful symbols used to express the unity of a group of people who share a common identity, whether in the domain of kinship, religion, or nationality. According to Schneider, blood is regarded as a 'natural substance', a 'shared biogenetic material'. It is a biological essence, an objective fact of nature, that is given at birth and that is often thought to constitute a permanent and unalterable aspect of a person's identity. By contrast, another aspect of a person's identity is that determined by law, by what Schneider calls 'a code for conduct', that is, a specific social relationship which is dependent for its continued existence on the performance of a particular social role (1968: 21–9). It is understood that this aspect of a person's identity is neither natural nor permanent, but that it can be either changed or terminated. In the conversations of immigrants from Florina to Melbourne, either of these two powerful symbols may serve as a criterion for determining a person's identity.

According to both Greek and Macedonian nationalist perspectives, national identity is something that is naturally and biologically given. It is determined first and foremost by 'blood' or by 'birth'. This biologised conception of national identity is expressed explicitly and metaphorically. A person of Greek nationality is 'Greek by birth' (*Ellinas to yenos*). Similarly a man from Florina who identifies himself as a Macedonian and not a Greek said: 'No one buys his nationality; no one chooses his mother. I inherited this nationality. It is my inheritance, the milk of my mother.'

Metaphors identifying the personified national homeland as parent also support this biologised conception of national identity. Greece is often referred to as the 'mother fatherland' (*mitera patridha*), while Macedonia is often referred to both as 'mother Macedonia' (*majka Makedónia*) and as the 'fatherland' (*tatkovina*). Macedonian nationalists frequently use biological metaphors equating the category of national identity with the category of biological species. When people from Florina who identify as Macedonians deny the legitimacy of the identity of their relatives and fellow villagers who identify as Greeks, they use images suggesting the immutability of biological species: 'Wheat is wheat, and corn is corn. You can't change one into the other. Even if you call it corn, it's still wheat. Its nature doesn't change.' As another Macedonian from Florina put it: 'A maple tree is a maple tree. You can't inject oak tree into it.' Macedonian nationalists often explain the incompatibility of Greeks and Macedonians by way of a proverb that also draws on the analogy between nationality and biological species. In commenting on the long history of conflict and hostility between Greeks and Macedonians, they say 'Sheep and goats don't mix.'

People from Florina who identify themselves as Macedonians and not Greeks argue that all Slavic-speaking people in northern Greece are 'really' Macedonians and not Greeks because their 'mother tongue' is Macedonian and not Greek. They contrast the 'natural' environment in which they learned Macedonian – at home, in the family, speaking with their parents and grandparents – with the 'artificial' environment of the educational system in which they learned Greek. 'Real Greeks,' they say, 'don't have grandparents who speak Macedonian'. They also attempt to undermine the legitimacy of the Greek national identity of people who speak Macedonian by making fun of them when they say in Macedonian: 'We are Greeks' (*Nie sne Grci*) or 'We Greeks are clever' (*Nie Grci sne eksipni*). From a Macedonian and even a Greek nationalist perspective such people may seem incongruous, their nationality suspect. From an anthropological perspective in which identity is a matter of self-ascription, however, the claims to Greek national identity of people who were born in Greece but who speak Macedonian and not Greek are just as legitimate as the claims to Macedonian national identity of people who earlier in their lives identified themselves as Greeks.

The contrast between a person's 'genuine' national identity, which is biologically given at birth, and a person's 'artificial' national identity, which is acquired somehow later in life, is conveyed by a humorous, if somewhat bitter, comment overheard by a Macedonian from Melbourne while visiting the village near Florina where he was born. A woman from southern Greece who had married a Slavic-speaking local Macedonian from the village told some men who had gathered in the village cafe that they were not 'real Greeks'. An old man, a local Macedonian, replied: 'That's right. You are a Greek with hormones. We are Greeks by injection.'

While the idea that national identity is a natural, biological given is a basic tenet of both Greek and Macedonian nationalist ideologies, in arguments among people from Florina over whether they are really Greeks or Macedonians, this position is most often taken by people who identify themselves as Macedonians. People who identify themselves as Greeks, on the other hand, are much more likely to argue that national identity is determined by what Schneider has called 'a code for conduct', that is, a particular relationship with the Greek state, which people enter into as they are socialised into Greek society and become members of Greek national culture. Through this process of socialisation people develop a commitment to the Greek state as well as a sense of being part of the Greek nation. From this perspective, being a part of Greek society and participating in Greek culture means that one is a member of the Greek nation. Given the identity of the Greek state and the Greek nation, the legal relationship between a Greek citizen and the Greek state, which involves the performance of a particular social role, is equated with membership in the Greek nation. People who are Greek citizens, in other words, must have a Greek national identity; people who were raised in Greek society must be Greek.

Immigrants from Florina to Melbourne who identify themselves as Greeks frequently argue that their relatives and fellow villagers who identify as Macedonians cannot 'really' be Macedonians on the grounds that there has never been a Macedonian state. When a Greek tells a Macedonian: 'You can't be a Macedonian because there's no such country (*kratos*)', he implies that because there is no Macedonian state as a legal entity and no Macedonian citizenship as a legal relationship, there can be no Macedonian nation and no Macedonian national identity. This argument, of course, ignores the fact that nations can and do exist which have no states to serve as national homelands (the Palestinians and the Kurds are two obvious examples), as well as the fact that the Republic of Macedonia has existed as one of the republics of the former Yugoslavia with its own government, educational system, flag, and nationality since 1944. It also ignores the fact that in 1991 the Republic of Macedonia declared its existence as an independent and sovereign state. Given the identity of state and nation in Greek nationalist ideology, Greece's refusal to recognise the Republic of Macedonia as an independent state can be seen as the equivalent of refusing to recognise the existence of the Macedonians as a distinct nation.

The Greek nationalist argument is more straightforward when it comes to asserting that people from Florina, people who were born and raised in Greece, must have a Greek national identity. A man from Florina who identified himself as Greek defended himself by saying: 'I was born under Greece, I went to school under Greece, I believe Greek, and I'll never change.' In an attempt to put an end to a long and frustrating discussion, another man said 'We're from Greece, so we're Greek. Let's just forget it.'

More specifically, people with a Greek national identity often argue that because many people from Florina who identify themselves as Macedonians have Greek, not Macedonian, names, because they attend the Greek, not the Macedonian, church, because they are literate in Greek, not Macedonian, and most importantly because they all have Greek, not Macedonian, passports, they must therefore be Greeks. Macedonians, however, refute these arguments by pointing out that many Aegean Macedonians have Greek names and are literate in Greek because of the assimilationist policies of the Greek government. They also point out that Aegean Macedonians have Greek passports because they are Greek citizens, emphasising once again that citizenship does not determine ethnic or national identity.

When confronted with the Greek argument that because they came to Australia on Greek passports they were therefore Greeks, many people from Florina who identify themselves as Macedonians simply say: 'No. We're Macedonians with Greek passports.' More argumentative Macedonians often reply: 'You say that we're Greeks because we were born under Greek rule. Does that mean that your grandfather was Turkish because he was born under Turkish rule?'

The relevance of Schneider's analysis of the symbols of blood and law to the present discussion of the construction of national identity among local Macedonian immigrants from Florina is clear from the analogies often drawn between trying to determine what a person's 'real' national identity is and who a person's 'real' mother is. At a village picnic in Melbourne, Sam, a man from a village near Florina who identifies himself as a Greek, tried to explain his Greek national identity metaphorically by comparing the Macedonian and the Greek nations to two mothers, one biological and one adoptive. 'My blood is Macedonian. My real mother is Macedonian. But my adoptive mother is Greece. And you can't spit in the face of your adoptive mother.' Faced with a clear choice, metaphorically speaking, between a relative to whom he was related by blood and one to whom he was related by law, Sam chose to place greater emphasis on the legal relationship and to remain loyal to his adoptive mother. In this way he explained the fact that he had a Greek national identity.

Ted, who was also from a village near Florina, but who identifies himself as a Macedonian and not a Greek, used the same metaphor, the metaphor of adoption, to explain how as an adult he had realised that he was actually a Macedonian, even though he had lived all his life as a Greek. 'I felt like an adopted child who had just discovered his real parents', he said. 'All my life had been a lie. I'd been a janissary; I'd betrayed my own people.' Ted, unlike Sam, however, chose metaphorically to privilege his relationship with his biological parents. In this way he justified his newly discovered Macedonian national identity.

As these two examples illustrate, immigrants from Florina can decide whether they are Greeks or Macedonians either by invoking the existence of a 'blood' tie or by invoking the existence of a social relationship. National identity, in this case, therefore, is a matter of choice, a matter of self-identification or self-ascription. Immigrants from Florina recognise the role of conscious choice and individual decision-making in their discussions of national identity, but only to a degree. They talk about people with a Greek national identity as people who 'want' or 'believe in' Greece. Conversely, they refer to people who have a Macedonian national identity as people who 'want' or 'believe in' Skopje. People who identify as Greeks or Macedonians are also described as being 'on the Greek side' or 'on the Macedonian side', as belonging to one 'political faction' (*parataksi*) or the other. This terminology suggests that whether immigrants from Florina identify themselves as Greeks or Macedonians is a matter of conscious political choice. People *are* Greeks or Macedonians because they *choose* to be Greeks or Macedonians.

Because a person's national identity can be defined as biologically determined or as acquired through a process of socialisation, and because a person's self-ascribed national identity (whether it is based on biology or socialisation) can either be accepted at face value or rejected in favour of another identity based on the other principle, the question of whether the Slavic-speaking people of northern Greece are Greeks or Macedonians is ultimately irresolvable. People from Florina will continue to argue about blood, place of birth, language, passports, consciousness, and belief as criteria of national identity. Parents and children, husbands and wives, brothers and sisters will continue to disagree about what they really are.

At a village dance in Melbourne a man who identified himself as Macedonian and not Greek told me a story about two brothers from a village near Florina. One had settled in Yugoslavia after the Civil War, the other had remained in Greece. Eventually they both came to Australia (one on a Yugoslav passport, the other on a Greek passport), where they lived together with their mother in the same house in Melbourne. They were constantly arguing with each other because one brother identified himself as Greek while the other brother identified himself as Macedonian. Finally they confronted their mother; they asked her how a woman could give birth to one Greek and one Macedonian. The narrator of the story did not tell me what the mother replied. Instead he offered his own answer to the question. 'It's not possible', he said emphatically. 'By blood, by birth, they're both Macedonians.'

I am sure that if the narrator of the story had been a Greek I would also have been told that it was not possible for a woman to give birth to one Greek and one Macedonian, but I would have been told that both brothers were *Greek*. As an anthropologist, however, I offer a different answer to this question. I suggest that it *is* possible for a woman to give birth to one Greek and one Macedonian. It is possible precisely because Greeks and Macedonians are not born, they are *made*. National identities, in other words, are not biologically given, they are socially constructed.

It is my hope that the detailed ethnographic material presented here has demonstrated the complexity of the process of identity formation as it takes place at the individual level among local Macedonian immigrants from Florina to Melbourne. This same complexity characterises the lives and identities of Macedonians in other parts of the world, as well as those of many other people who are members of ethnic minorities and diaspora communities in today's transnational world. These people are caught between mutually exclusive national identities. They are marginal participants in several national cultures and full participants in none, people who are struggling to construct a coherent sense of themselves from a complex, multilayered set of identities – class, religious, regional, ethnic and national. While these identities may coexist easily on some occasions, they conflict sharply on others, and this conflict often brings with it a great deal of uncertainty, alienation and pain.

It is also my hope that the analysis presented here has convincingly exposed the dangers of oversimplified nationalist ideologies, with their explanations of national identity in terms of some natural or spiritual essence. In addition, I hope it has exposed the weaknesses of earlier anthropological approaches to the study of identity, with their arguments that people are members of ethnic or national groups because they share some set of common cultural traits. Only by rejecting both these approaches are we in a position to understand the complex historical, political, social and cultural processes by which individuals construct and negotiate the identities that give meaning to their lives.

ACKNOWLEDGEMENTS

My research was carried out in Melbourne in 1991–2 and was generously supported by a Fulbright Scholar Award. I would like to express my appreciation to the members of the Department of Anthropology at the University of Melbourne for their kind hospitality. I would also like to thank the many people from Florina living in Melbourne who were willing to talk with me about the complex and emotionally charged issue of national identity and the Macedonian conflict. A grant from the National Endowment for the Humanities enabled me to spend the 1992–3 academic year working on *The Macedonian Conflict: Ethnic nationalism in a transnational world*, published by Princeton University Press in 1995. This chapter is a revised version of a portion of Chapter 8 of that book. Finally, I would like to thank several colleagues whose friendship, encouragement and constructive criticism I value very highly: Keith Brown, Jane Cowan, Victor Friedman, Michael Herzfeld, Gregory Jusdanis, Roger Just, Anastasia Karakasidou and Riki Van Boeschoten.

NOTES

1. The term 'Macedonian' has three basic meanings. It is used most frequently in this article and in general political, scholarly and journalistic discourse in a *national* sense to refer to people with a Macedonian national identity. According to this usage, 'Macedonian' and 'Greek' are mutually exclusive categories referring to people with two different national identities. 'Macedonian' is also used in a *regional* sense to refer to people with a Greek national identity who come from Macedonia. These people often refer to themselves as 'Greek-Macedonians'. Finally the word 'Macedonian' is also used with what I as an anthropologist would call an *ethnic* meaning to refer to the indigenous people of Macedonia (who may speak Greek or Macedonian or both), in contrast to the many other ethnic groups that live in northern Greece. For the sake of clarity, and because they also call themselves 'locals', I use the term 'local Macedonians' to designate this group.

   The term 'Slav-Macedonian' is generally used by Greeks who object to the use of the term 'Macedonian' for people who define themselves as Macedonians and not Greeks. Macedonians of the diaspora reject this term on the grounds that it denies the existence of a distinct Macedonian national identity. They point out that there are no Slav-Macedonians, any more than there are Slav-Russians or Slav-Bulgarians. Most Macedonian human rights activists in northern Greece reject the term for similar reasons. Some Macedonians in northern Greece, however, particularly those involved in the resistance movement during the Greek Civil War, do not object to this term and even use it as a term of self-ascription. (I would like to thank Riki van Boeschoten for her help in clarifying the use of this term.)

My statement that local Macedonians from Florina and nearby districts constitute a distinct ethnic group is based on extensive fieldwork carried out in Florina and among immigrants from Florina living in Melbourne. In their introduction to *Ourselves and Others* (1997: 21), Peter Mackridge and Eleni Yannakakis challenge my reference to 'local Macedonians' as 'the indigenous people of Macedonia' (Danforth, 1995: 7). I do not mean to imply that local Macedonians are the *only* 'indigenous people of Macedonia' or that they are '*more* indigenous' than *all* other groups. I simply use 'indigenous' as a formal translation of *dopii*, a category which contrasts primarily with the category of 'refugees' from Pontos, Thrace and Asia Minor. Georgios Agelopoulos (1997: 148) claims that *dopii* do not use 'Macedonians' to define themselves and cites my *Firewalking and Religious Healing* (1989: 65) in support of his claim. In fact, I state explicitly on the page he cites that these people refer to themselves as 'indigenous *Macedonians*' (i.e. *dopii Makedhones*). Jane Cowan (1997: 153) also states that *dopii* describe themselves as '*Makedones*'. Let me stress that the term 'local Macedonian' is used here in an ethnic, not a national sense, and that the majority of local Macedonians in Florina now have a Greek (not a Macedonian) national identity.

2. Bureau of Immigration Research (1990a: 3 and 36; 1991: 239) and Clyne (1991: 42).
3. Bureau of Immigration Research (1990a: 35; 1990b: 37; 1991: 261) and Clyne (1991: 37).
4. All the personal names used in this paper are pseudonyms. The narrative which follows is based on detailed notes taken during Peter Savramis' account of the exchange.

BIBLIOGRAPHY

Agelopoulos, Georgios. 1997. 'From Bulgarievo to Nea Krasia, from "Two Settlements" to "One Village": Community formation, collective identity and the role of the individual', in Peter Mackridge and Eleni Yannakakis. (eds) *Ourselves and Others: The development of a Greek Macedonian cultural identity since 1912*. Oxford: Berg, pp. 133–51.
Australian Bureau of Statistics. 1991. *The Overseas-born in Victoria*. Canberra.
Barth, Fredrik. 1969. *Ethnic Groups and Boundaries*. Boston: Little, Brown.
Bureau of Immigration Research. 1990a. *Community Profiles: Greece-born*. Canberra:Australian Government Publication Service.
—— 1990b. *Community Profiles: Yugoslavia-born*. Canberra: Australian Government Publication Service.
—— 1991. *Birthplace, Language, Religion 1971–86*. Canberra: Australian Government Publication Service.
Clyne, Michael. 1991. *Community Languages in the Australian Experience*. Cambridge: Cambridge University Press.
Cowan, Jane K. 1997. 'Idioms of Belonging', in Peter Mackridge and Eleni Yannakakis. (eds) *Ourselves and Others: The development of a Greek Macedonian cultural identity since 1912*. Oxford: Berg, pp. 153–71.
Danforth, Loring M. 1995. *The Macedonian Conflict: Ethnic nationalism in a transnational world*. Princeton, New Jersey: Princeton University Press.
—— 1989. *Firewalking and Religious Healing*. Princeton, New Jersey: Princeton University Press.
Gellner, Ernest. 1983. *Nations and Nationalism*. Oxford: Blackwell.
Handler, Richard. 1988. *Nationalism and the Politics of Culture in Quebec*. Madison: University of Wisconsin Press.
Hill, Peter. 1988. 'Macedonians', in James Jupp. (ed.) *The Australian People*. North Ryde: Angus & Robertson. pp. 685–91.

—— 1989. *The Macedonians in Australia*. Carlisle, Western Australian: Hesperian Press.

Hobsbawm, Eric. 1990. *Nations and Nationalism Since 1780: Programme, myth, reality*. Cambridge: At the University Press.

Jupp, James (ed.). 1988. *The Australian People*. North Ryde: Angus & Robertson.

Jusdanis, Gregory. 1995. 'Beyond National Culture?' *Boundary 2* 22(1), 23–60.

Mackridge, Peter and Eleni Yannakakis (eds). 1997. *Ourselves and Others: The development of a Greek Macedonian cultural identity since 1912*. Oxford: Berg.

Nagel, Joane. 1993. 'Constructing Ethnicity: Creating and recreating ethnic identity and culture', in Norman R. Yetman. (ed.) *Majority and Minority: The dynamics of race and ethnicity in American life*. 6th ed. Boston: Allyn and Bacon.

Pellizzi, Francesco. 1988. 'To Seek Refuge: Nation and ethnicity in exile', in Remo Guideri, Francesco Pellizzi and Stanley J. Tambiah. (eds) *Ethnicities and Nations: Processes of Interethnic Relations in Latin America, Southeast and the Pacific*. Austin: University of Texas Press. pp. 154–71.

Sahlins, Peter. 1989. *Boundaries: The making of France and Spain in the Pyrenees*. Berkeley: University of California Press.

Schneider, David. 1968. *American Kinship: A cultural account*. Englewood Cliffs, New Jersey: Prentice-Hall.

—— 1969. 'Kinship, Nationality, and Religion in American Culture: Toward a definition of kinship', in Robert F. Spencer. (ed.) *Forms of Symbolic Action*. Seattle, WA: American Ethnological Association, pp. 116–25.

—— 1984. *A Critique of the Study of Kinship*. Ann Arbor: University of Michigan Press.

Waters, Mary. 1990. *Ethnic Options: Choosing identities in America*. Berkeley: University of California Press.

Weber, Eugen. 1976. *Peasants into Frenchmen: The modernization of rural France 1870–1914*. Stanford, CA: Stanford University Press.

5 BLESSING THE WATER THE MACEDONIAN WAY: IMPROVISATIONS OF IDENTITY IN DIASPORA AND IN THE HOMELAND

Jonathan M. Schwartz

'TOO MUCH TALK ABOUT MULTICULTURALISM'

Since independence from Belgrade in September 1991, the Republic of Macedonia has undergone a series of what might be called 'crises of recognition', first by neighbouring Balkan states, then by the 'International Community' and finally by members of ethnic groups within the republic itself. This chapter will consider Charles Taylor's (1992) advocacy for multiculturalism, a 'politics of recognition' grounded in Canadian experience, within the specific context of the Republic of Macedonia and its citizens abroad. I shall be looking at two diasporic Macedonian communities: one in Toronto and the second, with which I am most familiar, in Copenhagen. These will be brought into comparison with the homeland community, the primary object of the article being to consider how people deal with identities and differences in diaspora and homeland.

The break-up of the Yugoslavian Federation has compelled ethnographers to pay attention to diaspora communities as political, as well as cultural forces. While the concept of 'diaspora' evokes ideas of active, loyal participation between inhabitants of the homeland and those in exile, in the case of Macedonia, with its multiple communities, one has to recognise a plurality of diasporas. Emigration from Macedonia, which began in the last decades of the Ottoman Empire and resumed after the Greek Civil War (1947–9), was described by its members as a temporary exile from the homeland. The hardships of emigration for economic gain (*pechalba*) only accentuated a nostalgic longing for 'return', yet for many exile was to stretch into a condition of permanent diaspora.

Who should be included in this category of 'Macedonians'? Firstly, 'Macedonian' can be argued to refer to members of a transnational ethnic community whose language and Orthodox liturgy are south Slavic. For such persons, the Macedonian homeland includes three regions: Vardar Macedonia[1] (the former Yugoslavian Republic), Pirin Macedonia (eastern Bulgaria) and Aegean Macedonia (northern Greece). These 'ethnic' or

104

'national' Macedonians have a well-documented history of emigration to North America and Australia since the late nineteenth century (Danforth 1995; Petroff 1995). Many also went to northern Europe following the Second World War.

'Macedonian' has a second, more recent sense, however, referring to a person holding citizenship in the homeland, the Republic of Macedonia. Uniquely among its former neighbours in the Yugoslav Federation, the multi-ethnic composition of the Macedonian Republic has survived the violent break-up of Yugoslavia. Citizens of the new republic include, in addition to ethnic Macedonians, smaller populations of Albanians, Turks, Rom, Vlachs, Greeks and Bosniaks. Some of these minorities have also migrated abroad and these Macedonian citizens must be included as actors within 'Macedonian' diasporas.

Despite the officially multi-ethnic character of the new republic, ethnic coexistence is constantly being put to the test. It has survived so far by dint of a Macedonian talent for both improvisation and creative crisis management. Tensions between ethnic Macedonians and ethnic Albanians have been resolved through often surprising coalitions of political parties. Hence, the current government consists of a (formerly) nationalist Macedonian party, a (formerly) nationalist Albanian party and a new multi-ethnic coalition party. By epitomising the stake which all communities had in the republic, that government was subsequently able to manage the severe shocks created by war in Kosovo and the arrival of Kosovar Albanian refugees in early 1999.

While there are many other meanings of 'Macedonian', this article will concentrate on ethnic Macedonians and Muslims who are citizens of the Republic of Macedonia. I will be speaking both of *membership*, by which I mean primary affiliation with one's ethnic group, and *citizenship* in an aspiring republic. Just as the hyphen in 'nation-state' can indicate ambiguity and disjuncture (Appadurai 1990), one might speak of hyphenated 'members-citizens' of the Republic of Macedonia (Schwartz 1996: 129). This admittedly awkward phrase implies that the present crises of recognition pertain to the divergent self-ascriptions within the political society. Thus, not all those who are 'citizens' feel equally, or equal as, 'members'.

For example, the celebration of Ilinden (Archangel Elias) Day on 2 August commemorates the abortive revolt of Macedonians against Ottoman Turkish rule in 1903. Although a national holiday in the Republic of Macedonia, ethnic Turkish citizens in the Republic of Macedonia cannot feel resonance with this historical event (Schwartz 1996: 34), which is in fact an expression of past Macedonian ethnic membership rather than present Macedonian political citizenship. Similarly, more improvised public events for demarcating identity seldom achieve a perfect congruence between membership and citizenship. Some people are bound to feel left out.

This is my enduring impression both from longer and shorter periods of fieldwork in Toronto, Copenhagen and in the Republic of Macedonia. If I seem to jump from one location to the other, with brief, deliberate pauses, the approach should be likened to that of crossing a mountain stream by foot, where one stone leads to another. Studying diasporas and homelands over distance and time has the structure of an improvised crossing of a turbulent mountain stream.

I have chosen occasions for the ritual blessings of water to explore my chosen themes. These blessings will be interpreted as ritual acts that symbolically summarise Macedonian cultural practices in diaspora and in the homeland. The anthropologist's predilection for ritual performances will be challenged, however, as the description and analysis proceed. Starting with a focus on *rites de passage*, I will shift to 'the *rights* of passage' in precarious political situations that make improvised solutions imperative.[2] We will start in Copenhagen's ethnically diverse diasporic communities and jump from there back to the homeland, in the arid tobacco country near Prilep. Revisiting previous ventures in Toronto's Macedonian diaspora, where the division between Hellenic and Slavic Macedonians is prominent, will complete the triadic compass of this chapter.

At moments in the narrative, the multi-ethnic elements of Macedonian society will seem to be eclipsed. Indeed, in the metropolitan, multicultural host societies, members of diasporic ethnic groups often do everything imaginable to avoid identification, or dialogue, with members of the other ethnic groups from the homeland. A failed attempt – with the agency of two anthropologists – to establish a multi-ethnic, Danish–Macedonian friendship association in Copenhagen will serve to highlight the vagaries of multiculturalist ideals.

If immigrant groups tend to keep sharp boundaries between their own ethnic and/or regional group and others, in the homeland close neighbours from different ethnic groups visit each other in their homes, especially on occasions like weddings. Donating and receiving labour power for house construction and harvesting (a south Slavic institution called *moba*) is also a way for crossing ethnic boundaries. In her detailed monograph on Albanian wedding songs in the Prespa Lake region, Jane Sugarman (1997) notes this difference in practices between Albanian, Macedonian and Turkish households in the home region, and within those communities living in North America:

> In Prespa in the early 1980s, it was not uncommon for Albanians from other districts or for Macedonian or Turkish neighbors to be included in home gatherings at weddings. By welcoming such families into their homes, Prespare were acknowledging that they and their guests shared some common moral ground. In North America, however, it is unusual for anyone except an Albanian or Turk from Prespa, or perhaps from the neighboring Bitola district, to be present at home gatherings. (Sugarman, 1997: 321)

I agree with Sugarman that distance-keeping is more typical of diaspora. In the villages interaction is still necessary for maintaining coexistence, even though the strain between Albanians and Macedonians is greater now than before the break-up of Yugoslavia.

As an anthropologist who has not chosen a single group for sustained study, I have become aware of the stereotypical, suspicious and sometimes antagonistic attitudes members of one group have towards those of other groups. The quasi-secret opinions that solidify one ethnic group against another are a dimension of what Herzfeld (1997: 170) calls 'cultural intimacy'. Of course, one should not claim that Balkan peoples are more prone to this abusive form of 'cultural intimacy' than peoples in other regions. There is indeed a tendency among some writers (for example, Kaplan 1993) to elevate Balkan conflicts to a grand geo-historical law. Concurring with Todorova (1994), I reject such reified notions of 'Balkan ghosts'.

Like most contemporary ethnogaphers, I consider actual practices more illuminating than rigid codes or norms. Multicultural policy in cities like Toronto or Copenhagen allows for, and even encourages, distance-keeping. It promotes the proverbial ethnic mosaic, allowing diverse communities to practice their own particular identities, while avoiding collisions with other groups.

In the homeland, on the other hand, activists in NGOs improvise projects that aim at the social and environmental improvement of multi-ethnic regions, but negotiations with local inhabitants often take place one ethnic group at a time. While the funding organisations in the metropoles stipulate multi-ethnicity as a pre-condition for targeting projects, project co-workers in the field focus on achieving concrete goals. 'Too much talk about multi-culturalism', one NGO staff-person said, 'is not good for a project'. Nevertheless, a successful project in one village can inspire neighbouring villages whose inhabitants consist of another ethnic minority group. In this way, a multi-ethnic pattern of change does occur.

BLESSING WATER IN COPENHAGEN AND TORONTO

The Orthodox Christian Macedonians in Copenhagen number just under 2000 people. Like the estimated 6000 Turks and Albanians also from the Republic of Macedonia, they have inhabited this city for nearly thirty years. The Orthodox community is still hoping to have its own church, but until that time comes it borrows a Danish church for special religious occasions.

On the evening of 19 January 1999, these Orthodox Christian Macedonians celebrated St John the Baptist Day with a traditional ritual blessing of the water. The liturgy was followed by a game-like part of the ritual in which boys rescued the crucifix that the priest had tossed into the sanctified water. In the homeland, retrieving the crucifix takes place in a lake or a stream. In diaspora, meanwhile, the body of water is smaller, usually symbolic – a plastic pool or a wash tub will do.

The liturgy on that winter evening, both chant and sermon, was in the Macedonian language. In spite of the 'foreign' style of the Danish church, its atmosphere soon became fully Macedonian. Although the Russian Orthodox church in the centre of Copenhagen celebrates the same ritual, and is well-attended by Russian, Greek and Serbian residents, the Macedonians preferred to hold their own religious service in the neighbourhood where they lived. Informant-friends told me three weeks in advance that I 'must' attend this special ceremony and even offered to drive me to the church if I could not find it on my bicycle.

Both through reading (Cowan 1990: 29–30) and through my own fieldwork in Toronto in winter 1991 (Schwartz 1996), I was familiar with the blessing of the waters. The general guidelines for the ritual and game are as follows: the priest and his assistants prepare the water in a series of rites which, upon completion, culminate with the priest tossing a crucifix into the water. The boys dive in after it, the one who retrieves it being considered lucky, often even blessed. Celebrants kiss the cross and make a gift of thanks to the church. In Macedonia, the ceremony takes place in mid-January at a customary site by the lake shore or on the bank of a river, that is, in a natural body of cold water. In the Prespa Lake district, the beach at Oteshevo, where families picnic and swim in the summer months is the preferred site. Intriguingly, 'nature' and 'nation' have the same roots. The blessing of waters within the nation's territory works on the assumption that the body of water is already potentially sacred.

Diasporic communities must improvise the ritual of the blessing of the water, especially if local nature is inhospitable. Because jumping into the thick ice of Lake Ontario would require an act of martyrdom beyond the call of normal ethnic and religious affiliation, Toronto ethnic Macedonians in 1991 used a plastic swimming pool, the kind found in many suburban back yards in the summer. In front of their church, St Clement of Ohrid, teenage boys playfully splashed to retrieve the crucifix, submerged, yet highly visible in one foot of tap water.

In Copenhagen, as mentioned previously, the rite took place in a Danish Lutheran church. Apart from a large painting over the altar, the church was bare, a stark contrast to the visual richness of an Orthodox iconostasis. The 'front-stage/back-stage' function (Goffman 1959) that the iconostasis usually provides for the rituals was also missing. The congregation of 40 thus had to 'make do' with a red plastic tub placed near the altar and a good imagination.

The priest, who had come specially from Sweden, gave a short sermon in which he named some of the places in the Republic of Macedonia where the blessing of the waters was occuring simultaneously. The audience was familiar with all of these places. In the service one heard that 'clean water' (*chist voda*) became 'holy water' (*svet voda)*. The priest then invited several boys and men to come up to the altar to take part in the game. Four men, myself included, went up to the table by the altar. I was tempted to participate in, as well as observe, the competition, but prudence prevailed.

First, the priest feigned the tossing of the cross, but on the third time he dropped it into the tub. Six arms plunged in after it, and much of the water spilled over the altar. The proud winner, the one I had hoped for, was a student of German literature at the University of Copenhagen. The man who almost got the cross, though, is a taxi driver in Copenhagen, about whom we will hear more at the conclusion of this chapter.

Significantly, it was not boys who fought over the cross but grown men. This must be understood in the context of diaspora. Though there are differences in diasporic practice, the primary intention seems to be to repeat the traditions of the homeland and thus confirm one's real identity. A minority status in exile renders these identities more vulnerable, while placing more pressure on people to assert their identities. Hence rituals are no longer mere 'child's play'.

Victor Turner's (1967: 95) keen distinction between 'transformatory ritual' and 'confirmatory ceremony' was manifest in the Danish church that evening. Turner explains:

> I consider the term 'ritual' to be more fittingly applied to forms of religious behavior associated with social transitions, while the term 'ceremony' has a close bearing on religious behavior associated with social states, where politico-legal institutions also have a greater importance. (1967: 95)

Some transformatory elements were indeed present: the Orthodox liturgy ritually transformed bread and wine into body and blood, and the water from ordinary 'clean' to 'sacred'. Yet the *confirmation* of the celebrants' Macedonian identity seemed the most valued aspect of the water blessing. The Lutheran church in Copenhagen became a vicarious location for a ritual which 'naturalised' the nation, while sanctifying it. The creativity of diasporic civic practice in marking that identity was striking: it involved making do with limited time and borrowed space, and most importantly 'doing it our way'. In the metropolitan diaspora, then, the blessing of water was geared toward asserting an ethnic-cum-national identity. In the rural homeland of the newly independent republic, the same ceremony had a different emphasis.

BLESSING WATER NEAR PRILEP: 'NEMA VODA, NISHTA!'[3]

Three months earlier, on 10 October 1998, I had observed a ritual blessing of water being performed in a small, arid village north of Prilep, in the Republic of Macedonia. The entire Prilep region is known for its tobacco cultivation, and the landscape was covered with the stalks of recently cut tobacco plants, wide arcs of tobacco leaves strung to dry on almost every wall. This ceremony did not occur on a regular holy day in the church calendar, but was the culminating event in the celebration of a newly constructed water system for a small municipality with five villages. A practical interest in clean water was thereby marked by an Orthodox religious ritual.

My entry to this village was through an NGO organisation, the Macedonian Centre for International Cooperation (MCIC). I first became familiar with the projects of the MCIC when I met Sasho Klikovski,[4] its programme director, at an international conference on Macedonia at the University of London in October 1994, organised by the FAEV. The MCIC has its main office in Skopje, and its chief funders include the World Council of Churches (Amsterdam office) and the Danish Church humanitarian and development aid organisation.

Multi-ethnic coexistence is the top priority of the organisation's mandate. The terms 'civil society' and 'empowerment' appear frequently in the Centre's newsletters and reports.[5] Significantly, MCIC has tried to attain these goals through attention to practical issues, such as organising local, rural communities around environmental and social improvement projects. Since its inception in 1993, the Centre has acted as a catalyst for several successful and low-cost, rural development projects, many of which involve fresh water supply and pollution control. My contact with Sasho Klikovski resulted in several visits to Skopje and two brief but productive encounters in rural areas where the Centre organised projects for clean water.

In April 1995, I accompanied a staff member to the Dolna Reka (Low River) region of western Macedonia, in the municipality of Gostivar. Water pollution control was high on the Centre's agenda (Schwartz 1996). The staff member, Herbie, drove the Land Rover along an unpaved road from which we had to remove large stones in order to continue the steep incline to a remote, highland village inhabited by Albanians.

An ethnic Albanian from Skopje, Herbie's discussions with the villagers were always in their mother tongue. He usually translated the gist of the conversations into English as he drove from one meeting on his schedule to the next. Herbie's main task in the all-Albanian village was to overcome the mistrust and isolation of the villagers, so as to incorporate them into the projects for improvement, in this case, the construction of a water tank a kilometre uphill from the village. Cooperation on such projects was much easier, Herbie noted, in multi-ethnic villages. Although the Centre was committed by its mandate to multi-ethnic projects, he had learned that 'too much talk about multiculturalism' was not the best way to get the villagers together. The best method was to find a village that could demonstrate concrete results and soon the neighbouring villages would follow suit.

In an attempt to check my experience in 1995 with more contemporary events in October 1998, I arranged to accompany two men from MCIC, Roman and Dimko, to meetings with residents in the villages north of Prilep. Our first stop was in a village at the home of a local leader for the water programme. A criterion for funding, as noted, is the multi-ethnic composition of the population in the region. Few regions in the republic could not qualify for projects, but some regions are more 'multi' than others. On each of my two excursions, there were three ethnic groups involved. In the Dolna Reka, there were Orthodox Macedonians, Muslim Macedonians and Muslim Albanians. In the Prilep region, there were Orthodox Macedonians, Muslim Bosniaks and Muslim Albanians.

Though this might be over-generalising, it does seem that an indigenous civil society is more accessible to an NGO when composed of a triad of ethnic groups, where one minority group occupies a mediating position. In the Dolna Reka, the Muslim Macedonians acted as the 'middle-men', or 'gate-opening' group. In the Prilep district, meanwhile, this same role was taken by the Muslim Bosniaks. They were the local coordinators of several water supply projects, mediating between Muslim Albanians and Orthodox Macedonians. This Bosniak minority in the Republic of Macedonia has a seldom-told history. In the 1950s and early 1960s, a party official named Rankovic pursued a vicious policy of ethnic cleansing against Muslim Yugoslavs, causing many to flee to Turkey.

Although Tito finally stopped Rankovic's repression and expulsion of Muslim Yugoslavs, opening – with Rankovic's imprisonment in 1966 – the period of socialist multiculturalism, the Muslim displacement had long-lasting consequences. Many Bosniaks decided to settle in the Prilep region of Macedonia, where today they have tobacco farms. The village leader whose home we visited was excited when he heard I was from Denmark. He gave me a small packet of tobacco, grown on the family farm, to deliver to his brother, now a Bosnian refugee in Denmark.

Besides working with village committees, the NGOs also meet with officials from municipalities and in state ministries. Reform legislation in 1995 subdivided several of the larger municipal governments, creating many smaller, rural units of local government. The opening of the water system in October 1998 in one of these small municipalities showed that the reform could bear fruit. Staff workers of MCIC said that they now had easier access to several of these small town governments. Despite there being many more such small municipalities with which they had yet to negotiate, this was a big improvement. Prior to the reform, the large, distant municipal authorities were often indifferent to the needs of the 'remote' villagers thirty kilometres away.

We arrived at the village town hall just as the official ceremony was starting. For the first time in history, residents in five neighbouring villages, including one nearly all-Albanian village, would have running water in their houses. The opening ceremony was the culmination of two years of difficult planning and construction in which the villagers, municipal officials, administrators from the Ministry of the Interior and, last but not least, NGOs combined forces to realise the project.

The day itself seemed auspicious. We learned that that particular October date coincided with the first mobilisation of the Prilep region's resistance movement against the Fascists and Nazis in 1941. Moreover, the first round of the national elections in the Republic of Macedonia was only one week away. Posters and flags of the Social Democratic Party were hung all around the site of the ceremony. The NGO co-workers complained to me about these. They did not think that the Social Democratic Party ought to take credit for the water project. 'Too much party politics!' one man commented.

The two staff members and I were shown to wooden chairs in the front row and the ceremonies began with a local orchestra playing Macedonian folk music. A group of young boys and girls wearing peasant costumes performed several dances, then a round of political speech-making commenced. Thanks were repeatedly offered to the MCIC, rounds of applause emerging each time this NGO was mentioned. As this was a celebration of Macedonian citizenship, all the speeches were in Macedonian. Even though the municipality included villages with Albanian inhabitants, the multi-ethnic composition of the district was not underscored here – perhaps in much the same way that the celebration of Ilinden Day highlighted the ethnic Macedonian community but kept the Turkish citizens in the shadows.

After the speeches came the ritual blessing of the water by two Orthodox priests at the outdoor faucet in the town hall yard. This ritual took me by surprise. I began to take close-up photographs, alongside others with video cameras. Finally, the faucet was officially opened and children and adults lined up to take their first drink from the cool, clean water. I wondered why a Muslim *hodja* was not present at the ceremony and decided to ask the staff members why later. The opening ceremony was now complete and we were invited to a large luncheon served inside the municipal hall for officials and special guests. Roman made a brief speech and proposed a toast. Almost immediately after, we joined several people at a cafe in a neighbouring village for a final drink, before heading back to Prilep.

In the car I was able to ask many questions as we sped by the tobacco fields. In the two-year period of the project, Roman and Dimko had made twice-monthly visits to the Prilep region to assure that progress was being made. The biggest problem, they said, had been an Albanian village, whose inhabitants had not wanted to have the pipeline running through their town, because they thought they would be cheated of their water. At one critical point the police came from Prilep to ensure that the construction work could take place. When the villagers threatened them with pick-axes and hoes, however, the police left. After many negotiations with MCIC staff, the Albanian villagers finally agreed to let the construction work continue. They provided labour, as originally planned, and are now linked up with the entire system, which provides 50 litres of water per household per day.

I then asked why there hadn't been any Muslim *hodja* at the ceremony. 'Because there are no Albanians living in the village where the celebration took place.' Dimko's answer suggested that the event we had just attended was not conceived as a *multicultural* celebration which thus might be represented equally by clergy from the two neighbouring faiths. Those trying to develop 'civil society' in Macedonia regard multi-ethnic coexistence as a primary, though often tacit, goal. Perhaps as an outsider from the metropole, I was prone to what might be called 'multi-ethnocentrism'. I would have thought it a valuable, symbolic gesture to have invited a *hodja* to participate in the community's celebration.[6] This was not on the agenda, however, and the coordinators had not pressed for such a symbolic action. 'Too much talk about multiculturalism', and the pieties often associated with it, did not seem in keeping with current local practice. So the liturgical blessing of water was done in the Orthodox way alone.

The very concept of 'civil society' implies a measure of trust between its different members, who often are unequally positioned (Seligman 1992; Hann and Dunn 1996; Verdery 1996). Since the concept's origins in the eighteenth-century 'Republic of Letters', it has always been evident that organisations of civil society build upon, and can sometimes generate, a modicum of trust only through persistent effort. The pipeline went through the Albanian village and left some good water on the way. This 'right of passage' is more important than the *rite de passage* we anthropologists customarily focus upon. Indeed, while the performance of exotic rites has been the perennial interest of anthropology, there is also a pressing need to enquire into how civil rights are attained and maintained. In this specific case, an organisation of 'civil society' had a pivotal role in the completion of a needed hydraulic project.

DIVISIONS OR DIALOGUE IN DIASPORA?

Not every day is there a blessing of water. In Denmark, 'civil society' is often synonymous with specific social and cultural work in voluntary associations (*frivilligt foreningsarbejde*). Civil society is as local as it can be, and if there are sharp differences between members, the typical solution is to split into two or three associations. Nobody describes Danish society as 'Balkanised', however. Segmentation is taken for granted and is a fact of associational life, because agreement *(enighed)* among members has almost a sacred status. The term 'Balkanisation', on the other hand, stigmatises diversity and finds violence imminent at every moment.

At the same time that I began studying the civil society organisations in the Republic of Macedonia, I also began observant participation in diverse Macedonian organisations in Copenhagen. I helped to start a Danish–Macedonian friendship association (*Dansk–Makedonsk Venskabs-forening*, or *DAN-MAK*). Preliminary meetings took place in autumn 1994 and we formally initiated the organisation in February 1995. Among the regular participants in the founding committee were one ethnic Turk, one ethnic Albanian, one ethnic Rom, several ethnic Macedonians, one ethnic Danish woman and one ethnic American man – the latter two both anthropologists. The shortage of Danes in the friendship association's organising committee did not seem to be a problem. In fact, hyphenated ethnic 'friendship associations' typically have very few Danish members. A great deal of discussion, however, was about the inflections of the word 'Macedonian' in the organisation's statement of purpose. The result of the discussion, in which the anthropologists were influential, was that 'Macedonian' in *DAN-MAK* became defined by citizenship. Potential members of the association were 'people from Denmark and Macedonia' with the implicit prefix, 'Republic of'.

Thus, the proposed charter did not emphasise having 'Macedonian culture and identity'; rather, citizenship in a newly independent, and ethnically unstable, republic. We anthropologists argued that a friendship association should mean precisely a friendship that *included* different ethnic groups, without having to name all of them. The ethnic Macedonians in the planning committee accepted this important stipulation, perhaps a bit grudgingly. Much like their counterparts in the republic, the members in diaspora frowned upon 'too much talk about multiculturalism'.

The initiating committee sent out invitations in early January 1995 to the addresses of the diverse ethnic clubs in Copenhagen. On the first Sunday in February, a convening meeting was scheduled in a well-known recreation hall, the Grøndal Centre, in Nørrebro. This sprawling, multipurpose structure, financed in part by the European Union's social funds, houses many cultural, sports and other leisure activities, all of which are under the auspices of clubs and voluntary organisations. *DAN-MAK* held its first meeting in one of the two adjacent meeting rooms that 'Makedonija', the ethnic Macedonian club, had already reserved for Sunday afternoon folk dancing. Nearly 70 persons attended, including a group of 20 Albanian men seated together in the front rows. The boys and girls performed their dances, then I, sitting at the head table, read the Danish statement of purpose for the association, while Hasim, the Turkish committee member, read it in Macedonian. Texts of the by-rules were likewise copied in Danish and Macedonian.

A spokesman from the Albanian group questioned why the word 'Albanian' was not mentioned in the text. I answered that the committee did not think it was necessary to list all the ethnic affiliations in our organisation's statute. Rather, our view was that all people 'from Macedonia' were welcome, and that the most important word was 'friendship' (*venskab*). This interchange, like most of the discussion, was in Danish. My remarks were met with applause from the majority. A second Albanian speaker stated that there were many other Albanian clubs that had not received invitations to the meeting. Hasim answered that we had sent invitations to all the clubs whose addresses we had at our disposal. The man then requested a postponement of the organisation's establishment until all the clubs were informed. I opposed the proposal and asked for a show of hands. After the overwhelming rejection, the Albanian men left, one arguing with me on the way out.

Those who remained unanimously voted acceptance of the proposed by-laws and then elected a steering committee. I became chairman and Hasim, from the Prespa Lake region, became vice-chairman. The Albanian man who had been on the planning committee, also from the Prespa region, was elected to the board. All the persons who planned the organisation were elected to posts, and the remaining positions were taken by ethnic Macedonians. Forty-four persons signed membership cards and paid their dues.

DAN-MAK was thereby launched, with more hope than history. The level of activity was never high. In May 1996, for its third cultural event since its founding in February 1995, I proposed a celebration of Djordjiden (George's Day), sometimes called in folkloric texts 'Green George's Day' (Stoianovich, 1967). Djordjiden is one of the unofficial holidays in the Balkans which, though a Christian Saint's day, can be multi-ethnic in practice. Indeed, Tone Bringa (1995: 225–6) has pointed out that Muslims in Bosnia participated in the celebration. Similarly, during my fieldwork in Resen in May 1995, Muslims and Christians alike marked the coming of spring by placing sprigs of fresh willow on doorways and windows.

In Copenhagen, about 40 persons came to the *DAN-MAK* George's Day programme, held in a school classroom in Nørrebro. I gave a short talk and introduced the main speaker, a Danish colleague from the university whose field is Balkan geography but whose interest is mostly political. He chose to deliver a speech that defended the Albanian university in Tetovo. He condemned the Macedonian state for its repression of Albanians (see Brown, this volume). There ensued an intense argument, and one of the Macedonians on the steering committee looked at me bitterly while criticising the guest speaker. As host and chairman, I tried to moderate the conflict but to no avail. George's Day ended joylessly, and it proved to be the last event in *DAN-MAK*'s brief history. Attempts to summon the steering committee to meet failed again and again. When I was reviewing this episode with Hasim at his home in October 1998, he revealed that the Macedonians have never forgiven me for inviting that particular speaker. I admitted that it was an extremely naïve thing for me to do.

Since the demise of *DAN-MAK* in 1996, I have persistently followed, though separately, diverse diasporic organisations in greater Copenhagen. Bringing all the groups together in a multi-ethnic 'dialogue' has not turned out to be feasible, however. In large metropolitan societies with multicul-turalist policies, it is possible for different ethnic groups from the same region to keep their distance from one another, that is, to avoid dialogical situations.

WHERE AND WHEN WILL THEY STILL BE DANCING?

My research approach since 1996 has been to visit the groups in their own, often temporary, spaces. I have been lucky in that many of the ethnic organ-isations use the same suburban municipal hall in Ballerup for their dance and dinner parties. In this section, I will repeat the question that Carl-Ulrik Schierup and Aleksandra Ålund posed in their study of Yugoslavian emigrants in Scandinavia: 'Will They Still Be Dancing?' (Schierup and Ålund, 1987). One of the key topics of their fieldwork was the celebration of the Yugoslavian national holiday, 29 November, in a Danish provincial town near Copenhagen. They express very well the meaning of dancing the *ore* among emigrants:

The *ore* is not just folklore. It is an important part of ongoing social life; a scene for the unfolding of multiplex social life in a migrant community. It is a scene which reflects interests, conflicts, and dilemmas in a total field of migrant experience. (Schierup and Ålund, 1987: 205)

Interestingly, Schierup's photographs from the dance are from 1981, that is, the year after Tito's death, when his memory was still a strong unifying force. Their commentary applies to the present, however, in unexpected ways. Refugees from the former Yugoslavia have since joined the immigrants in Scandinavia. The different forms of *ore* now underscore the ethnic specificity of the dancers, who are no longer citizens of the same nation-state, Yugoslavia.

In the 1970s, Ballerup, a suburb 15 kilometres west of Copenhagen, became one of the earliest settlements of Yugoslavian 'guest workers'. In 1998, the town's listing of voluntary organisations included two Albanian clubs, one Montenegrin, one Serbian and one Macedonian. Although these clubs celebrate separately, with different ethnic and commercial sponsors, they all use the municipal hall, Tapeten (meaning 'wallpaper' in Danish), located in one of the public housing districts of Ballerup. The hall can accommodate 400 people, seated at long tables, with space left for the chain dances (*ore*). At these celebrations, tables empty as guests join in a single chain, the orchestra and singer often performing non-stop for half an hour or more. Each ethnic group has its distinctive melodies and songs, and its particular style of dancing the *ore*.

Since 1996, many dances have been held in Tapeten. I attended the four to which I was invited. These included a party in March 1996 sponsored by the club 'Makedonija' (where my wife and I were special guests because of our work in *DAN-MAK*) and a party in May 1996 which followed the opening of the Albanian club house in Ballerup. (The invitation to the second party was proferred to us not by the club, but by the Danish butcher who allowed Albanians from Ballerup to graze their sheep at his farm before the religious holiday of Bayram.) The two most recent dance events (September 1998 and January 1999) are most relevant for this article.

The 5 September 1998 celebration commemorated the seventh anniversary of the Macedonian Republic's independence from Milosevic's regime in Belgrade. It was planned by an *ad hoc* group of Macedonians led by George, my *DAN-MAK* friend, who hoped to revive our defunct organisation at the independence day party. When George and I arrived at

Tapeten, we noticed that the wall behind the orchestra stand was decorated by adjacent Danish and Macedonian flags, with a logo of stylised folk dancers and an inscription: 'Danish–Macedonian Friendship'. There also hung a portrait of Goche Delchev, who inspired the abortive independence movement against Ottoman Turkish rule in August 1903. A band of five musicians, 'Grom', had come from Göteborg and a well-known singer, Blagoja Gryevski, had flown in from Skopje for the occasion. Sitting at a table with George and a young ethnic Turkish man, I recognised almost all the people at the party as ethnic Macedonians. The ambassador from the Republic of Macedonia, an ethnic Albanian, sat with his wife at the table for guests of honour facing the orchestra. He gave a short speech wishing the party success. However, once the music and dancing were well under way, I noticed that he and his wife did not join the chain dance.

There were between 200 and 300 people present that night and, to me, they appeared to be enjoying themselves. Yet according to George, the evening was 'a catastrophe'. What he meant was that members of the other ethnic communities in the republic, though invited, had not come. He was disappointed that they had not felt like celebrating their common citizenship. Perhaps he was recalling with nostalgia the Yugoslavia of the 1970s, when migrant workers in western Europe met at large dances twice a year (the national holiday, 29 November, and Women's Day, 8 March).

It is true that, apart from the ambassador, the Albanians were definitely absent. I had visited the Albanian club-house in Ballerup in July to find out whether its members would be coming and was informed in no uncertain terms that they wouldn't. The men recalled how I had not postponed the founding of *DAN-MAK*, which to them proved that I was on the side of the Macedonians. They were deeply involved in supporting the cause of Albanians in Kosovo and the illegal university in Tetovo and mistrusted the Macedonians, one man saying of them that they were of 'the same Slavic blood' as the Serbian enemies. Another man referred to 'the Prespa Mafia' which sponsored the dance party. This was an expression not just of *ethnic* but also of *regional* loyalties. The Albanians from the Tetovo region, who are that region's majority population and in this respect have a similar position to the Kosovar Albanians, consider the Albanian minority in the Prespa region as too conciliatory and passive.

If George felt discouraged that the Albanians did not attend the dance party, my private feelings were those of relief. What if a huge fight had broken out in Tapeten between Albanians and Macedonians? It is not unknown among members of hostile diasporas. My guess is that George too was not surprised at the absence of Albanians. In Copenhagen, diasporas were, until now, 'low profile' affairs. The equal, cultural space of Tapeten was shared by different and opposing groups, though never on the same Saturday night.

The Albanians in Ballerup and Copenhagen were absent on 5 September. So too were the Turkish families. The fourth dance which I and my wife attended at Tapeten was sponsored by 'Prespa Club' on 30 January 1999 to celebrate Bayram, the holiday after the completion of the fasting during Ramadan. This party resembled the others I had seen in Ballerup. The room was filled to its capacity, and most of the people had driven to Ballerup from Nørrebro or other parts of Copenhagen, since few ethnic Turks from Macedonia live in Ballerup.

'Prespa' is not an ethnic category, but rather the name of the lakes located on the borders of Albania, Greece and ex-Yugoslavia. In the early years (1970s) after arriving in Denmark, the 'Prespa Club' was located in Copenhagen's multi-ethnic, slum neighbourhood of Vognmandsmarken (Schwartz 1985). In those days, regional affiliation predominated over the ethnic; there were Albanian, Macedonian and Turkish members of the club when it started in 1974. Soccer further united the Prespa Club members, as did the mobilisation for better housing conditions. When Vognmandsmarken was finally torn down in 1979 and the tenants were rehoused and scattered, the ethnic Turkish members gradually became the majority of Prespa Club. Albanians and Macedonians formed their own associations with definite ethnic labels.

'Prespa' in Copenhagen and in Malmö (Sweden) are today almost entirely ethnic Turkish. A member of 'Prespa' told me at the club's annual party in November 1992 that 'the Macedonian and the Albanian clubs are political. Ours is social.' Being 'social' and not 'political' makes a significant difference to the Turkish community from Macedonia. I had hoped that the Prespa Club might mediate between the Albanians and the Macedonians in Copenhagen's diasporas, just as I had seen a 'group in the middle' mediate in the republic, but the accusation of 'Prespa mafia' by a militant Albanian in Ballerup belies that likelihood. The Albanians suspect the Turkish minority of siding with the ethnic Macedonians. The appeal to provide humanitarian aid to the people of Kosovo – which hung prominently on the bulletin board of the Prespa Club – suggests otherwise however. The Turks are 'in the middle' in Copenhagen, just as they are in the Prespa region. In the ethnic diasporas, however, separateness dissipates the possibility of mediation.

At the ethnic Macedonian dances, the lottery numbers are read in Macedonian and then in Danish. The Albanians follow the same procedure with numbers called out in Albanian and Danish. Likewise, Prespa Club's lottery numbers are read in Turkish and then in Danish. The allocated, municipal space in Ballerup for ethnic dancing is a good place for observing the segmentary practices of multiculturalism.

CONCLUSION: INTERFACE BEHIND THE BOWLING ALLEY

In my Copenhagen fieldwork I have visited local, all-male spaces, as well as the occasional dance parties. As mentioned, the Albanian club has its own quarters in Ballerup, having raised funds to purchase and repair a dilapidated house for the organisation. The Turkish-dominated Prespa Club, too, has its own large hall in a former factory. The Macedonians, meanwhile, deplore the fact that they do not have their own space, and we noted at the opening of this chapter that they borrowed a Danish church for the blessing of the water.

On Sunday afternoons, the Macedonian men meet at three tables behind the noisy bowling alleys in Grøndal Centre. There they talk, play cards, drink beer and eat snacks. Macedonians, well aware that the Muslim groups from the republic have their own facilities, have often told me that they would like to have their own club house. Demographically, the Albanian and Turkish groups are twice the size of the ethnic Macedonian community. This is exactly the inverse of the population figures in the republic, which is two-thirds Orthodox Macedonian and one-third combined Muslim Albanians and Turks. Becoming an ethnic minority in diaspora may heighten one's home-sickness, or at least one's longing to be part of the majority once more.

When I came to the Macedonian meeting place behind the bowling alleys for the first time in November 1998, the taxi driver (the same man who just missed grabbing the crucifix at the church) yelled, 'Here's the guy who loves Albanians!' I immediately told him that the Albanians thought of me as the guy who loves the Macedonians. 'You just can't win', I added. He laughed, obviously getting the point. He became more friendly. 'You are a journalist,' he said, 'who does not write behind our backs'. I took this as a compliment. I wonder now if what I have written above can be construed as 'behind the backs' of the many informants. Whether we 'look over the shoulders' of the informants, as if they were writing (Geertz 1973: 452) or write behind their backs, we must have a certain degree of trust in our informant-friends, as they must have a mutual trust in us.

My informants in diaspora and in the homeland do not have many secrets about each other. Stereotypes about the 'others' are deeply rooted, if not always uttered. In fact, the presence of an ethnic triad implies that each group knows what the others think about the other two. This is literally an experience of 'interface'. One should recall that the term 'interface' is used by traffic engineers for exits and entrances onto super-highways (Wallman 1978). 'Interface', Wallman observed, is the point of maximum danger where each driver must be aware of the others' intentions.

Ethnic coexistence is a process like the interface on freeways. To pursue my initial preference for attention to 'rights of passage' over *rites de passage*, I can conclude that interactions in the multi-ethnic homeland are commonly prepared by interfacing. Real collisions are usually avoided. Negotiations can take place, but most often the different ethnic groups maintain the principle of Robert Frost's farmer in 'Mending Wall': 'Good fences make good neighbors.' Likewise, in diaspora, distance-keeping is enhanced by the surrounding society, in this case, the tolerance of Danish society. Whether it is a blessing of water or a dancing of one's *ore*, the issue of 'rights' is felt to be primary. Each group strives to maintain its rights to practise its identity. Sometimes, as I have shown in Ballerup, the differences actually resemble each other. In my descriptions and analyses, I have placed the rites of 'blessing water' in the foreground, but only to emphasise the wider context of the ongoing contest for the civil rights of passage.

Finally, one could describe, with not a little irony, the formations of ethnic communities in diaspora as 'more Balkan than in the Balkans'. At a distance the memory of the homeland becomes pristine and pure (Kontos 1988). Moreover, the multiculturalist environment in the diasporas curiously inhibits the interethnic practices of the homeland. Nationalisms and antagonisms flourish in the hot houses of multiculturalist nation-states. There, one remembers only the pure-bred nation, forgetting the neighbourly exchanges of baklava at Bayram and Easter.

ACKNOWLEDGEMENTS

I am grateful for the editorial comments made by two anthropologists in Copenhagen, Sally Anderson and Kirsten Rønne. The MCIC has been extremely hospitable to my field research. I also thank Jane Cowan for her astute comments and intensive editorial labour. Kirsten, my wife, has accompanied me on much of the fieldwork in Macedonia, Denmark and Canada, so her witnessing has frequently corrected my faulty observations and inferences.

NOTES

1. To give an example of the contested symbolic inflections of Macedonia, 'Vardar' is the river which flows through Skopje, though when it crosses the Greek border north of Thessaloniki, its name changes to Axios.
2. For a comparable use of the pun 'rites' and 'rights' see Cohen (1996).
3. 'No water, Nothing.' This is a remark I heard exclaimed several times while helping clear the small irrigation channels to apple orchards in the Prespa Lake region, July 1982.
4. The names of most of the informants are authentic, not fictive. When they have preferred not to be named in the text, I have respected that wish.
5. 'Civil society' is one of the organisation's key terms, especially used in its contacts with the funders in northern Europe. I have noted several times that although 'cooperation' (*sorabotka*) is the word in the organisation's title, 'help' (*pomosh)* is the word spoken by the villagers when they thank the staff workers.
6. My question to the NGOs in Prilep, in retrospect, was provoked by an experience in Bosnia in May 1997. To celebrate the construction of a new bridge in Mostar, a multi-faith peace walk across the river took place with Roman Catholic, Muslim, Orthodox and Jewish religious leaders. The manifestation was initiated by the American ambassador and was organised by an OSCE staff person from the Republic of Macedonia (Schwartz 1999).

BIBLIOGRAPHY

Appadurai, Arjun. 1990. 'Disjuncture and Difference in the Global Cultural Economy', in M. Featherstone (ed.) *Global Culture: Nationalism, globalization, and modernity.* London: Sage.

Bringa, Tone. 1995. *Being Muslim the Bosnian Way: Identity and community in a Central Bosnian village*. Princeton: Princeton University Press.

Cohen, Anthony. 1996. 'Personal Nationalism: A Scottish view of some rites, rights, and wrongs'. *American Ethnologist* 23(4), 802–15.

Cowan, Jane K. 1990. *Dance and the Body Politic in Northern Greece*. Princeton: Princeton University Press.

Danforth, Loring M. 1995. *The Macedonian Conflict: Ethnic nationalism in a transnational world*. Princeton: Princeton University Press.

Geertz, Clifford. (ed.). 1973. *The Interpretation of Cultures*. New York: Basic Books.

Goffman, Erving. 1959. *The Presentation of Self in Everyday Life*. Middlesex: Penguin.

Hann, Chris and Elisabeth Dunn. (eds). 1996. *Civil Society: Challenging Western models*. London: Routledge.

Herzfeld, Michael. 1997. *Cultural Intimacy: Social poetics in the nation-state*. London: Routledge.

Kaplan, Robert. 1993. *Balkan Ghosts: A journey through history*. New York: Vintage.

Kontos, Alkis. 1988. 'Memories of Ithaca', in I. Angus (ed.) *Ethnicity in a Technological Age*. Edmonton: Canadian Institute of Ukrainian Studies.

Petroff, Lillian. 1995. *Sojourners and Settlers: The Macedonian community in Toronto to 1940*. Toronto: University of Toronto Press.

Schierup, Carl-Ulrik and Aleksandra Ålund. 1987. *Will They Still Be Dancing? Integration and ethnic transformation among Yugoslavian immigrants in Scandinavia*. Göteborg: Almkvist and Wiksell.

Schwartz, Jonathan M. 1985. *Reluctant Hosts: Denmark's reception of guest workers*. Copenhagen: Akademisk Forlag.

—— 1996. *Pieces of Mosaic: An essay on the making of Makedonija*. Højbjerg: Intervention Press.

—— 1999. 'Tomorrow's Anthropology: NGOgraphy'. *Anthropology in Action* 6(1), 16–17.

Seligman, Adam. 1992. *The Idea of Civil Society*. New York: Free Press.

Stoianovich, Traian. 1967. *A Study on Balkan Civilization*. New York: Knopf.

Stubbs, Paul. 1996. 'Creative Negotiations. Concepts and Practice of Communities in Croatia', in R. Jambresic and M. Povrzanovic (eds) *War, Exile, and Everyday Life*. Zagreb: Institute of Ethnology.

Sugarman, Jane. 1997. *Engendering Song: Singing and subjectivity at Prespa Albanian weddings*. Chicago: University of Chicago Press.

Taylor, Charles. 1992. *Multiculturalism and 'The Politics of Recognition'*. Princeton NJ: Princeton University Press.

Todorova, Maria. 1994. 'The Balkans: From discovery to invention'. *Slavic Review* 53(2), 453–82.

Turner, Victor. 1967: *The Forest of Symbols: Aspects of Ndembu ritual*. Ithaca: Cornell University Press.

Verdery, Katherine. 1996. *What was Socialism, and What Comes Next?* Princeton: Princeton University Press.

Wallman, Sandra. 1978. 'The Boundaries of "Race": Processes of Ethnicity in England'. *Man* 13(2), 200–18.

6 IN THE REALM OF THE DOUBLE-HEADED EAGLE: PARAPOLITICS IN MACEDONIA 1994–9

K.S. Brown

In the break-up of Yugoslavia in the early 1990s, international law and understandings of sovereignty were put under considerable strain when parts of the federal state sought to secede. When the European Commission set up the Badinter Commission to evaluate the cases for autonomy made by various different entities within the federal republic, high on the agenda for the applicants was the protection of minority rights. In January 1992 the Commission ruled that the Republics of Slovenia and Macedonia met the criteria for immediate recognition. The Republics of Croatia and Bosnia-Hercegovina were deemed to fall short of the desired standards in minority rights guarantees. The case put by the province of Kosovo was deemed unreceivable, as the right of secession was granted only to existing republics.[1]

As is well known, the Commission's recommendations were outweighed by other political considerations. Croatia found powerful allies within Europe and was recognised at the same time as Slovenia. Macedonia, by contrast, fell foul of an opponent within the European Community, Greece. Particular attention was paid at the time to the particular objections lodged by Greece that key symbols of the Republic of Macedonia – its new flag and constitution, and indeed its very name – conveyed indirect and implicit but nonetheless efficacious claims to Greek territory and heritage.

At that time the dispute between Greece and the new Republic of Macedonia was a major focus of international attention. Anthropologists strove to illuminate some of the issues involved and were for their pains drawn into wider, politicised theoretical debates (Danforth 1993, 1995; Karakasidou 1993, 1994). The various twists and turns in the saga of Macedonia's Greekness, and some Greeks' Macedonianness, have turned the Florina region of northern Greece into an ethnographic boomtown, with around a dozen social or cultural anthropologists pursuing active research there by 1998 (Agelopoulos, n.d.). One of the most visible sites of dispute was the issue of the flag, a 16-pointed star. In an article published in *Antiquity* (Brown 1994), I suggested that the question of the flag did not just illuminate a quarrel between two history-obsessed Balkan states: rather, it pointed to the struggle for internal legitimacy that was already in train within the new state. In this chapter, I revisit the argument of the 1994 paper, and suggest that while the particular tensions between the new Republic and Greece have eased, what I would now term parapolitics – the realm in which state and non-state actors compete to define the relationships between culture, politics and identity, and thus invest symbols with material consequence – remains a vital dimension to our understanding of the Republic of Macedonia's uneasy path towards sovereign statehood.

SEEING STARS, 1991–4

The device around which much of the issue apparently revolved was the 16-pointed star or sun (Figure 6.1), which was chosen to appear on the new republic's flag in mid-August 1992. It took the place of the *petokratka*, or five-pointed star, a symbol freighted with the republic's association with the socialist ideals of the federal Yugoslavia. The process by which the 16-pointed star or sun was chosen and approved by the new Macedonian parliament has not been fully investigated; what drew rather more international attention, almost immediately, was the strong sense of outrage that the flag seemed to provoke in Greece.

Figure 6.1 Emblems of the two flags: the five-pointed star of the Yugoslav period, and the 16-pointed sun/star of Macedonia

The grounds of Greek hostility to the new republic's recognition under the name of Macedonia, and carrying this symbol on its banner, have been extensively explored. At the heart of much of the rhetoric in Greece, which appeared to mobilise large-scale support, was a particular view of ancient history as national patrimony that underpins rights to exclusive ownership of symbols and territory in the present. The 16-pointed star was associated with Philip II of Macedon, father of Alexander the Great – an association enshrined by the archaeological work of Manolis Andronikos at Vergina, in northern Greece. Philip's kingdom had been situated not on the territory of the former Yugoslavia, but within the borders of modern Greece. The attempt by the former Yugoslav Republic of Macedonia to achieve sovereign status as Macedonia, and display the star of Vergina as its own, was thus read as a claim on both a territory and a history celebrated as inalienably Greek.

RIVAL SYMBOLS

The analytical focus on the Greek–Macedonian dispute which evoked such strong passions, though, distracted attention from other elements of the story of the flag. While much was made of the replacement of one symbol with another, less noted was the fact that the visual style of the republic's flag remained unaltered, preserving the form of a red background inscribed with a yellow or gold device. In debates at the time within the republic, then, the choice of symbol was not the only element that carried the weight of collective representation: so too did the frame in which the symbol stood.

The focus on the emblem and the international problems that its choice prompted, also overshadowed the possible exploration of counterfactuals: the emblems not chosen, and the problems that their rejection perhaps averted. Among symbols that have emerged to replace the communist *petokratka* in other sites is the Christian cross; also enjoying a renaissance on banners is a lion rampant. In the context of modern multi-ethnic Macedonia, though – a Macedonia, it might be stressed again, whose juridical–legal institutions were in 1992 recognised by the European community as providing adequately for the protection of minorities – such symbols represent potential divisions rather than grounds for civic unity. In the first place, the republic's new leadership resolutely sought to maintain the division between religion and state that Yugoslavia had embraced. In the second, leaders recognised that symbols have their own historical associations. The lion had positive significance only for some of the Slav-speaking Orthodox majority of the population and, as such, offered no potential to achieve appeal across the lines of language and religion.

Attention to such alternatives shifts the debate over the choice of a symbol from its external consequences to its internal dynamics. The apparent political and popular consensus within the republic on the choice of the 16-pointed sun suggested that it was seen as a rare marker of solidarity across the internal boundaries of ethnic group and religion that dominated most discussions. It had resonance for various groups in the republic: Vlachs or Aroumanians, for example, have flown an 8-pointed star and claim descent from Philip II by various dubious arguments, one being that the Greek name for their people – *Koutsovlachs* – arose because Philip II was lame (*koutsos*). Albanian parties, by contrast, have claimed Alexander because he was the son of Olympias, the Illyrian queen, and they claim descent from the Illyrians. Alexander's Macedonia – according to Greek historians as well as to the Oxford English Dictionary in its account of how *macédoine* came to mean fruit salad – was an empire of mixed traditions and heritages. The spirit of the selection of the 16-pointed star by a parliament drawn from different ethnic groups seems to evoke this past diversity. Although in the Greek view the flag appears to make exclusive claims about identity, within the republic it remains one of the more inclusive symbols from the past. In this respect, again, the republic's use of the flag represents a continuity with Yugoslav Macedonian rhetorics about the past, as explored by Neil Silberman (1989).

Such symbols are in demand because of the very real social and economic differences that exist in the Republic of Macedonia, and the way in which those differences are experienced and narrated by individuals in ways that serve to separate communities from one another. I sought to describe the contours of difference, especially as they are perceived by members of the Macedonian majority in the republic, in my previous article (Brown 1994). In brief, although most Macedonians still trace descent to one or more villages (in this respect, not necessarily emphasising patrilineage) and acknowledge the key role played in their national history by rural activism, their own adult lives are bound up with the opportunities presented by urban life. Ties with the land that were once established and maintained through agricultural practice, and close neighbourhood and kin relations formerly embedded directly in economic and social life, are now mediated by larger-scale institutions, many created by the agency of the former socialist state. The reconstruction of Skopje after the earthquake of 1963 presented residents with a modern urban landscape in which the past was inscribed only in certain preserved or newly built monuments; much of the lived environment for Macedonians was wholly new.

In this regard, a sharp distinction was sometimes made by Macedonians between their own situation and that of their fellow citizens of other linguistic or religious groups, in particular Albanian Muslims. The latter were perceived often as occupying the physical and imagined territory of the countryside from which Macedonians left in the time of socialist Yugoslavia. This identification of Albanians clearly represented a negatively charged stereotype, imbued with certain qualities of alleged 'backwardness'. Yet also, ironically, in the aftermath of the break-up of Yugoslavia, the economic crisis, and the struggle to establish the legitimacy of the Macedonian nation and state in the international arena, some Macedonians seemed to want to reclaim the (imagined) ground of heritage for themselves. When citizen organisations or the Macedonian government sought to have an impact on the physical landscape of rural Macedonia, though, they often found themselves dealing not with an abandoned space awaiting reclamation, but with a territory occupied and imbued with cultural meanings by people with whom they shared citizenship, but little else. The stage was set, then, I argued, for a potentially violent confrontation between an increasingly politicised minority and a majority anxious, in the last resort, to maintain control of a territory they celebrated as their own.

THE DISAPPEARING GREEK DIMENSION

Since 1994, a number of things have changed. In the first place, the dispute between Greece and the Republic of Macedonia over the flag came to an end. In the light of the blockade imposed at the Macedonian border by Greece on 17 February 1994, the pressure on the republic to reach some form of compromise became unendurable: by September of that year, Boutros Boutros-Ghali named tensions with Greece as one of the most serious threats to the republic's stability (Shea 1997: 220). In the following year, Richard Holbrooke and Christopher Hill brokered a deal in which Kiro Gligorov ceded use of the flag, and Andreas Papandreou called off the blockade. After the deal was signed in early September, the republic finally stopped using the flag on 13 September 1995 and the introduction of a new flag was approved by Parliament on 5 October 1995. The vote was 110 members for, one against, with four abstentions (Holbrooke 1998: 122–6; Shea 1997: 308).

Strikingly, the new flag continued the same visual tradition of previous Macedonian republican flags, which had been noted in Macedonian newspapers as early as 1992 (Brown 1994: 786).[2] It is a golden sun on a red background, with rays shooting outwards. In this regard, the new design represents an ingenious resolution of the problem posed by the alteration of a freighted symbol. For while the visual impact is undoubtedly very different from that of the Vergina sun/star, when the new design is described in words as the 'Macedonian sun' one might imagine that the republic has made no compromise. It is almost as if the utopian solution to the Macedonian–Greek dispute so earnestly pleaded by Danforth (1993) has come true, and the two sides somehow co-occupy the same symbolic space, each illuminated by its own symbol, the one a sun, the other a star.

From this point onwards, the standoff with Greece which had so dominated discourses in the first years of the republic became less important. The settlement over the flag was accompanied by a growing reaction from Greek intellectuals in particular, who stated that Greek opposition to the new state's progress had in fact been detrimental to Greece's status in the international sphere. Some tensions continue over the issue of visas to Macedonians with republic passports seeking vacations or hoping to visit relatives or birthplaces in Greece. The name issue, too, has yet to be resolved. Although meetings between Greek and Macedonian leaders have been held, as of the middle of 1999 no compromise had been found. Nonetheless, Greek investment is now playing a major part in the privatisation of Macedonian industry (Holbrooke 1998: 127; Perry 1998: 120). This has not occurred without opposition on both sides. It has nonetheless proceeded, and has a symbolic significance of its own.

INTERNAL DYNAMICS

That the dispute between Macedonia and Greece has come to be viewed as an aberration, and has been succeeded by the building of ties in the formal realm of interstate relations, seems to buttress the view that there was more (or less) at stake than two countries squabbling over the interpretation of history. Yet the end of the symbolic standoff was not divorced from political realities of a far more brutal kind. Two days before the vote on the flag in the Macedonian parliament, the president of the republic, Kiro Gligorov, narrowly survived a bomb attack in which his driver was killed and he lost an eye. Those responsible for the assassination attempt have not been arrested; it seemed a clear attempt to destabilise the republic in a direct way. Gligorov himself had come to stand as a symbol of the path the new state had chosen. The attack put to the test the constitutional machinery of the republic, and it survived.

Other challenges to Macedonia grew in salience, especially those which arise from the internal issues described in some detail in the previous chapter. What has become still clearer is commitment, both from within the republic and outside, to recognise and represent the citizen body's ethnic and religious diversity. This was reflected in the way in which the defining practice of the modern nation-state, the census, was carried out in 1994. Questionnaires were prepared in six languages – Macedonian, Albanian, Turkish, Rom, Serbo-Croatian and Vlach – to cater for the linguistic diversity of the population. The returns from the census indicated that self-identified ethnic Macedonians, mostly Orthodox Christian, constitute a dominant majority in the state as a whole (1,228,330 or 66.5 per cent), while the largest single other group comprises self-identified Albanians, predominantly Muslim (442,914 or 22.9 per cent) (Friedman 1996: 90).

The polarisation between these communities, and their association with different parts of the landscape, was the main subject of my original article in 1994, where I argued that the grounds of legitimate residence claimed by the two groups were made in different registers. Urban Macedonians evoked a myth of origin which stressed rural roots, but had little to do with the countryside: it had also been invested in certain charged symbolic sites and events. Albanian presence, by contrast, appeared in a more quotidian round, in neighbourhoods and private homes, not memorialised in any coordinated way. Since the article's publication in 1994, the battle-lines of legitimacy have been renegotiated. The article stressed what in Perry Anderson's terms could be read as an acute ethnic Macedonian investment in *identity*, as opposed to an infusion of the domestic landscape of Macedonia with Albanian *character* (Anderson 1992). Recent years, however, have seen a more conscious and deliberate set of practices in which sections of the Macedonian-Albanian population have engaged in what Easton (1965) and Tambiah (1989) call 'parapolitics'. This describes the realm of activities apparently conducted with another purpose, but which nonetheless entail

a challenge to the state's legitimacy. In the years since Macedonia's
declaration of sovereignty, numerous such confrontations between the
Albanian minority and agents of the Macedonian state have occurred. At
Bit Pazar in Skopje in 1992, police sought to crack down on cigarette dealing
by Albanian teenagers, and a gun battle confrontation ensued in which four
people were killed in the exchange of fire. In November 1993, a number of
Albanians, including the deputy minister of defence, were arrested on
charges of gun-running, and conspiring to create a paramilitary organisation (Vickers and Pettifer 1997: 176–7). In trying to halt illegal traffic across
the Albanian–Macedonian border, Macedonian security forces have shot
and killed civilians and, on occasion, Albanian military personnel (Roskin
1993–4: 92). Street fights have taken place between Macedonians and
Albanians, which led in at least one case to a fatal stabbing. Bomb explosions
in urban centres during 1998 prompted the arrest by Macedonian police of
Albanian students with suspected links to the Kosova Liberation Army.
Every such incident, although not directly political, has the potential to be
read as such by people in Macedonia. For much of the past five years, their
readings have increasingly coalesced around exclusive positions which are
easily associated with ethnic collectivities, and demonstrate the salience of
a single issue: the future relationship between nation and state in the
Republic of Macedonia.

NAROD, NARODNOST, NACIJA

Within Yugoslavia, groups that might otherwise be considered as ontologically equivalent 'ethno-nations' were categorised and hierarchised.
Macedonians, as a Slavic-speaking group who constituted the majority in
one of the republics, were classified as a *narod*, or people, one of the
constituent peoples of the federal republic. Albanians, although more
numerous than either Macedonians, Montenegrins or Slovenians within
Yugoslavia as a whole, were divided between republics. Because they were
perceived as having a 'kin-state' outside Yugoslavia, they were classed as a
narodnost, or nationality. Within Yugoslavia, then, Macedonians were
arguably more 'at home' in the Republic of Macedonia than Albanians.
Although all were Yugoslav citizens, differential status seemed to suggest
different stakes in the survival of the country.[3]

  In post-Yugoslav Macedonia, the category of *narod* has endured, while
that of *narodnost* is now considered a part of the Yugoslav past. Opinions
differ, though, as to how those citizens who identify themselves as Albanians
should be designated. For some, no designation should ever have been
sought. They argued that all Macedonian citizens – whether ethnically
Macedonian, Albanian, Turkish, Serb, Rom, Vlach, or Egyptian – should
enjoy equal status.[4] Many ethnic Macedonians, however, translated the old
term *narodnost* straightforwardly into *malcinctvo*, or minority, thereby appro-

priating a term from standard Western ethno-national discourse, which allowed them to preserve a conceptual scheme which in turn drew an invidious distinction. For while within Yugoslavia all citizens were notionally equal in the eyes of the federal state, the new-found authority of formerly republican governments provoked nervousness among those citizens who now found that their ethnic affiliation – whether to a *narod* or *narodnost* – did not match that of the republic in which they now lived. This was, of course, the problematic by which Serbs in Croatia and Bosnia justified their opposition to the secession of those republics. In an interview after the Bit Pazar incident in November 1992, a Macedonian Albanian evoked that precedent to a British journalist, saying that international recognition of the new Republic of Macedonia would be seen as a provocation to his people and that: 'We'll put up barricades just like the Serbs did in Croatia; we're fed up with being cheated' (Chazan 1992: 12 col. 4). Such responses complicate the notion that the standoff between Greece and Macedonia was the only reason for the delay of international recognition.

Among Albanians, too, some have persistently called for a move beyond the politics of group affiliation, and the creation of a state closer to the 'civic' ideal so beloved of theorists. Increasingly dominant, though, are the voices of those Albanian political parties within Macedonia which have agitated for greater recognition of the Albanian community as a political subject in its own right. Their end goals vary, some advocating a federal-type solution with greater autonomy for areas with a local Albanian majority, while others call for a 'two-nation' state, with equal recognition and support for Albanian and Macedonian languages, without ties between the state and one religion. There has also been a more radical discussion of partition, and the possible future creation of a greater Albania.

Political tactics too have differed: Albanian voters boycotted the referendum on Macedonian autonomy in 1991, and party leaders have at different times operated in coalition with and opposition to Macedonian-led governments. What these political parties share, though, is a commitment to equalising the status of the Albanian and Macedonian communities within Macedonia. Their goal is to impress upon their community, the Macedonian state and the international community that Albanians in Macedonia constitute a *narod* and, as such, should have a significant collective voice in determining the shape of the state in which they live.

THE NEW ZONES OF ENGAGEMENT

A key arena of action in pursuit of this goal has been western Macedonia and, specifically, two townships where Albanians are in a local majority: Tetovo and Gostivar. The former has been described as a 'regional capital for the Albanians' (Vickers and Pettifer 1997: 171), while in the latter – which has a 65 per cent Albanian population – the more radical of the Albanian political parties came to power in local elections in December 1996 (Abrahams 1998: 7). The two cities were the sites in 1995 and 1997 respectively of major incidents which demonstrated both Albanian will to obtain the recognition of cultural rights and Macedonian governmental determination to oppose what are seen as illegal and nationally destabilising initiatives. Ostensibly at stake were rights to higher education and issues of local autonomy; both incidents were fraught with wider significance, whose theoretical import will be discussed.

A key concern in Albanian political activism within Macedonia has been the place of the Albanian language in the state. In particular, Albanian politicians have consistently campaigned to give Albanian a more prominent place as a language of instruction in the educational system, arguing in particular that the unavailability of higher education through the medium of Albanian discriminates against the Albanian-speaking population.[5] Although the Macedonian government made some concessions during 1994 and 1995, activists on the Albanian side of the debate took more direct action and in February 1995 an Albanian language university was opened in Mala Rechica, in the Tetovo area. Present at the celebrations were members of the Albanian international diaspora, as well as large numbers of local residents. When Macedonian police moved in to close down what was declared an illegal educational establishment, violence broke out, in the course of which one man was killed and around 20 people were injured. Albanian politicians intervened to calm the situation, but tensions were rekindled when prominent local leaders, arrested for their part in the demonstrations, were sentenced.

This incident generated a diverse array of analyses. The Macedonian government emphasised the university's illegality, while Albanian politicians emphasised police violence. But the debate quickly moved beyond a stark account of oppressive state intervention in cultural matters and an attempt to prevent an illegal institution from operating to highlight the role of outside actors. Serbian slogans were found on walls close to the scene, and this fuelled theories of Serbian involvement. The president of the municipality accused the police of being pro-Serb (Shea 1997: 266), while Macedonian sources asserted that the university rector, Fadil Suleimani, was a KOS (Serb Secret service) agent. Opposition politicians, from the party then considered as Macedonian nationalists, the Internal Macedonian Revolutionary Organisation/Democratic Party of Macedonian National Unity (*VMRO-DPMNE*), suggested the whole affair was orchestrated by the state and signalled Gligorov's long-term plan to re-annex Macedonia to Serbia (Shea 1997: 269). Serbian sources within Macedonia instead saw the university's attempted foundation as an extension of Kosovar-led militancy to western Macedonia.[6]

At first glance, this polyphony is bewildering, and threatens to paralyse analysis. The accusations of Serb involvement on both sides, though, represent a shared vision that Serb influence operates only through state structures inherited from the Yugoslav period and threatens to destabilise Macedonia. What further links the various interpretations is an overall conviction that events at Tetovo were the pursuit of politics by other means. The ability to determine the medium in which disputes are negotiated and politics conducted is, for a nation-state, a key test of its authority. By contesting that medium, local political actors assault not just a particular regime, but the legitimacy of an order. Conversely, as documented by theorists of nationalism, state-builders frequently strive to promote a standardised language with the precise goal of generating underlying unity, even among factions that might disagree on policy. Macedonians frequently complain that Albanians make no effort, or refuse to learn or speak Macedonian, the language of the state. The radical Albanian response, that there is no fundamental reason why Macedonian should be the language of state, challenges a sacred tenet of nationalism – the existence of a single dominant medium of communication. The additional fact that in townships in western Macedonia it is perfectly practicable for a Macedonian citizen to live without ever needing to use Macedonian is testimony to the long-standing social divisions between the two communities. Parallels can be made between western Macedonia and Kosovo, as regions whose indigenous minority is denied access to state resources and where as a consequence parallel institutions have been developed. In Kosovo, it is clear that this outcome was primarily caused by Yugoslav and then Serbian behaviour. In western Macedonia, though, in addition to social exclusion, one can detect a process of determined and wilful withdrawal from the public realm, with the aim of destabilising the republic.

A more dramatic symbolic showdown was the confrontation between Albanian demonstrators and Macedonian police in Gostivar on 9 and 10 July 1997. *Human Rights Watch* devoted an issue to the police violence in which three people were killed and at least 200 injured. The trigger on this occasion was the display of flags outside the town hall. After the new mayor, Rufi Osmani, came to power in December 1996, signs were posted in Albanian and Turkish, and both national flags flown.[7] Following the flags' forcible removal by 'some individuals' (Abrahams quoting Mayor Osmani, 1998: 7), 20,000 Albanians mounted a demonstration and, on 27 May, the flags were rehoisted and guards posted by the local government. This was in apparent defiance of a Macedonian constitutional court ruling, that declared the flying of foreign flags a violation of sovereignty. Late on 8 July, the national parliament passed a new law on foreign flags, which decreed they could be flown on private property at any time and on state holidays in front of town halls. In the early morning of 9 July, police arrested Osmani; when demonstrators gathered to protest, force was unleashed. In the aftermath of the violence, again, interpretations differed. Representatives of the government condemned Albanian political activism and saw the police reaction as justified. Kiro Gligorov, for example, while expressing condolences for those who lost their lives, said that a state could (and should) protect its national symbols (Abrahams 1998: 14). According to Perry, Albanians argue that the flag is not primarily a marker of the Albanian State, but a possession of the Albanian nation (Perry 1998: 123), thus positioning it as a cultural artifact rather than a political one. Osmani defended the display of the flag under an article in the constitution which grants members of nationalities 'the right freely to express, foster and develop their identity and national attributes' (Abrahams 1998: 7). When he was sentenced to almost 14 years in prison, on the charge of 'inciting national, racial and religious hatred', the opposition party *VMRO-DPMNE* condemned the verdict, arguing that it betrayed a double-standard – Macedonian students demonstrating earlier in the same year had used far more inflammatory language, but had never been prosecuted.

More so even than events at Tetovo, where language was the issue, the crisis provoked by the display of a red rectangle of cloth outside a building in Gostivar can be read as an indication of a broadening of the 'zone of engagement' (Anderson 1992) between ethnically differentiable populations in Macedonia. Those sympathetic to the radicalised Albanian position recall the discriminatory practices of the formerly Yugoslav Macedonian state, and see the recent confrontations as evidence that the state remains fundamentally unreconstructed. Some commentators go so far as to suggest that an 'apartheid' mentality persists, evoking as evidence the apparent and unthinking racism towards Albanians expressed by Macedonians in everyday settings. Police responses in Tetovo and Gostivar represent for such commentators further examples of state-sponsored terrorism, perpetrated with the support of a racist majority against a minority seeking only to exercise its cultural rights. The presence of large numbers of demonstrators at Gostivar, as at Tetovo, is viewed as a product of aggregative, individual decisions on the part of citizens to express their solidarity in the face of oppression. Hoisting a flag is in this view an extension of more mundane practices, not substantively different from preferring a particular house style, speaking a particular language or favouring a certain kind of dress. The primary reference of the double-headed eagle flag is a culture-hero of the fourteenth century, Skanderbeg, whose ownership by Albanians is not in dispute. Pride in this heritage is understandable and a commitment to making it public a sign of shared purpose, authorised in the constitution.

An alternative view would label such a position, which relies on a notion of national character, as naïve at best. Macedonian commentators in particular, while acknowledging Albanian cultural distinctiveness, deplore what they see as a political offensive directed against the Macedonian state. From this point of view, the demonstrations at Tetovo and Gostivar are not spontaneous expressions of national character; rather, they are choreographed displays in the realm of identity politics. In the context of the republic's own difficult path towards recognition and ongoing economic and political fragility, they represent additionally an existential threat to the Macedonian nation, whose members are primary stakeholders in the republic's future. Rather than perceiving the demonstrations as the work of a victimised domestic minority, Macedonian interpreters are more prone to see them as the product of transnational agitation. They note the links between political leadership in the Albanian community in Macedonia and in Kosovo, as well as the evidence that Macedonian Albanians have access to resources overseas through long-established labour migration networks. By attributing agency and malign intent to shadowy, criminal organisations imagined along the lines of the Kosova Liberation Army, Macedonians see in incidents like those in Tetovo and Gostivar parts of an initiative to build a greater Albania. They find evidence for such plans in other parapolitical fields, such as the publication by the Albanian Academy of Sciences of a 'Platform on the Resolution of the Albanian National Question', which appeared in 1998.[8]

ELECTORAL DEVELOPMENTS

In the period 1994–8, then, tensions rose between Macedonians and Albanians within Macedonia, which drew international attention at symbolic sites like Tetovo and Gostivar. For much of this period, nationalist parties within each community were held to be responsible for the ethnic polarisation of society as a whole. After elections in 1994, the social democratic alliance, or Social Democratic Alliance of Macedonia (*SDSM*), formed the government, in coalition with the most popular party among Albanian voters, the Party of Democratic Prosperity (PDP). But PDP leaders were accused from within their party of not doing enough to advance the interests of Albanians within Macedonia, and a radical faction emerged which was to become the nucleus of a new party, the Democratic Party of Albanians (DPA), under the newly dominant politician Arben Xhaferi.[9] Conversely, SDSM came under constant fire from their main rivals for Macedonian votes, *VMRO-DPMNE*, for making concessions which hurt the national interest. *VMRO-DPMNE* was, for example, opposed to the 1995 accord with Greece (Burg 1996: 64). During the run-up to the 1994 presidential elections, the *VMRO-DPMNE* candidate, Ljubisha Georgievski, famously said with regard to Albanian influence within the state: 'We will let the eagle fly, but we will cut off its talons first' (Schwartz 1996: 90).

The memory of such rhetorics obscured the fact that from the party's relaunch at a meeting in Kichevo in May 1995, and even before, *VMRO-DPMNE* had become far more pragmatic. After boycotting the second round of elections in 1994, it operated outside parliament, largely through local politics and a campaign of media responses to government initiatives. The party also operated in coalition with Albanian political parties in Tetovo from mid-1995. Increasingly the party presented itself as a centre-right party, and stressed its opposition to the government not for its ethnic policies, but for its corruption and close ties to Milosevic's Serbia. Although it can be argued that 'Yugonostalgia' has been a powerful sentiment among certain generations in post-independence Macedonia (Brown 1998; Thiessen 1999), one can also trace in Macedonia the view that some positions of power and influence in Yugoslavia were gained by illegitimate means, and were used for personal advantage by their holders. In the difficult economic conditions of Macedonia in the mid-1990s, when public companies found their way into the hands of a new business elite recruited, it seemed, from among party cronies, *VMRO-DPMNE*'s message found support in new and broader Macedonian circles. The shift in Albanian support from PDP to DPA can be seen in similar terms: not necessarily as towards ethnic extremism, rather, as against corruption and rule by elites perceived as old communists. On the Albanian side too, there was recognition of the change in the political landscape. In May 1995 a minister speaking Albanian in parliament had accused leading (SDSM) Macedonian politicians of being pro-Serbian and anti-Albanian and suggested therefore that Albanian parties should join forces with *VMRO-DPMNE*, as the only Macedonian national party (Shea 1997: 273, 276).

Recognition of the grounds for a shared agenda between Macedonian citizens from different communities helps make sense of the otherwise surprising turn of events in Macedonian politics since 1998. After outperforming their respective rivals in the elections of 1998, *VMRO-DPMNE* and DPA announced that they would form a coalition government. *VMRO-DPMNE* had made a pre-election agreement with a smaller new centre-party, the Democratic Alternative, under the leadership of Vasil Turpurkovski.

The post-election pact, between parties that had before the election staked out seemingly irreconcilable positions, was nonetheless a shock to many members of the Macedonian electorate, as well as to international observers. One result has been a vertiginous reorientation in nationalist rhetorics on the Macedonian side. Once *VMRO-DPMNE* claimed that the *SDSM* coalition was in thrall to its Albanian allies: that accusation has now been turned on its head. Graffiti in Skopje in the summer of 1999 dubbed Ljubco Georgievski, *VMRO-DPMNE* leader and prime minister, a *schiptarski zet* – an Albanian son-in-law – suggesting he had married into and thereby thrown in his lot with the Albanian community. Arben Xhaferi's undoubted personal charisma, and his ability to mobilise near-unanimous Albanian support, further reinforces the view that he, and not Georgievski, holds the strings of power.

The interethnic cooperation between political parties in Macedonia's government has been taken as a positive sign for the country's future. It was certainly remarkable, given the variety of pressures on the country and its population, that Macedonia was able to weather the influx of over a quarter of a million Kosovar Albanian refugees in the spring and summer of 1999. There are various signs that a new spirit of accommodation is at work in the activities of sections of the media (Borden and Mehmeti 1998) and NGOs (Fraenkel 1996; Petroska-Beshka 1996) to open channels of communication between different groups. A recently produced television series for children, *Nashe maalo* (*Our neighbourhood*), supported by Search For Common Ground, has been greeted as an exemplary project which can teach tolerance and mutual respect.

All such projects, though, are predicated on a model of ideal and existential equality which, for many ethnic Macedonians at least, represents in itself a theoretically difficult step. As I sought to lay out in 1994 and to recapitulate above, the pragmatics of the current situation dispose many ethnic Macedonians to see their security as vested in a state that their language often represents as exclusively 'theirs'. Fears regarding Albanian influence in the republic are mostly expressed in the future tense and coalesce around two claims. Some people point to the differential demographic structure of the two communities and say that in time the Albanian population will outnumber the Macedonian. Without constitutional privilege for the Macedonian language, flag and other symbolic artifacts of identity, they say, and operating from a view which sees majority rule as inevitable, the state will simply take on Albanian character. Others see the danger in more immediate terms, describing the current Albanian population of Macedonia as invested in creating a greater Albania and loyal to that virtual entity rather than to their state of citizenship. Both views recognise the dynamics of political process and bespeak a suspicion of arguments couched in terms of universal, moral principles that the Macedonian state should embrace.

These concerns resonate with the history that most Macedonians have learned either in school or from older family members, of a people who have repeatedly been incorporated into the state projects of powerful and more numerous others. Yet they are also a specific product of the Macedonian experience of Yugoslavia, wherein the Macedonian *narod* did enjoy a privileged position within the republic at the expense of other groups. The combination of circumstances makes the Macedonian population of the Republic of Macedonia potential victims of what Milica Bookman (1994) describes as 'the sense that well-being is a zero-sum game in which one group gains at the expense of another' which, she adds, increases in economically hard times (1994: 86). She terms this phenomenon 'nationalist bankruptcy': its effects, one might argue, were most recently visible in the near-victory of the *SDSM* presidential candidate in the 1999 elections on a platform which sought to mobilise anti-Albanian resentment among ethnic Macedonian voters.

Albanians in Macedonia, in parallel, have become increasingly politicised and declare an investment in the state of which they are citizens. This was demonstrated most vividly by the large turnout among Albanian voters in the final round of the presidential elections to vote for the *VMRO-DPMNE* candidate and against *SDSM*. It appears to represent striking progress from their boycott of the referendum on Macedonian sovereignty in 1991. Albanian politicians represent voters who continue to consider themselves the targets of discrimination and victims of social exclusion, especially in the fields of educational opportunities and state employment. Their energies now, though, are concentrated on acquiring greater representation and access to resources through electoral means. They operate as stakeholders in the state's survival and can therefore be argued to seek, albeit implicitly, to challenge the ethnically exclusive meaning of being Macedonian.[10]

The interplay of different orders of symbolic economics in Macedonia over the past decade demonstrates the complex workings of the politics of nationalism in a single-state setting, where communities coexist, yet have limited interaction. The problem of relations with Greece, which once loomed so large, has since 1995 been sidelined by the more enduring issue of relations between Macedonians and Albanians, a problem with domestic and international dimensions. Analysis of the 'flash-points' of the issue – the clashes in Tetovo and Gostivar – reveal the extent to which the lines that separate politics and culture are blurred. What is an educational issue is simultaneously political, and cultural markers cannot easily be stripped of state-level significance. Part of the constant balancing act that leaders must negotiate in such a setting is when to assert political agency, and to whom, and when to present a choice as untainted by political considerations. Those who emerge in such a setting are not only astute politicians, but also deft parapoliticians. To succeed, they have mastered the art of translating between the rhetorics of character and identity to trade in the currencies of culture and politics.

ACKNOWLEDGEMENTS

I would like to thank a number of people whose positive reactions to earlier work on this theme provided encouragement. These include Michael Herzfeld, Yannis Hamilakis, Michael Dietler and Rozita Dimova. I would also like to thank Jane Cowan and Sarah Green for specific comments. This chapter was written while the author was a senior fellow at the United States Institute of Peace, and I would like to thank Rebecca Kilhefner for research assistance. The illustration on page 123 first appeared in Brown, 1994. I am grateful to the editors of *Antiquity* for their permission to reproduce it here.

NOTES

1. For an account of the set-up of the Badinter Commission, see Weller (1992).
2. Because the remainder of this paper deals primarily with the FY Republic of Macedonia, and there is thus little risk of confusion, I henceforward refer to the republic simply as Macedonia. Within the republic, there are no more than a few people, mostly elderly, who would identify themselves as Greeks. There is, of course, a much larger population that have family links to northern Greece, many of whom harbour memories of displacement and loss after the Greek Civil War. These people, sometimes referred to as *Egejci* or as coming from 'the Aegean part of Macedonia', represent a diverse group, among whom are many who passionately resist any

imputation that they are Greek, and instead insist upon the Macedonian character of their villages of origin.

The adjectival form 'Macedonian' presents greater possible confusion. It has both, in Gellner's terms (1983), a political meaning connected to the republic, and a cultural meaning referring to a particular language and sense of identity deriving from the 'assumed givens' (Geertz 1973: 259) of language, religion, kin connection and social practice. Rather than freight this chapter with a host of potentially maddening qualifiers, I rely in most cases on readers' goodwill and sensitivity to context.

3. A description of the significance of these categories in Bosnia is given by Bringa (1995). The other numerically significant former *narodnost* in Macedonia is the Turkish community, which continues to have a complicated relationship with the larger Albanian community, as it did in the Yugoslav period (Poulton 1991: 91–3). The Serbian community in Macedonia, formerly classified as a *narod*, constitutes a second type of new minority, with close ties to a newly separate neighbouring state whose majority population are perceived by many ethnic Macedonians as being close relatives in the Slavic community of nations. A third classification, *etnichka grupa* or ethnic group, was assigned to those groups that did not have a recognised 'kin-state' elsewhere: in Macedonia, Roma and Vlachs occupied this category.

4. For a description of the Egyptian community, see Duijzings (1999).

5. A minority rights group report stated that in 1992, of 22,994 registered students in higher education in Macedonia, only 386 were Albanian (Vickers and Pettifer 1997: 174). For different accounts of the events in Mala Rechica, see Schwartz (1996: 89–97) and Shea (1997: 259–72). A good account of the division of interpretation is given in Burg (1996: 66–70).

6. 2000 students at the university in Skopje demonstrated under the slogan 'Let the damned *schiptars* [a derogatory term for Albanians] know the Macedonian name will never die' (Shea, 1997: 270). The Skopje student council and national government distanced themselves from this stark and adversarial understanding of the situation.

7. The dynamics of relationships between Turkish and Albanian minorities in Macedonia continue to be complex and to vary by city. Gostivar and Tetovo are in some sense rival cities: old residents of both agree only that Albanians in Gostivar have been Turkified and Turks in Tetovo Albanified (Burcu Akan, personal communication). For an excellent and nuanced discussion, see Akan (2000).

8. I learned about this document in a visit to Skopje in June 1999. The Macedonian Academy of Sciences had just published its response, dated April 1999.

9. The naming of this party remained in dispute even after the elections of 1998, as it has not received formal recognition. Its formation is described briefly by Ackermann (2000: 60), who provides a good account of political developments in the republic, focusing on efforts to prevent conflict in Macedonia. Her book became available only as this paper was going to press: since it was written, a new faction has occurred within *VMRO-DPMNE*, yielding a fledgling party that claims the same acronym but a different name, the 'True Macedonian Reform Option'. Similar cases of schism and regeneration may already have occurred by the time this volume reaches publication.

10. It is, perhaps, the correlation between this implicit project and the ideological preferences of the international community that drives the high profile enjoyed outside the country by moderate Albanian political leaders, who are perceived as holding the key to a secure state organised on 'civic' rather than 'ethnic' lines.

BIBLIOGRAPHY

Abrahams, Fred. 1998. 'Police Violence in Macedonia: Official thumbs up'. *Human Rights Watch Report* 10(1).

Ackermann, Alice. 2000. *Making Peace Prevail: Preventing violent conflict in Macedonia.* Syracuse, New York: Syracuse University Press.

Agelopoulos, Georgios. n.d. 'Three years of living in the margins: Between auto-ethnography and fieldwork in Florina'. Paper presented as part of the symposium, *Negotiating Boundaries: The Past in the Present in South-Eastern Europe.* Lampeter, Wales, September 1998.

Akan, Burcu. 2000. 'Shadow Genealogies: Memory and identity in the lives of Turkish-speakers in Macedonia'. Ph.D. dissertation: School of International Service, American University.

Anderson, Perry. 1992. 'Fernand Braudel and National Identity', in *A Zone of Engagement.* London: Verso.

Anderson, Perry. 1992. *A Zone of Engagement.* London: Verso.

Bookman, Milica. 1994. *Economic Decline and Nationalism in the Balkans.* London: Macmillan.

Borden, Anthony and Ibrahim Mehmeti (eds). 1998. *Reporting Macedonia: The new accommodation.* London: Institute for War and Peace Reporting.

Bringa, Tone. 1995. *Being Muslim the Bosnian Way: Identity and community in a Central Bosnian village.* Princeton NJ: Princeton University Press.

Brown, K.S. 1994. 'Seeing Stars: Character and identity in the landscapes of modern Macedonia'. *Antiquity* 68,784–96.

Brown, K.S. 1998. 'Macedonian culture and its audiences: An analysis of *Before the Rain*', in F. Hughes-Freeland (ed.) *Ritual, Performance, Media.* London & New York: Routledge.

Burg, Steven. 1996. 'The Field Mission', in B.R. Rubin (ed.) *Toward Comprehensive Peace in Southeast Europe: Conflict prevention in the South Balkans.* New York: Twentieth Century Fund. pp. 47–80.

Chazan, Y. 1992. 'Minority threatens Macedonia split'. The *Guardian*, Tuesday, 17 November, p. 12.

Danforth, Loring M. 1993. 'Claims to Macedonian Identity: The Macedonian question and the breakup of Yugoslavia'. *Anthropology Today* 9(4), 3–10.

Danforth. Loring M. 1995. *The Macedonian Conflict: Ethnic nationalism in a transnational world.* Princeton NJ: Princeton University Press.

Duijzings, Gerhardt 1999. 'The making of Egyptians: The politics of identity among Gypsies', in *Religion and the Politics of Identity in Kosovo.* London: Hurst.

Easton, David. 1965. *A Framework for Political Analysis.* Prentice-Hall: Englewood Cliffs N.J.

Fraenkel, Eran. 1996. 'International NGOs in Preventive Diplomacy and Early Warning: Macedonia', in Robert I. Rotberg (ed.) *Vigilance and Vengeance: NGOs preventing ethnic conflict in divided societies.* Washington DC: Brookings Institute/World Peace Foundation.

Friedman, Victor. 1996. 'Observing the Observers: Language, ethnicity and power in the 1994 Macedonian census and beyond', in B.R. Rubin (ed.) *Toward Comprehensive Peace in Southeast Europe: Conflict prevention in the South Balkans.* New York: Twentieth Century Fund Press. pp. 81–96.

Geertz, Clifford. 1973 [1963]. 'The Integrative Revolution: Primordial sentiments and civil politics in the new states', in *The Interpretation of Cultures.* New York: Basic Books.

Gellner, Ernest. 1983. *Nations and Nationalism.* (ed.) C. Geertz. Ithaca, New York: Blackwell.

Holbrooke, Richard. 1998. *To End a War.* New York: Random House.

Karakasidou, Anastasia. 1993. 'Politicizing Culture: Negating ethnic identity in Greek Macedonia'. *Journal of Modern Greek Studies* 11(1), 1–28.

—— 1994. 'National Ideologies, Histories and Popular Consciousness: A response to three critics'. *Balkan Studies* 35(1), 113–46.

Perry, Duncan. 1998. 'Destiny on Hold: Macedonia and the Dangers of Ethnic Discord'. *Current History*, March. 119–26.

Petroska-Beshka, Violeta. 1996. 'NGOs, Early Warning, and Preventive Action: Macedonia', in Robert I. Rotberg (ed.) *Vigilance and Vengeance: NGOs preventing ethnic conflict in divided societies.* Washington DC: Brookings Institute/World Peace Foundation.

Poulton, Hugh. 1991. *The Balkans: Minorities and states in conflict.* London: Minority Rights Publications.

Roskin, Michael G. 1993–4. 'Macedonia and Albania: The missing alliance'. *Parameters: US Army War College Quarterly* 23(4), 91–9.

Rotberg, Robert. I. (ed.). 1996. *Vigilance and Vengeance: NGOs preventing ethnic conflict in divided societies.* Washington DC: Brookings Institute/World Peace Foundation.

Schwartz, Jonathan M. 1996. *Pieces of Mosaic: An essay on the making of Makedonija.* Højbjerg: Intervention Press.

Shea, John. 1997. *Macedonia and Greece: The struggle to define a new Balkan nation.* Jefferson NC: McFarland.

Silberman, Neil. 1989. *Between Past and Present: Archaeology, ideology and nationalism in the modern Middle East.* New York: Henry Holt.

Tambiah, Stanley. 1989. 'Ethnic Conflict in the World Today'. *American Ethnologist* 16(2), 335–49.

Thiessen, Ilka. 1999. 'T'ga za Jug – Waiting for Macedonia: The changing world of young female engineers in the Republic of Macedonia'. Ph.D. thesis, London School of Economics.

Vickers, Miranda and James Pettifer. 1997. *Albania: From anarchy to a Balkan identity.* New York: New York University Press.

Weller, Marc. 1992. 'The International Response to the Dissolution of the Socialist Federal Republic of Yugoslavia'. *American Journal of International Law* 86, 569–607.

7   POLITICAL PRACTICES AND MULTI-CULTURALISM: THE CASE OF SALONICA

Georgios Agelopoulos

'Multiculturalism' was a relatively unknown term in Greece until the mid-1980s. During the 1980s the discourse of multiculturalism was gradually introduced in Greece by the use of the term 'multicultural' in fashion magazines, in discussions about interior decoration and in articles examining new trends in music published in magazines and daily journals. In a second stage, 'multiculturalism' appeared in a number of studies conducted by sociologists, teachers and researchers within the education field. It was only in the 1990s that the word came into wider use as an analytical or descriptive term in an attempt to understand the current changes in Greek society.[1]

'Multiculturalism' (in Greek, *polypolitismikotita*) is not a native Greek concept. It has been introduced into Greece by scholars, journalists, NGO activists and policy-makers who are aware of the multicultural societies of North America, Australia and western Europe. Although it is clear that even in these societies 'there are as many multiculturalisms as there are political arenas for collective action' (Werbner 1997: 264), a number of commonly accepted features are related to the various discourses of multiculturalism both as an analytical category and a political project. To start with, multiculturalism is strongly related to the flow of ideas, images, people, finance and commodities embodied in the globalisation process of late modernity. Second, multiculturalism recognises the coexistence of different cultures in the same society (Kahn 1995). Third, societies which embrace multiculturalism as a political project actively encourage, through specific social, cultural and educational policies, the reproduction of the various cultures (Rex 1995).

Multiculturalism acquired a significant importance in public discussions among intellectuals and policy-makers in Salonica in the late 1990s. Various factors contributed to this phenomenon:

- the arrival of a great number of immigrants, mainly from Albania but also from other Balkan and eastern European countries, created new social and educational policy issues

- the undertaking of the 1997 Cultural Capital of Europe (CCE) by Salonica encouraged discussions regarding multiculturalism in the past and the present of the city
- the emergence of a discourse about minorities inside Greece, supported by groups of Greek citizens who describe themselves as culturally or nationally different, contributed to the development of questions regarding the issue of multiculturalism.[2]

This chapter examines the development of the discourse of multiculturalism in Salonica during the last decade and the challenges it raised for Greek society and the Greek state. I will focus my analysis on two main factors that contributed to the development within Salonica of the discourse of multi-culturalism: the 1997 CCE activities and the national policies towards illegal migration. I do not disregard the importance of the minorities discourse in the process of identity politics in Greece and in the Greek diaspora. However, I consider the influence of the minorities discourse to operate at the local level of specific regions (Thrace and some areas of western Greek Macedonia), in parts of the Greek diaspora (in Canada and in Australia) and in the think-tank centres working on foreign policy issues in Athens. In that sense, it is mainly an external factor to the development of the local discourse of mul-ticulturalism in Salonica. Furthermore, I consider its influence to be rather limited compared with the grandiose 1997 CCE activities and the phenomenon of 100,000 immigrants currently living in the city.

Arguments and hypotheses put forward regarding the discourse of mul-ticulturalism in Salonica can, to a certain degree, be generalised for the whole of Greece. Nevertheless, such a task is beyond the limits of the present analysis.[3] It should be noted that this study focuses mainly on the discourse of multiculturalism as perceived and presented by intellectuals, politicians, journalists and policy-makers. The various versions of multiculturalism among intellectuals and policy-makers are interpreted within the framework of a still dominant, and still hegemonic in Greece, value on national homogeneity. Focusing the analysis at this level does not limit our under-standing of the subject. As already explained, the introduction of the discourse of multiculturalism is strongly related to discussions among intel-lectuals and policy-makers.

A central aspect of the 1997 CCE agenda was to expose and celebrate 'the multicultural character of Salonica'. In order to succeed in this endeavour, the 1997 CCE promoted a specific perception of the city's past and present as multicultural. Emphasis was given to the coexistence of the 'different' populations of the city during the Byzantine and the Ottoman periods. It is beyond any doubt that cultural plurality, in its broad definition,[4] has been a dominant characteristic of the population of Salonica throughout the previous centuries. However, I will argue that the coexistence of what some intellectuals today consider as culturally different populations does not, in itself, permit us to posit a multicultural domain in

Salonica's past. Multiculturalism is only a historically recent and quite specific form of organising cultural plurality.

An examination of the process of multiculturalising the city's past also has two important purposes. First, it highlights the essentialism inherent in the dominant version of multiculturalism. Such a version of multiculturalism basically accepts the common-sense view that 'each culture has a unique, fixed essence that can be grasped independently of context or inter-cultural relations and which makes an ethnic group act the way it does' (Modood 1997: 10). I suggest that embracing this understanding of multiculturalism contains the danger of an institutionalisation of cultures in the public spheres, a freezing of cultural differences and a reifying of cultural 'communities' (Caglar 1997: 179). Second, an examination of the multiculturalising of Salonica's past contributes to an understanding of the various ways the pre-existing forms of political, social and cultural pluralities, such as the Byzantine and Ottoman eras in this case, shape particular representations of present-day multiculturalisms (Samad 1997: 241).

The case of illegal and legal immigrants who settled *en masse* in the city, as in the rest of Greece, during the last decade, is investigated in order to emphasise that the form cultural pluralism takes is connected to issues of political order (Grillo 1998). The mere fact that 100,000 immigrants settled in the city during the last decade does not in itself make Salonica 'multicultural', contrary to what is often claimed by the media. Nevertheless, I will argue that the presence of immigrants raises political questions regarding the basis on which the Greek society and the Greek state are constituted.

CULTURAL PLURALISM IN SALONICA'S PAST

The Byzantine and the Ottoman administrations in the Balkans stimulated various people and cultures that were previously separated and produced an amalgamation of populations out of which new social groups emerged. The present population of Salonica is mainly the result of population movements and population exchanges that occurred in the context of the Ottoman Empire, during and soon after its dissolution. In the Ottoman state the administration of non-Muslim populations was organised according to the *Millet* system. Non-Muslims were divided into religious communities comprising Orthodox Christians, Armenian Christians, Jews and, after 1849, Orthodox Christian followers of the Bulgarian Exarchate. Each *Millet* had its own organisation under its religious leaders and bodies. The *Millet* was defined by religious affiliation, but its autonomous administration was concerned with secular matters, such as the allocation and collection of taxes, education, and intracommunal legal matters such as marriage, divorce and inheritance (Petrovich 1980: 385). Until 1849, all the Orthodox Christians inside the Ottoman Empire, irrespective of cultural background, constituted the Orthodox *Millet*.

In the context of the *Millet* system, as in other pre-modern states, culture rarely assumed any political significance at all (Gellner 1983: 75). Grillo calls such societies patrimonial and points out that although 'cultural and ethnic difference was not absent from these societies, it was never crucial to their operation' (Grillo 1998: 3). In the context of the Ottoman state, religion was the main determinant of identity (Kitromilides 1990: 25; Kofos 1990: 104). Religion may be considered as a cultural idiom itself but obviously it was not the only one available.[5] The Ottoman *Millet* system, which Kymlicka calls 'the most developed model of non-liberal religious tolerance' (1995: 158), produced in Salonica some very interesting, extreme and (with respect to our modern standards) peculiar phenomena. The amalgamation of linguistic, socioeconomic, kinship, political and religious domains led to unique forms of syncretism. The existence of Greek-speaking Muslims and the existence of a Ladino-speaking (Judeo-Spanish) Muslim community (former Jews who converted to Islam in 1666, the *Donmedes*) are among the most striking cases. We should also note the existence of populations which cut across the *Millet* divisions, such as the Muslim Gypsies and the Orthodox Christian Gypsies.

It is obvious that in this context any classification of the city's populations according to a single cultural criterion, as in the case of modern multicultural societies, is an arbitrary one. Defining Ottoman Salonica as a multicultural society implies projecting our own modern standards onto a society that was organised on a different basis. The multiculturalisation of Salonica's past fails to take into account the various forms that cultural plurality took in history.

The situation in Ottoman Salonica changed under the influence of the various nationalist movements in the early nineteenth century. Modern nationalism requires the existence of exclusive and unique identities (Gellner 1983). The Greek nation, as other eastern European nations, mainly developed on the basis of what Anthony D. Smith calls 'ethnic nationalisms' (1986). In this model of national ideology, cultures are nationalised and culture becomes a criterion of national identification and mobilisation. However, models of cultural nationalism failed in their attempt to divide the population of Salonica and Macedonia in general into well-defined nations according to their criteria. This became evident when politicians, policy-makers and state officials attempted to use sociocultural, linguistic and historical criteria in order to divide the population into distinctive national groups. They failed to understand that at the local level, the decision to embrace a nationality during the late nineteenth/early twentieth century was a political choice very often irrelevant to the sociocultural identity and linguistic practices of those who took this decision.[6] The inability of policy-makers and state officials to comprehend the national identification process led to the problematic practice of imposing cultural nationalisms over local populations. As a result, they forced the silence and the assimilation of those local identities that could not comply with the national homogenising process (Agelopoulos, 1997a; Cowan, 1997; Karakasidou, 1997).

CULTURAL PLURALISM IN THE 1990s

The end of the Balkan Wars and the First World War established the present-day northern frontiers of Greece. As a part of the Greek state territory, Greek Macedonia experienced all the significant social, demographic and political changes that took place in the region. Until 1922, when the compulsory exchange of populations between Greece and Turkey took place, the society of Salonica was composed of a variety of populations: Jews, local Greeks (including Vlachs), Turks, small numbers of other Muslim populations, Bulgarians and Gypsies. Macedonian-speaking populations were not settled in the city, since they lived exclusively in rural areas.[7] The departure of the Muslim (mainly Turkish) population in 1922 was followed by the arrival of almost 200,000 Greek Orthodox Christian refugees of various cultural and linguistic backgrounds[8] from Turkey. As a result of all these population movements, Salonica ended up having a variety of people living inside the city or in the nearby villages. The Jewish community of Salonica, which comprised at least one-third of the city's total population before 1922, was deported to concentration camps during the Second World War. Only a small number of Jews returned to the city in the late 1940s. Parts of the small Bulgarian community of the city were assimilated into the wider population and some left for Bulgaria.

These movements did not influence the ideological basis of the Greek state. The Greek state remains a national state following the ethnic model of nation-states established in the nineteenth century. The range of strategies adopted by some state institutions towards any kind of 'difference' remained the same, although their intensity varied according to international and domestic political developments. They included assimilation, incorporation, the imposition of silence, yet also a narrow recognition of 'difference' in response to obligations imposed by international treaties (as in the case of the Muslims in Thrace). It is widely accepted that the large majority of the population of Greek Macedonia has been assimilated into the Greek national ideology (Cowan 1997; Danforth 1995).

The above-mentioned policies aimed at homogenising diverse local populations within the Greek state. However, since the mid-1980s Greek society has experienced a new situation: the sudden arrival of a great number of immigrants as well as political and economic refugees. The first immigrant communities were established in Athens during the early 1980s from workers coming from Egypt, Pakistan and some Asian countries (Iosifides 1997). Their numbers were limited and the first significant migration movement was the 'repatriation' of Pontic Greeks from Russia, Georgia, Kazakstan, Armenia and other former USSR Republics (Voutira 1991).[9]

Most of them settled in Athens and Salonica. The post-1989 political changes in eastern Europe escalated the migration process and within a few years about 700,000 immigrants had settled in Greece.[10]

Enormous differences exist between illegal and legal immigrants. Until 1997 the only legal immigrants were the Pontic Greeks from the former USSR. They have been acknowledged as Greek nationals; consequently, they have been able to follow a repatriation process, in which they receive a certain degree of state support and are given Greek citizenship. Thus Pontic Greeks are usually legally employed and receive salaries equivalent to those of local Greeks. On the other hand, most illegal immigrants work in dirty manual jobs and are poorly paid (King, Iosifides and Myrivili 1998: 169–70). According to Lianos, the wage of an illegal migrant worker is 60 per cent of that of a native worker (1998: 541). This situation has created a number of social and educational policy problems. Until recently, illegal immigrants were not able to register their children in schools and were not eligible for any kind of social protection provided by state institutions. It became obvious that to prevent serious social problems a new legal context was necessary (Karydis 1996; Sitaropoulos 1992). Two ministerial decrees were issued in 1997 and 1998 (359/1997 and 358/1998) and a new migration law has been announced as under preparation for discussion in parliament (February 2000).

The two ministerial decrees established specific registration procedures for all those immigrants living in Greece but, as a result of this process, new problems have arisen. The registration mechanisms proved to be rather slow and bureaucratic. According to the latest available data of the Greek Organisation for the Employment of Human Resources (*OAED*) reported in June 1999, about 370,000 immigrants applied for a Green Card (legalisation certificate) and 225,691 of them submitted all the necessary documents. By the end of June 1999 about 40,000 applications were reviewed by the Greek state authorities. Out of the 40,000 reviewed applications a total number of 35,000 Green Cards were issued.

Many immigrants were not able to register because they had been convicted for crimes in Greece.[11] In addition, the registration process does not guarantee legalisation for those who have been registered. This is due to the various preconditions required for the completion of the legalisation process. Immigrants are required to have 40 days' worth of social security stamps[12] in order to complete the legalisation process. Since most employers prefer to have immigrants as a workforce precisely in order to avoid the registration process – and thus payment of taxes and social security contributions – immigrants face a dilemma. In order to acquire a permanent legal working permit they need to be legally employed but most employers do not offer them jobs on that basis. This is what King, Iosifides and Myrivili call 'the complex relationship between their illegal status, their exploitation on the labour market and their social and spatial marginalisation' (King, Iosifides and Myrivili 1998: 171). In addition, the ministerial decrees have not taken into account the fact that immigration is still continuing. In other words, the deadlines for submitting the documents necessary for legalisation have expired; immigrants who currently enter the country are thus, by definition, considered illegal. In early February 2000, the Secretary of the Ministry of Internal Affairs announced that the new immigration law will provide a permanent, continuous operating framework for the legalisation of immigrants. Since the new law, at the time of writing, had not yet been discussed in parliament, it is not possible to predict future developments.

Meanwhile, the institutional context established to regulate the life and work of immigrants who arrived in Greece in the 1990s failed to build up an infrastructure sensitive to immigrants' social and linguistic needs. This fact became evident in the everyday life of immigrants: they have found that bureaucratic papers and documents used in hospitals, schools, police stations, municipal authorities and employment offices are rarely translated into languages other than Greek. They have found very few reception classrooms in schools that offer courses in the native languages of the immigrant children. They have encountered an absence of political represent- ation of immigrant communities, the non-existence of Greek language courses for immigrants[13] and of specialised interpreters in courts. However, the main problem has been the legalisation process itself, since it creates an illegal status for the large number of immigrants who cannot comply with its bureaucratic procedures.

One can understand why a number of immigrant community represent- atives argue that the two ministerial decrees created more problems than they solved. The immigrants' problems, as well as the problems of Greek society, obviously arise from the political management of immigration (the legalisation context) and not from the 'cultural difference' of immigrants as such. Immigrants themselves are well aware of this situation. This is evident in the fact that, as the legalisation process has continued, some immigrant communities have become divided. Legal immigrants have established their own close and well-organised communities and have differentiated themselves from the rest who failed to receive the Green Card.

Immigrant communities continue to grow. In the case of Salonica, the vast majority of the immigrants come from Albania (King, Iosifides and Myrivili 1998). This is due to the geographical proximity of Greek Macedonia and Albania. The rest of the recently settled immigrant population of the city is mainly composed of Pontic Greeks from the former USSR. Lianos estimates that about 8 per cent of Salonica's population was composed of illegal and legal immigrants in 1993 (1998: 538). The dramatic rise in migration from Albania after the 1997 political violence has certainly increased this number. Given that the population of the wider area of Salonica is about 1 million people,[14] it seems likely that about 100,000 immigrants currently live in the city and in the nearby villages.

The presence of immigrants is more obvious in specific areas of the city. A number of immigrants from the former USSR have rented houses in the old centre of the city. Albanian workers and their families live in some of the working-class neighbourhoods to the east of the city suburbs, but they socialise in the streets and coffee houses around the main railway station. In 1998 the first exclusively Albanian coffee house opened up at Anageniseos Street close to the main railway station. Over the past decade, though, a number of racist reactions to the immigrants began to appear. These reactions most often took the form of what is today called in Greece *Albanophobia*, that is, collectively accusing the immigrants for the increase of criminality in the country.[15] Such attitudes contributed to the appearance of police round-up operations (called *skoupa*, 'sweeps'), where special police units take into detention all immigrants walking in the streets in order to check their documents. Most racist reactions are encouraged by a few populist politicians, mainly active at the local authorities level, and by extreme right-wing groups.

Given this situation, the introduction of the term 'multiculturalism' in the political rhetoric of Greek politicians lacks any meaning and value for the immigrants. Even though the Greek Prime Minister Konstantinos Simitis, in his speech on the celebration of the 1998 Year Against Racism, stated that 'Greece is becoming a multicultural society', multiculturalism has not acquired the status of a political project for the reconstruction of the Greek state institutions. Recently arrived immigrants have no alternative apart from becoming members of an expanding group of low-paid illegal workers.

MULTICULTURAL REFERENCES AND THE 1997 CULTURAL CAPITAL OF EUROPE

The case of illegal immigrants coming to Greece testifies to the inability of state institutions to cope with an issue that requires that the ideological context of the ethnic model of the nation-state be overcome. In Salonica the pursuit of a multicultural society was further encouraged by the activities of the 1997 CCE. The CCE is an institution sponsored by the EU and lasting one year, which takes place in a different EU member state every year. Although there is no fixed agenda of activities, each organising city is expected to promote art events related to the city's history and culture as well as activities bringing together artists and scholars from various European and non-European countries. The EU provides the necessary funds to construct or reconstruct the infrastructure needed for art events.

The case of the 1997 CCE clearly demonstrates the important role that intellectuals play in the construction of culture. In order to understand the contribution of the intellectual community, it is important to know the context that led the intellectuals of Salonica to produce and consume the new image of multicultural Salonica (Kahn 1995: 148). The intellectual community of the city is well aware of the cultural plurality of Salonica's past. Indeed, one of the most important characteristics of literature produced by writers and poets of Salonica has been its acknowledgement of the multilingual, culturally mixed society of the city (Abatzopoulou 1997; Mackridge 1997; Yannakakis 1997). This has become a popular way to differentiate Salonica from Athens and to signify the 'character' of the city. Not only in literature but also in music and other arts, in architectural reconstructions of parts of the old city as well as in everyday discourses such as the local cuisine and night life entertainment, this unique 'character' of the city is often promoted (Moutsou 1994).

The stress on the cultural plurality of the city's past was part of the 1997 CCE agenda since its very beginnings. The 1997 CCE administration clearly stated that 'the promotion of the multicultural character of the city, which in its long history has been a meeting place for different nations, is among the basic targets of the 1997 CCE programme' (CCE 1997: 1). A great number of cultural events stressed the image of Salonica as a Mediterranean port, as one of the oldest and most important cities in the southern Balkans. Such activities included traditional dance performances with groups coming from Syria, Lebanon, southern Italy, France and Spain, literature presentations from Balkan writers, folk music concerts by ensembles from the eastern Mediterranean and the Middle East. However, this emphasis on what was called a 'multicultural programme' of art events coexisted with more Hellenic-oriented cultural activities, such as the exhibition about Alexander the Great and the exhibition of ancient Greek technology. Indeed, as the Greek Minister of Culture Evangelos Venizelos argued, the 1997 CCE agenda attempted to find a compromise between two distinctively opposite views: the Hellenic and the 'cosmopolitan' (multicultural) one (Venizelos, 1998).

The CCE administration, composed of local intellectuals and bureaucrats, decided that a focus on Byzantium[16] was the ideal compromise between the two views for the 1997 CCE agenda. Hence, as Ioannou argues, the focus on Byzantine Orthodoxy was nothing more than an attempt to find a middle ground (Ioannou, 1999). Both the opening ceremony of the 1997 CCE and the most important exhibition of the 1997 CCE (The Mount Athos Treasures exhibition) clearly referred to the Byzantine heritage of Salonica. However, even this presentation of Byzantium was in its own way Greek-centred, since it emphasised Greek Orthodoxy as the most important element of the Byzantine era. Such developments attracted a number of critiques.[17]

The 1997 CCE model of multiculturalism was therefore dominated by a stress on Byzantine Greek Orthodoxy and an exclusion of Islam, other Christianities and syncretisms and, to a lesser degree, Judaism. Thus, the attempt to capitalise on the cultural plurality of Salonica's past did not include a balanced presentation of the populations which created this cultural plurality in the city's history. In addition, there was very little emphasis in the 1997 CCE activities on the cultural plurality of Salonica in the present day. To my knowledge, among the few 1997 CCE activities related to the cultural plurality of the city in the 1990s were the organising of an academic conference, the publication of a pamphlet titled *The ABC Against Racism*, the activities of the 'Red Thread' programme[18] and the coordination of an international festival of folk music and 'traditional' food. The participation of the immigrant communities of present-day Salonica was evident only in the case of the international festival where they performed 'folk dances' and cooked their 'traditional' food. Overall, the 1997 CCE promoted representations of multiculturalism that failed to fully incorporate the non-Greek elements who created the cultural plurality of the city, both in the past and in the present.

WHICH MULTICULTURALISM FOR SALONICA?

Multiculturalism has become an ambiguous term in present-day social sciences as well as in many political contexts. According to Modood: 'it is only through specific case studies that we can analyse how integration and multiculturalism are worked in different ways in different local and national settings' (1997: 5). This paper has attempted to present the development of the discourse of multiculturalism in Salonica during the 1990s, and the challenges it posed for the Greek state and society. As already explained, two parallel processes were taking place in the city. On the one hand, the arrival of about 100,000 immigrants and their inability to integrate highlighted the need for the establishment of multicultural institutions or, at least, institutions able to cope with the particular social and linguistic needs of its increasingly heterogeneous populations. At the same time, the 1997 CCE capitalised almost exclusively on pre-existing forms of cultural plurality in the city's past, ignoring to a great degree this newer heterogeneity, in order to present its own version of multiculturalism. In addition to forces in the local context that have turned Salonica into a multicultural site, there are also, of course, wider influences contributing to the development of multiculturalism, such as the minorities discourse. However, what is striking here is the way the two local factors that served to establish the multicultural domain in the city were perceived as unconnected in most of the local discussions. This was basically a consequence of the refusal of the 1997 CCE organisers to make the exploration of the serious social and educational issues of the present immigrant communities part of the 1997 CCE agenda. The failure to bring Salonica's past and present cultural plurality into a single framework meant that a crucial opportunity to envisage and explore, critically, the future of the city's cultural plurality was lost.

It should also be noted that the dominant discourses of multiculturalism coexist in Salonica with a less visible but developing critical approach to the present-day cultural heterogeneity of the city. During the last few years, young artists and writers of Salonica have been exploring issues related with the presence of 'others' in the city. This can be seen, for example, in the work of a number of young photographers, who participated at the 'Photo Syngiria' exhibitions in the 1990s. In such approaches, the presence of 'others' is located at the centre of everyday Salonica life, the syncretisms and social dynamics between groups being clearly manifested. An alternative critical exploration of identities may develop out of these attempts, although this is not yet clear. However, the work of most of these young local artists and writers had a limited presence in the 1997 CCE projects. Reportedly, this had to do with the agenda set by the 1997 CCE administration, which focused on well established, internationally recognised artists and their work.[19]

The multiculturalisation of the city's past, as encouraged by the 1997 CCE agenda, followed a folkloric approach to cultures. This is not a unique case, since similar phenomena have occurred in multicultural contexts in other parts of the world (Castles, Kalantzis and Cope 1990; Goldberg 1994). In such cases, cultures become commodities and there is a form of cultural difference 'to suit every taste' (Kahn 1995: 125). The consumption of cultural commodities allows us to construct our perceptions of selfhood, our relationships to the world and to 'others' (Caglar 1997: 182). This is why the presence of illegal immigrants was minimised in the 1997 CCE version of multiculturalism; illegal immigrants would create unpleasant perceptions of who we, the citizens of Salonica, are.

In order to become commodities, cultures have to be homogenised. Homogenisation is necessary in order to present distinctive cultures in dance performances, in 'traditional' food festivals and folk music concerts. Such an essentialist representation of culture is contradictory to an understanding of culture as an open-ended, changing, creative and unbounded process involving relations between insiders and outsiders. In its own way, the homogenisation of cultures has significant consequences on individuals. Individuals are by definition perceived as members of cultural collectivities (Delafenetre 1997). Culture is not perceived as an outcome of social relations but as a definite and essential form of demarcation of the self (Strathern 1995: 154–6). Individuals are free to choose 'their culture' but this limits their ability to construct a polycentric, multiple and unsituated self beyond cultural stereotypes (Turner 1993: 419).

It is not an exaggeration to argue that versions of multiculturalism such as the one promoted by the 1997 CCE may contribute to imposing limits on individual freedom. Under these conditions dynamic and unbounded idioms of identification created in everyday discourses will obviously continue to exist. However, in order to become established in the 'official scene', similar idioms of identification will have to abandon their open-ended, continuously changing qualities. The freedom to construct identities without the limitations of stereotypes will therefore be located beyond and outside the society of Salonica. Individuals and groups following such a process will practically face the denial of their existence at the public scene. Is it possible to recognise the existence of 'others' without applying an essentialist definition of identity? This is the crucial political question that needs to be addressed.[20]

The introduction of multiculturalism in Salonica is currently posing a deeply political challenge for its present inhabitants and for Greek society and the state. The discourse of multiculturalism is now spreading and developing beyond the discussions of intellectuals. It is presenting challenges to, and highlights dilemmas of, the present situation. There are new calls for the establishment of multiculturalism as a political project. The Greek nation-state is attempting to respond to these challenges within a context that cannot be disregarded: the wider European context in which various western European versions of multiculturalism are operating. In order to respond to all these pressures the ethnic model of the Greek nation-state will have to be revised, but it is still not clear what will succeed this model. The case of Salonica illustrates that already some versions of multiculturalism are available in Greece. There exists a Western cosmopolitan model; there is also a more native version of multiculturalism dominated by the ideology of Byzantine Greek Orthodoxy and, finally, there are fragments of native critical explorations that have not yet been materialised into an alternative proposal. Whatever the future developments, it is clear that in order to establish a democratic polity, Greek society also needs to take into consideration immigrants' views on the issue of cultural plurality.

ACKNOWLEDGEMENTS

I am most grateful to Jane Cowan for her contribution in writing this chapter and to Sarah Green, Dimitra Gefou-Madianou, Makis Makris, Sophia Avgitidou and Efi Voutira, who offered important comments on earlier drafts.

NOTES

1. A number of papers, books and edited volumes published in Greek during the last decade examine various aspects of multiculturalism (see, for example, Agelopoulos 1997b; Chiotakis 1999; Dragona-Monachou 1999; Gefou-Madianou 1999; Lavdas 1999; Katsikas and Politou 1999; Katsoulis 1999; Papageorgiou 1997; Paparigopoulos 1999; Skourtou 1999; Vryzas 1997). In addition, a number of well-known books on multiculturalism and multicultural education have been translated and published in Greek (for example, Cummins 1999; Modgil *et al.* 1997; Taylor 1997).
2. For an analysis on the emergence of a minorities discourse in Greece, see Tsitselikis and Christopoulos (1997); Gounaris, Michailidis and Agelopoulos (1997) and Danforth (1995).
3. Although immigrants from other countries can be found throughout Greece, settlement patterns are uneven. Thus, while many immigrants in Athens come from Asian or African countries, these kinds of immigrant communities are virtually non-existent in the north of Greece. The immigrants living and working in Salonica come almost exclusively from Albania, Bulgaria and the former USSR. Furthermore, a number of populations living in the north have very little presence in the south.

4. I use the term 'cultural plurality' following Grillo's understanding of cultural pluralisms (1998).
5. The issue of the dynamics, hierarchies and syncretisms between the populations of Ottoman Salonica is beyond the limits of the present analysis.
6. For a detailed analysis, see Agelopoulos (1995); Cowan (1997); Gounaris (1993); Karakasidou (1997); Vereni (1996) and Vermeulen (1984).
7. Brailsford points out that since the years of the Ottoman empire the population of the cities of Serbia, Bulgaria and Macedonia was ethnically different from the population of the nearby rural areas (1906: 86). The distinction between bourgeois Bulgarians of Salonica living in the urban centre and Macedonian Slavs living in the rural areas of Macedonia is important. A great number of urban Slav-speaking populations of Macedonia had acquired a Bulgarian national identity by the end of the nineteenth century. The Macedonian national movement was established in the early twentieth century, at a point when two generations of bourgeois Slavs in Macedonia had developed a Bulgarian national identity.
8. Among the Greek Orthodox refugees who settled in Salonica in 1922–3 were a number of Pontic Greeks from the Black Sea coast of Turkey (Greeks speaking the Pontic Greek dialect), bourgeois Greeks from the cities of the Turkish Aegean Sea coast and Turkophone Greeks from highland villages of central Turkey.
9. The political changes of the 1980s and the 1990s in the former USSR caused the migration movement of Pontic and other Greeks from the former Soviet Republics to Greece (Voutira 1991).
10. Estimates regarding the number of immigrants in Greece vary from 400,000 to one million persons. My own figures (700,000) represent a conclusion based on official statistics, existing studies (Iosifides 1997; King *et al.* 1998; Lianos 1998) and discussions conducted with the representatives of immigrant communities and anti-racist organisations participating in the Network of Social Support to Immigrants and Refugees. My estimate refers to those immigrants who live and work in Greece throughout the year.
11. Non-Greek citizens who have been convicted for crimes committed in Greece prior to the legalisation process are not eligible to receive a Green Card.
12. Every full-time, legally registered worker in Greece receives a social security stamp for each working day.
13. A very limited number of reception classes and Greek language courses are established in some schools of the larger cities of Greece (*Scholeia Palinostounton*, literally, 'schools for repatriates'). These courses were initially created for the Pontic Greek repatriates from the former USSR. At a later stage they accepted immigrant children of any background.
14. According to the 1991 census, the prefecture of Salonica had a population of 977,528 persons.
15. It is beyond any doubt that immigrants have contributed to the increase of criminality in Greece. Most of the immigrants' criminal activity has to do with petty crime related to their social marginality. However, some immigrants were engaged in extreme forms of criminal activities such as the two incidents in June–July 1999 in which two desperate Albanian illegal immigrants hijacked two public buses and took all the passengers as hostages. Both incidents had tragic outcomes and three persons died. In any case, it should be made clear that the majority of crimes in Greece are committed by Greeks and that the majority of immigrants are not engaged in criminal activities (Fakiolas 1994; Karydis 1996). Furthermore, as Fakiolas points out, Albanian immigrants are over-represented in the statistics on arrests due to their social visibility, by police targeting of known areas of Albanian concentration (such as the railway and bus stations and specific neighbourhoods in Salonica) and by their problematic legal status as illegal immigrants (1994).

16. The Byzantine heritage has often been proposed as a way out from the so-called 'failure of the modern Greek nation', that is, its inability to solve the Hellenic–Romeic dilemma imposed on modern Greeks by Western modernity (Herzfeld 1986). During the last decade a number of scholars have argued that the Byzantine Orthodox cultural heritage and its context (that is, the Balkans) can contribute to a postmodern construction of Greekness. Most of these scholars, such as Christos Giannaras and Kostas Zouraris, are influenced by the so called neo-Orthodox movement. As Ziakas clearly puts it 'our country has to participate in the postmodern quest by capitalising upon its pre-modern cultural deposits', referring to the Byzantine Orthodoxy as 'our pre-modern cultural deposits' (Ziakas 1998: 52).

17. A collection of papers highly critical of the activities of the CCE was published in *Entefktirion* (vol. 42–3). *Entefktirion*, a periodical published in Salonica, invited a large number of intellectuals and politicians to review the activities of the 1997 CCE and produced a special volume published in 1998.

18. The 'Red Thread' ('Kokini Klosti') programme organised a number of high quality activities (music, dance, games, story-telling, exhibitions, parties, happenings) aimed primarily at children's education and entertainment. Most of these activities incorporated strong multicultural references.

19. See the various papers at *Entefktirion* (vol. 42–3).

20. I am grateful to Sarah Green for her thoughtful remarks on this point.

BIBLIOGRAPHY

Abatzopoulou, Fragiski. 1997. 'The Image of the Jew in the Literature of Salonica', in Peter Mackridge and Eleni Yannakakis (eds) *Ourselves and Others: The development of a Greek Macedonian cultural identity*. Oxford: Berg.

Agelopoulos, Georgios. 1995. 'Perceptions, Construction and Definition of Greek National Identity in Late Nineteenth–Early Twentieth Century Macedonia'. *Balkan Studies* 36(2), 247–63.

—— 1997a. 'From Bulgarievo to Nea Krasia, From "Two Settlements" to "One Village": Community formation, collective identities and the role of the individual', in Peter Mackridge and Eleni Yannakakis (eds) *Ourselves and Others: The Development of a Greek Macedonian cultural identity*. Oxford: Berg.

—— 1997b. 'Ethnotikes Omades kai Taftotites'. *Synchrona Themata* 63, 18–26.

Brailsford, Henry. 1906. *Macedonia, its Races and their Future*. London: Methuen Press.

Caglar, Ayse. 1997. 'Hyphenated Identities and the Limits of "Culture"', in Tariq Modood & Pnina Werbner (eds) *The Politics of Multiculturalism in the New Europe*. London: Zed Books.

Castles, Stephen, Mary Kalantzis and Bill Cope. 1990. *Mistaken Identities: Multiculturalism and the Demise of Nationalism in Australia*. Sydney: Pluto.

Chiotakis, Stelios. 1999. 'I "Polypolitismikotita" Enantion tis Polypolitismikotitas? Anastaltikoi Paragontes tis "Anoichtis Koinonias"'. *Epistimi kai Koinonia* 2–3, 105–44.

Cowan, Jane K. 1997. 'Idioms of Belonging: Polyglot articulations of local identity in a Greek town', in Peter Mackridge and Eleni Yannakakis (eds) *Ourselves and Others: The development of a Greek Macedonian cultural identity*. Oxford: Berg.

Cultural Capital of Europe (Salonica 1997). 1997. *Alfavitari kata tou Koinonikou Ratsismou*. Salonica: a 1997 Cultural Capital of Europe Publication.

Cummins, Jim. 1999. *Taftotites ypo diapragmatefsi*. (Greek translation of *Negotiating Identities*). Athens: Gutenberg.

Danforth, Loring M. 1995. *The Macedonian Conflict: Ethnic nationalism in a transnational world*. Princeton: University of Princeton Press.

Delafenetre, David. 1997. 'Interculturalism, Multiculturalism and Transculturalism'. *Nationalism and Ethnic Politics* 3(1), 89–109.

Dragona-Monachou, Myrto. 1999. 'Ithiki kai Thriskeia yia mia Pankosmia Polypolitismiki Koinonia: To Aitima mias Koinis Ithikis'. *Epistimi kai Koinonia* 2–3, 145–70.

Fakiolas, R. 1994. 'Metanastefsi Apo kai Pros tin Ellada', in *Meletes pros timi tou Konstantinou G. Drakatou.* Athens: Papazisis.

Gefou-Madianou, Dimitra (ed.). 1998. *Anthropologiki Theoria kai Ethnografia.* Athens: Ellinika Grammata.

———. 1999. *Politismos kai Ethnografia.* Athens: Ellinika Grammata.

Gellner, Ernest. 1983. *Nations and Nationalism.* Oxford: Blackwell.

Goldberg, Theo David (ed.). 1994. 'Multicultural Conditions', in *Multiculturalism: A critical reader.* London: Blackwell.

Gounaris, Basil, Iakovos Michailidis and Georgios Agelopoulos. 1997. *Taftotites sti Makedonia.* Athens: Papazisis.

Gounaris, Vasilis. 1993. 'Ethnotikes Omades kai Kommatikes Parataxis sti Makedonia ton Valkanikon Polemon', in *Ta Ogdonta Chronia ton Valkanikon Polemon.* Athens: E.L.I.A.

Grillo, Ralph. 1998. *Pluralism and the Politics of Difference: State, culture and ethnicity in comparative perspective.* Oxford: Oxford University Press.

Herzfeld, Michael. 1986. *Ours Once More: Folklore, ideology and the making of modern Greece.* New York: Pella.

Ioannou, Andreas. 1999. 'Katanalonontas ti threiskia. Simeioseis Schetika me tin Ekthesi Thisavroi tou Agiou Orous'. *Dokimes* 8, 24–39.

Iosifides, Theodoros. 1997. 'Immigrants in the Athens Labour Market: A comparative survey of Albanians, Egyptians and Filipinos', in Russell King and Richard Black (eds) *Southern Europe and the New Immigrations.* Brighton: Sussex Academic Press.

Kahn, Joel. 1995. *Culture, Multiculture, Postculture.* London: Sage.

Karakasidou, Anastasia. 1997. *Fields of Wheat, Hills of Blood.* Chicago: Chicago University Press.

Karydis, Vasilios. 1996. *I Egklimatikotita ton Metanaston stin Ellada.* Athens: Papazisis.

Katsikas, Christos and Eva Politou. 1999. *Ektos 'Taxis' to 'Diaforetiko'?* Athens: Gutenberg.

Katsoulis, Ilias. 1999. 'Antistaseis stin Polypolitismikotita'. *Epistimi kai Koinonia* 2–3, 53–104.

King, Russell, Theodoros Iosifides and Lenio Myrivili. 1998. 'A Migrant's Story: From Albania to Athens'. *Journal of Ethnic and Migration Studies* 24(1), 159–75.

Kitromilides, Paschalis. 1990. 'Imagined Communities and the Origins of the National Question in the Balkans', in Martin Blinkhorn and Thanos Veremis (eds) *Modern Greece: Nationalism and Nationality.* Athens: ELIAMEP.

Kofos, Evangelos. 1990. 'National Heritage and National Identity in Nineteenth and Twentieth Century Macedonia', in M. Blinkhorn and Thanos Veremis (eds) *Modern Greece: Nationalism and nationality.* (eds) Athens: ELIAMEP.

Kymlicka, Will. 1995. *Multicultural Citizenship: A liberal theory of minority rights.* Oxford: Clarendon Press.

Lavdas, Kostas. 1999. 'I Polypolitismikotita kai i Theoritiki Klironomia tou Ethnikou Kratous'. *Epistimi kai Koinonia* 2–3, 27–52.

Lianos, Theodoros. 1998. 'Kinonikes Anisotites kai Kinonikos Apoklismos', in *Praktika tou ektou sinedriou tou Idrimatos Saki Karagiorga.* Athens: Exantas.

Mackridge, Peter. 1997. 'Cultivating New Lands: The consolidation of territorial gains in Greek Macedonia through literature', in Peter Mackridge and Eleni Yannakakis (eds) *Ourselves and Others: The Development of a Greek Macedonian Cultural Identity since 1912.* Oxford: Berg.

Modgil, Sohan, Gajendra Verma, Kanka Mallick and Celia Modgil. 1997. *Polypolitismiki ekpaidefsi: Provlimatismoi, Prooptikes.* (Greek Translation of *Multicultural Education: The interminable debate*). Athens: Ellinika Grammata.

Modood, Tariq. 1997. 'Introduction: The Politics of Multiculturalism in the New Europe', in Tariq Modood and Pnina Werbner (eds) *The Politics of Multiculturalism in the New Europe*. London: Zed Books.

Moutsou, Christina. 1994. 'Urban Definitions of Greekness: Selective Turkish fragments in Salonican popular expressions'. Unpublished M.Sc. dissertation, Department of Social Anthropology, London School of Economics. London.

Papageorgiou, Konstantinos. 1997. 'Proloyiko Simeioma', in Charles Taylor (ed.) *Polypolitismikotita. Exetazontas tin Politiki tis Anagnorisis*. (Introductory Notes to Greek Translation of *Multiculturalism and 'The Politics of Recognition'*). Athens: Polis.

Paparigopoulos, Xenofon. 1999. 'I Polypolitismikotita os Sygchrono Provlima'. *Epistimi kai Koinonia* 2–3, 1–26.

Petrovich, Milan. 1980. 'Religion and Ethnicity in Eastern Europe', in Peter Sugar (ed.) *Ethnic diversity and conflict in Eastern Europe*. Oxford: ABC.

Rex, John. 1995. 'Multiculturalism in Europe and America'. *Nations and Nationalism* 1(2), 243–59.

Samad, Yunas. 1997. 'The Plural Guises of Multiculturalism: Conceptualising a fragmented paradigm', in Tariq Modood and Pnina Werbner (eds) *The Politics of Multiculturalism in the New Europe*. London: Zed Books.

Sitaropoulos, Spyros. 1992. 'The New Legal Framework of Alien Immigration in Greece: A draconian contribution to Europe's unification'. *Immigration and Nationality Law and Practice*, 69(3), 89–96.

Skourtou, Eleni. 1999. 'Eisagoyi', in *Taftotites Ypo Diapragmatefsi*. (Introduction to Greek translation of *Negotiating Identities*). Jim Cummins (ed.) Athens: Gutenberg.

Smith, Anthony D. 1986. *The Ethnic Origins of Nations*. London: Blackwell.

Strathern, Marilyn (ed.). 1995. 'The Nice Thing About Culture is that Everyone Has it', in *Shifting Contexts. Transformations in Anthropological Knowledge*. London: Routledge.

Taylor, Charles. 1997. *Polypolitismikotita. Exetazontas tin Politiki tis Anagnorisis*. (Greek translation of *Multiculturalism and 'The Politics of Recognition'*). Athens: Polis.

Tsitselikis, Konstantinos and Dimitris Christopoulos. 1997. *To Meionotiko Fenomeno stin Ellada*. Athens: Kritiki.

Turner, Terence. 1993. 'Anthropology and Multiculturalism: What is anthropology that multiculturalism should be mindful of it?' *Cultural Anthropology* 8(4), 411–29.

Venizelos, Evangelos. 1998. 'Mia Protognori kai Exairetika Plousia Empeiria'. *Entefktirion* 42–3, 62–6.

Vereni, Piero. 1996. 'Boundaries, Frontiers, Persons, Individuals: Questioning "identity" at national borders'. *Europea* 2(1), 77–89.

Vermeulen, Hans. 1984. 'Greek Cultural Dominance Among the Orthodox Population of Macedonia During the Last Period of the Ottoman Rule', in Anton Bloch and Hans Driessen (eds) *Cultural Dominance in the Mediterranean Area*. Amsterdam: Katholieke Universiteit Nijmege.

Voutira, Efi. 1991. 'Pontic Greeks Today: Migrants or Refugees?' *Journal of Refugee Studies* 4, 27–8.

Vryzas, Konstantinos. 1997. *Pagkosmia Epikoinonia, Politistikes Taftotites*. Athens: Gutenberg.

Werbner, Pnina. 1997. 'Afterword: Writing Multiculturalism and Politics in the New Europe', in Tariq Modood and Pnina Werbner (eds) *The Politics of Multiculturalism in the New Europe*. London: Zed Books.

Yannakakis, Eleni. 1997. 'Resurrecting Greek Macedonian Culture: Pentzikis, the dead man and the resurrection', in Peter Mackridge and Eleni Yannakakis (eds) *Ourselves and Others: The development of a Greek Macedonian cultural identity since 1912*. Oxford: Berg.

Ziakas, Theodoros. 1998. 'To Noima tou Thesmou'. *Entefktirion*. 42–3, 48–52.

CONTRIBUTORS

Georgios Agelopoulos is Lecturer in European Anthropology at the Department of Social Anthropology, Panteion University, Athens. His research interests focus on nationalism and ethnicity, migration and identity-building in the southern Balkans (Greece, Bulgaria, Macedonia). His main publications include 'Perceptions, Construction and Definition of Greek National Identity in Late 19th-Century Macedonia' (*Journal of Balkan Studies*, 1995) and 'From Bulgarievo to Nea Krasia: Community Formation, Collective Identities and the Role of the Individual' in *Ourselves and Others: The development of a Greek Macedonian cultural identity since 1912*, edited by P. Mackridge and E. Yannakakis (1997). He co-edited *Taftotites sti Makedonia* (*Identities in Macedonia*, 1997).

K.S. (Keith) Brown is Lecturer in the Department of Anthropology at the University of Wales, Lampeter, and Assistant Professor (Research) at the Thomas J. Watson Institute of International Studies at Brown University, Providence, Rhode Island, US. He has undertaken archival and ethnographic research at various sites in the Republic of Macedonia, Greece, and the US on national and local memory, labour migration, humour and cultural politics. His publications include a number of articles and chapters on these themes. He is currently completing an ethnography of the post-Yugoslav transition in Macedonia.

Jane K. Cowan is Senior Lecturer in Social Anthropology at the School of Cultural and Community Studies at the University of Sussex at Brighton, England. She is author of *Dance and the Body Politic in Northern Greece* (1990), Winner of the 1991 Chicago Folklore Prize, and co-editor (with Marie-Bénédicte Dembour and Richard A. Wilson) of a volume on *Culture and Rights: Anthropological perspectives* (forthcoming). She has published numerous articles on gender relations, ritual, popular music, the politics of 'tradition' and the formation of complex identities in contemporary Greece. She is currently undertaking archival research on the League of Nations' supervision of minority treaties in the southern Balkans in the interwar period, focusing on the minority petition process.

Loring M. Danforth is Professor of Anthropology at Bates College in Lewiston, Maine. He is the author of *The Macedonian Conflict: Ethnic nationalism in a transnational world* (1995), which received Honourable Mention in the competition for the American Ethnological Society's Senior Book Award, *Firewalking and Religious Healing: The Anastenaria of Northern Greece and the American firewalking movement* (1989), Winner of the 1990 Chicago Folklore Prize, and *Death Rituals of Rural Greece* (1982). He has written, in addition, numerous articles on Greece and Macedonia.

Iakovos D. Michailidis is Research Associate at the Centre for Macedonian History and Documentation in Thessaloniki. His main work is 'Slav-speaking Emigrants and Refugees from Macedonia and Western Thrace' (unpublished Ph.D. dissertation, University of Thessaloniki 1996, in Greek). He co-edited *Taftotites sti Makedonia (Identities in Macedonia,* 1997), and has published many articles on Balkan minority issues. They include 'Traditional Friends and Occasional Claimants: Serbian claims in Macedonia between the wars' (*Journal of Balkan Studies,* 1995) and 'Minority Rights and Educational Problems in Greek Interwar Macedonia: The case of the primer "Abecedar"' (*Journal of Modern Greek Studies,* 1996).

Jonathan Matthew Schwartz has taught social science at the University of Copenhagen since 1970, when he emigrated from the US to Denmark. He is the author of *Reluctant Hosts: Denmark's Reception of Guest Workers* (1985), *In Defense of Homesickness: Nine essays on identity and locality* (1989) and *Pieces of Mosaic: An essay on the making of Makedonija* (1996). In 1998 he edited a collection of articles on the reception of Bosnian refugees in three Nordic countries, *Det Midlertidigt Liv (The Temporary Life)*. Schwartz started his study of immigration and emigration in Detroit and has continued it in Denmark.

Riki Van Boeschoten is a translator at the Council of Ministers of the European Union, Brussels. Since 1975 she has undertaken field research in Northern Greece in the areas of social history, oral history and ethnicity. She has published three books on the social history of the 1940s in Greece: *Anapoda Chronia: Sillogiki Mnimi kai Istoria sto Ziaka, Grevenon, 1900–1950 (Unruly Years: Collective memory and history in the village of Ziaka, district of Grevena, 1900–1950,* 1997), *Perasame Polles Bores, Koritsi mou... (We've Gone Through a Lot, My Girl...,* 1999) and (with Roberto Cipriani, Vittorio Cotesta and Nikos Kokosalakis) *Il Villaggio Armonioso: Tradizione, Modernità, Solidarietà e Conflitto in una Communità Greca (A Harmonious Village: Tradition, modernity, solidarity and conflict in a Greek community,* 1999). She has also published numerous articles in various European languages.

Piero Vereni has held research and teaching positions at the School of Anthropological Studies of the Queen's University of Belfast, at the University of Venice Ca' Foscari, and at ISH (*Institutum Studiorum Humanitatis*) in Ljubljana, Slovenia. He has undertaken fieldwork in Greek

Macedonia (1995–7 and 1999) and Ireland (1998–9), where he examined the construction and perception of ethnic and national identities along the political borders of nation-states. His publications include 'Il Vocabolario degli Antropologi: Alcune idee sull'etnicità' ('The Vocabulary of Anthropologists: Some reflections on ethnicity', *Il Mondo*, 1994) and 'Boundaries, Frontiers, Persons, Individuals: Questioning "identity" at national borders' (*Europaea*, 1996).

INDEX

Compiled by Auriol Griffith-Jones

Index

European Commission, Badinter
commission, 122
European Union
and Cultural Capital institution,
147
and minority rights, 14
Exarchate (Bulgarian Orthodox
church), 68, 74, 75

family
and allegiance, 73–4, 92, 93
and personal identity, 52–3
zadruga (extended family), 52
flags
foreign, 131–2
new version of Macedonian, 126
symbolism of, 18, **123**, 124–5,
126
Florina region (western Greek
Macedonia), 14, 15–16, 48,
122
compared with Assiros, 40–1
disputed national identity, 90
economy, 33–4
emigrants in Australia, 92–4
ethnic composition of rural
population, 32–4, **32**
ethnic divisions, 28–9
illegal Albanian immigrants, 33
relations with Republic of
Macedonia, 53–4
see also Khristopoulos, Leonidas
Forum Against Ethnic Violence
(FAEV), x, xi, 19
FYROM (Former Yugoslav Republic
of Macedonia) (alternative
name), xiii, 4, 23nn, 53–4,
70–1, 79, 124, 136n
see also Macedonia, Republic of

Gatsos family, 52, 53, 55, 60–1, **61**,
62, **63**
Georgievski, Ljubco, 134
Georgievski, Ljubisha, 133
Gladstone, W.E., 1
Gligorov, Kire, 4, 126, 127
and Gostivar incident, 131–2
globalisation
and locality, 64
and multicultural discourse, 140
rights discourses, 13, 14

Gostivar (Macedonia), 110, 129–30
Albanian flag incident, 131–2
Gramadikovski, Mihail, 78
Great Britain, and Macedonian
Question, 1
Greece, 1, 5
Aegean Macedonia, xiii–xiv, 104
and compulsory population
exchange with Turkey, 11, 29,
36–7
and concept of multiculturalism,
18–19, 140–1, 150–1
economic blockade of Macedonia,
x, 42, 126
emigration from, 37
financial investment in Macedonia,
126
German Occupation of, 68, 70
historiography on Macedonia,
71–2
immigrants in, 5, 42, 140–1,
144–7, 151n, 152n
immigration procedures, 145,
146, 147, 152n
local government, 42, 43, 44n
nation-building policies, 1, 11–12,
23n, 36–8
national unity concerns, 5–6, 141
new nationalism, 41–2, 144
opposition to Republic of
Macedonia, x, xiii, 4, 5–6, 53–4,
98
political allegiances, 37, 38, 44n,
59
political centralisation of, 33–4
racism against Albanian
immigrants, 146–7
Slavic dialects in, xiv, xv
state policies on minorities, 37–8,
42–3
and symbolism of flag, 18, 122–4,
126
see also Florina region; Greek Civil
War (1946–49); Salonica
Greek Civil War (1946–49), 7, 16
personal history and, 58, 70–1
and Prespa region, 33
state repression after, 37–8
Greek Communist Party (1940s), 73
Greek Orthodox Church, 148
in Australia, 94